Karl Ganzhorn Sergio Faustoferri (Eds.)

Bridging the Information Gap

for Small and Medium Enterprises

Proceedings of the Seminar
"Distributed Database Systems
for Small and Medium Enterprises",
Beijing, China, May 8–12, 1989

With 54 Figures

Published for and on behalf of the
United Nations with the support of the Commission
of the European Communities and UNESCO

Springer-Verlag
Berlin Heidelberg New York London
Paris Tokyo Hong Kong Barcelona

Prof. Dr. rer. nat. Dr.-Ing. E. h. Karl Ganzhorn
Gluckstraße 1, W-7032 Sindelfingen, FRG

Dr. Sergio Faustoferri
International Centre for Science and High Technology (ICS)
Via Grignano 9, Adriatico Palace
P. O. Box 586, I-34100 Trieste, Italy

United Nations
Centre for Science and Technology for Development
New York, NY 10017, USA

Commission of the European Communities
Directorate General XIII – Telecommunications,
Information Industries and Innovation
Rue de la Loi, B-1049 Brussels, Belgium

United Nations Educational, Scientific
and Cultural Organisation (UNESCO)
7, Place de Fontenoy, F-75007 Paris, France

ISBN 3-540-52706-0 Springer-Verlag Berlin Heidelberg New York
ISBN 0-387-52706-0 Springer-Verlag New York Berlin Heidelberg

Library of Congress Cataloging-in-Publication Data
Seminar "Distributed Database Systems for Small and Medium Enterprises" (1989: Peking, China)
Bridging the information gap for small and medium enterprises / Karl Ganzhorn, Sergio Faustoferri, (eds.). p. cm.
„Proceedings of the Seminar 'Distributed Database Systems for Small and Medium Enterprises', Beijing, China, May 8-12, 1989" – T.p. verso.
"Edited on behalf of the United Nations with the support of the Commission of the European Communities and UNESCO."
ISBN 3-540-52706-0 (Berlin) – ISBN 0-387-52706-0 (New York)
1. Small business – Information services – Congresses. 2. Distributed data bases – Congresses. 3. Data base management – Congresses. 4. Small business – Information services – China – Congresses. I. Ganzhorn, Karl, 1921- . II. Faustoferri, Sergio, 1960- . III. United Nations. IV. Commission of the European Communities and UNESCO. V. Title.
HD2341.S46 1989 658'.05–dc20 90-10202

2145/3140-543210 – Printed on acid-free paper

Preface

The process of social and economic development is likely to be increasingly influenced by the role played by Small and Medium size Enterprises (SMEs).

A proper and healthy development of SMEs will require a number of support services among which the development of infrastructural information services is a key element. This fact is clearly evident from the analysis of modern economic and productive systems.

It is interesting to notice how the life of the SMEs in an economy is characterized by a strong interdependency among the various actors of the economic world. The growth and the success of many entrepreneurial activities depend more and more on the availability of reliable and up-to-date information about market situation and opportunities, about new technologies and industrial processes as well as legislation and facilities for the enterprises. At the same time the lack of in-house expertise in developing information systems or even in accessing the existing commercial ones frequently hampers the continuity of many SMEs. However, the use of existing reliable and low cost information technologies could greatly help to meet the needs of the SMEs. A low degree of complexity of these technologies and their cost-effectiveness could be a suitable solution for the present needs of the SMEs and an incentive for the future broader use of computerized information management.

The use of the information systems available through the various national and international networks is an expanding phenomenon almost all over the world. The efforts of many public sector organizations as well as private companies in creating new information systems are producing prodigious effects. A large number of data-bases are presently available which provide mainly bibliographic and research related information. In this overall framework, there is a general lack of information relevant to the SMEs and their productive activities. Even from the conceptual point of view it is not possible to find any data-base structure designed specifically to meet the needs and the potentials of the SMEs.

Initially an International Seminar on Distributed Data-Base Systems for Small and Medium Enterprises was organized mainly to explore the various issues associated with the information gaps of the SMEs. The overall goal was to explore operational concepts and develop, through the collaboration of eminent experts, the structure of an information system particularly suitable for SMEs together with a series of recommendations for the implementation of a pilot project in China and other interested developing countries.

Even though the papers and the final report in this volume refer to China it is important to note that the concepts and the methodology expressed have a broader range of applications. With the proper modifications and consideration of the specific local conditions, these ideas can be applied in other developing countries as well as in many developed countries.

We recognize that almost no publications are available on this specific topic and we hope this one may be a good beginning for fruitful development work in this area. We expect that researchers working on distributed data-base management systems could be stimulated by this publication towards further conceptualization of new architectures which could better fill the existing voids in the information systems for the use of the SMEs. These enterprises have characteristics which differentiate them from larger corporations, and therefore it is desirable that the information systems which will serve them are tailored specifically for their use.

This volume is organized into five sections. An overview of the outcomes of the Beijing seminar appears in the first section together with a series of recommendations for the implementation of a pilot project. The second section addresses issues related to the needs of the SMEs and user considerations. Information system principles and design, together with practical advice on information system development and maintenance, are grouped in the third section. The fourth section deals with communications technologies and techniques supporting information systems. An overview of the status of computerized information systems in China and a survey of users' needs in the county where the pilot project will be implemented form the fifth and final section.

We thank the Commission of the European Communities for the substantial contribution which has made this seminar possible; the Institute of Scientific and Technical Information of China for their kind hospitality and valuable intellectual contributions; our colleagues at the United Nations Centre for Science and Technology for Development who perceived the importance of this topic and organized the seminar; Dr. Faustoferri, at that time associate expert at the Centre, for his extensive and able contributions in editing these proceedings; and finally Dr. Ganzhorn, member of the Advisory Committee on Science and Technology for Development, for his able and energetic guidance in all phases of this endeavour.

New York   Sergio C. Trindade
August 1990   Executive Director
                                                                      United Nations Centre for Science
                                                                      and Technology for Development

Executive Summary

Industry and especially Small and Medium Enterprises in all industrializing countries have a great need for technical/scientific, product and market information and particularly for factual and numeric data. However the SMEs do not usually have sufficient professional staff and the necessary communications infrastructure to make direct use of existing modern information systems and services. With the rapid progress of computer technology, powerful workstations and personal computers have become available at decreasing costs. This has opened up new venues of using these and other appropriate technologies for a distributed system of data-bases where relevant information can be stored and accessed locally.

The international seminar on Distributed Data-Bases for Small and Medium Enterprises held in Beijing, China, has identified a number of specific steps in support of the development of infrastructural information services for Chinese industry and in particular for Small and Medium Enterprises (SMEs) or Township and Village Enterprises (TVEs) and with wider possibilities of applications in other developing countries.

The recommendations of the seminar include a design for a pilot system of distributed data-bases and consultancy services which can be built up in several steps, each step representing a self-consistent and operational approach so that practical user experience grows along with further system development.

A major recommendation of the seminar is to use appropriate available technologies at any point in time rather than to buy most advanced technologies. They should be used in such a way as to provide early user involvement. Conventional and less sophisticated technologies should be also taken into account, including such technologies as paper, facsimile transmission, local personal computers with diskette or fixed disk files, and mailing of diskettes for transporting data-base information.

Skills of "information agents" acting as links between local PCs and county/regional/central data-bases should be established. Eventually in future stages of development the PC at an information agency can become an on-line terminal and thus a part of a larger information and data-base system.

It was recognized that the user involvement should include participation in all stages of the system development process and that an awareness must be created that information is a valuable good which is not freely available but has a price.

Table of Contents

1 Overview: the Beijing Seminar

Working groups' recommendations introduced and edited by:

Karl Ganzhorn, Sergio Faustoferri

Summary'

The overview of the essential features of the information support for SMEs is based on the outcomes of the Beijing Seminar. The recommendations are grouped according to the steps of the information system development process, and include a practical approach for a pilot system to be implemented in China.

Although the concepts expressed refer to the specific case of China, they can easily be adapted to different national situations. The layered structure drawn for the information systems in China is valid in other economical and political settings as well.

In order for these ideas to be easily grasped by enterpreneurs and policy makers, as well as by information-management experts, we tried to keep specialized technical expressions to the minimum in the overview. Specific technical issues are extensively addressed in other sections of this publication.

1.1 Introduction

Industry and especially Small and Medium Enterprises in all industrializing countries have a great need for technical/scientific, product and market information and particularly for factual and numeric data. At the same time they produce substantially useful information which could be of mutual benefit for themselves. Contrary to large scientific institutions or industrial companies SMEs[1] usually do not have sufficient professional staff and the necessary communication infrastructures to make direct use of existing modern information systems and services. This is also true in many industrialized countries. Therefore they must approach the use of modern technologies in consecutive stages while they build up trained manpower resources.

With the rapid progress of computer technology powerful workstations and Personal Computers have become available at decreasing costs. This has opened up new venues of using these and other appropriate technologies for a Distributed System of Data-Bases where relevant information can be stored and accessed locally, i.e. close to a cluster of SMEs. Initially such data-bases may be operated as small stand-alone systems which will be periodically updated from a central institute like ISTIC. Such update information may well be delivered on paper or diskettes in the initial phase. But it requires already the systematic approach of future Distributed Data-Bases. In subsequent steps such Distributed Data-Bases may be connected via telecommunication links when appropriate network technologies become available. Stepwise development of on-line updating, interactive inquiries and upward information collection can then be approached.

Such a concept is favored by the evolutionary trends of information technologies. These are:

- a rapidly increasing processing power at the workstation and Personal Computer level;
- a new category of sophisticated user orientation and friendliness in systems and application software and network infrastructure.

Yet many SMEs do not have enough expertise to make direct use of an information system, even when it is locally accessible, not to talk of accessing large national and international information services. Therefore one of the primary requirements is to develop the capacity to perform specific interface functions through trained personnel such as consultants (or week-end engineers) who serve as interpreters between users and data base systems. These consultants can act as "information brokers" or as "information agencies". They should facilitate the information flow between users and information systems by interpreting requirements and offerings. Surprisingly this concept is presently taken up in industrialized countries as well and there are cases where information agencies for SMEs have become self-supporting and even profitable commercial services.

With the deepening development of China's economic structural reform a transformation process from unitary planned economy to a market oriented

---

1   See sec. 6.2 for a list of abbreviations and acronyms used.

commodity economy in China is taking place. Such an economy has many interdependencies and requires awareness of market opportunities, industrial, technical and scientific resources and data, as well as access, to relevant information sources inside and outside the country.

In order to support the development of infrastructural information services for the Chinese industry and in particular for Small and Medium Enterprises (SMEs) or Township and Village Enterprises (TVEs), an International seminar on Distributed Data-Bases for Small and Medium Enterprises was organized in Beijing, China, from 8 to 12 May, 1989. The seminar was a joint undertaking of ISTIC, UNCSTD, CEC and UNESCO. The Commission of the European Communities (Directorate General DG XIII) provided major and background support. ISTIC, as the host, provided many outstanding speakers as well as efficient organization support. The objective of the seminar was to develop recommendations for a system of Distributed Data-Bases and consultancy services which can be built up in several steps. Each step should represent a self-consistent and operational approach so that practical user experience grows along with further system development.

In order to lead the transformation process of the economy and industry a number of surveys have been undertaken in China between 1981 and 1986. They indicate the primary needs of SMEs very clearly, namely:

- much information needs, not so much bibliographical information but market, industry, product, resources, factual and numeric data and scientific information;
- very widespread personnel education and training;
- means of technology transfer;
- information on and access to patents and standards;
- equipment, etc.

China presently has a substantial number of data-bases and information retrieval systems under development and in operation. They are in many cases aimed at scientific and bibliographic usage and in this respect are well ahead. Many of them have links and access to international networks and information retrieval systems. They are far ahead of the needs of industry and especially SMEs users. Yet it will be necessary to extend their offerings to the non-scientific types of needed information described earlier. In doing this they can be further developed to become information sources for SMEs as well. Early contacts between national and provincial data-bases and the industrial user periphery are necessary in order to guide their extension in this direction. Even assignment of some of their experts to an industrial "information agency" should be planned.

A general observation with the present data-base development is that the involvement of the user and application side is rather low and also late in the development process. Market requirements and user needs must be an integral part of all system development in every phase. They represent a moving target and the development process must be adjusted in every phase to them.

Data-bases for SMEs for a long time to come do not represent "Distributed Data-Bases" in the professional sense (i.e. with transparent access and consistent data updating and management protocols). They must be understood as a distribution of information systems and data-bases which are geographically spread and can be updated and supplemented in batch mode periodically from central institutions.

The seminar gave priority attention to user orientation of data-base development and to early implementation of pilot cases using appropriate technologies in various overlapping stages of system design of data-bases for SMEs.

A major conclusion of the seminar was that at any point in time, an efficient use should be made of appropriate available technologies rather than buying most modern technologies or waiting for future ones. In China many appropriate technologies for data-bases as well as the associated communication means are available or can be provided economically. They should be used in staged approaches in order to provide early user involvement. Conventional and less sophisticated technologies should be also taken into account. Such technologies are paper, facsimile transmission, local Personal Computers with diskette or fixed disk files, mailing of diskettes for transporting data base information. CD-ROM technology may be used for archieval type information in a central data-base, from where segments of information can be downloaded on diskettes and mailed or transmitted. With developing transmission technologies and skills of "information agents" telecommunication links between local PC's and county/regional/central data-bases can be established. They will allow downloading of new and update information as well as upward information collection. In further steps on-line inquiries can be established. Eventually in future stages of development the PC at an information agency can become an on-line terminal and thus a part of a larger information and data-base system.

The seminar also pointed out that an awareness must be created throughout industry and economy that information is a valuable good which is not freely available but has a price. User involvement should not be limited to their needs and desires but should encourage their participation in the entire system development process, sharing costs and having their own personnel engaged in the build-up of skills. In this way their interests can best be sustained.

1.2 User Considerations

1.2.1 Market Research

It is necessary first to discover which enterprises are potential users of information and in each of them to identify a person with whom the information exchange will take place. It is necessary then to find out how they handle information now and how they will handle it when there are more input sources through the information agent. In addition information on the end-product produced by the enterprise should be collected.

The "potential users" consist of a variety of persons in the SMEs such as designers, production managers, sales and purchasing people and others. The term "information handling" relates to the manner of passing the appropriate pieces of information to others in the enterprise, and sometimes to other enterprises and how and why the potential users will ask for more information.

The end-product may be a finished article for sale to a consumer for example a bicycle or a shirt. It may equally be an intermediate product sold to another SME to turn into a finished product for example a bicycle.

The information agent will make the collection of data that will form a local data-base and will have to keep it up-to-date by periodic visits to check the content. The agent will discover where the SMEs find the information they use now, who provides it and how it is passed on to the user of the information. The form of the information used at present and any transformations made, e.g. English into Chinese, words added to pictures, etc. should be noted. The agent in making visits will discover some information that the SMEs do not know how to obtain and which can be provided. By doing this a relationship will be built up between the agent and the SME. Sometimes the agent will also realize that there is information that the SME ought to have and does not know about. This may be particularly true of regulations, standards, patents and commercial information. Good agents will become persons trusted by the SMEs and will have to respect the trust placed in them because they will come to know much about the enterprises.

1.2.2 Awareness

How do users discover what products are wanted either in other parts of China or in other countries? Governments abroad often publish lists of items required by them ranging from super-computers to buckets. Trade journals and newspapers are sometimes a useful source. If this service does not exist in China it should be developed both at the level of the province and nationally. If it does exist, does it get to the right people in the SMEs?

Through what process do the SMEs find out where information is available at present in China? The knowledge and dissemination of this process becomes an important feature of the chain. The relationship between the national and provincial sources of information and the information agent must be strong and interactive. It requires that the national agencies provide both general information as well as the detail, for example a data-base of data-bases in China as well as downloading sub-sets of the information in the data-bases.

Greater awareness will be achieved by full training of the information agents and by a short term exchange of the staff on assignments between the local, county, provincial and national centres. By this means, both sides will understand each other better and become more actively connected. These exchanges need to be refreshed at intervals, perhaps yearly, or as particular needs arise.

Whilst the information agent will receive many pieces of information in the form of abstracts, usually the only form useful to the SME will be a fuller but not necessarily complete text with illustrations and diagrams etc. What the user receives must be tailored to his needs, neither too little nor too much. This can be done by the information agent only if he is aware of both the needs for and the availability of information. The cost of information is another aspect of the awareness step that needs to be transmitted from the beginning.

The awareness programme must be monitored to ensure that it is cost-effective and may become self-supporting in the longer term. The build up of the local data-base is one criteria and the number and kind of questions asked and responses made will provide more data in addition to the normal accounting procedures. The user must be shown the section of the local data-base that concerns him so that he may change and add to it as necessary. This will also help to build his confidence in the system. An understanding of the use he makes of information supplied will help the agent to provide better packaged information on subsequent occasions.

1.2.3 Market Segmentation

The information packages provided at all levels from the national centres down to the local level must be tailored for specific user needs. Chemical Abstracts provide one form for organizations such as ISTIC and the large chemical companies to buy and several smaller packages for smaller companies with specific needs. The smallest establishments use CA output only through agents such as on-line services or organizations such as ISTIC who will do searches on their behalf. In the same way other information packages must be cut down and tailored to match the users requirements.

Those buying chemicals in bulk and repacking them for sale do not need to know about the latest research in chromatography but may need information on the health hazards of crop sprays or the ways of keeping salt for the restaurant table dry, free-flowing and fit to eat.

Segmentation may be by product eg. clothing, chemicals, office equipment etc. It may also be by production method, by the country in which the product will be used or by aspects such as standards, health and safety regulations, legal and commercial requirements.

1.2.4 People

In the end only people create and receive information. Computers, paper and electronic transmission systems of all kinds are only intermediaries and as yet far from perfect. Unless for some of the time one person talks freely and openly to another the information will not be properly transmitted.

1.2.5 Some General Experiences

At present only part of SMEs throughout the world have computers, large or small, and if so these are mostly used for accounting, word processing and local data storage.

Only few data-bases are commercially profitable. Those that make any profit only do so because of additional value-added services or because they sell hard-copy forms of their information. Data-bases are sometimes very expensive to build up and always need continuous updating and maintenance in order to provide saleable services.

1.3 Systems Design and Development Principles

Information handling problems are addressed through wide range of approaches from manual systems through totally computerized capabilities. Computers are being used more extensively in the preparation and delivery of information products and services. Because of the rapidly developing technological environment and the need to respond to increasingly demanding user requirements, much design attention should be given to positioning for the deployment of new technologies as they become available. Several of the design approaches that are critical to the stepwise development of computer-based information processing systems are described in the following paragraphs.

1.3.1 Establish a Vision and Implement Stepwise

In building an information-handling system, attention must be given to designing for change. The system needs to be extensible for future purposes, but also has to handle past and current needs. It is important to establish a general direction, because information services will evolve from the manually-based printed products to a totally computerized, on-line, interactive, and distributive environment. Normally, the information products from the earlier stages will continue to meet some customer needs, and new products will provide additional service delivery mechanisms. During the system evolution, there will be many changes in the requirements, the capabilities, and the technology. The system should be implemented in small, user-meaningful, manageable stages consistent with the desired long-term directions.

1.3.2 Establish a Development Methodology

A rigorous well-defined development methodology must be established. This methodology must ensure that:

- an overall project evaluation (e.g. a cost/benefit analysis) is conducted and periodically updated;
- the development progress is monitored, reviewed, and controlled;
- the users are actively involved in every stage of the development process.

Disciplined testing and strict software management procedures must exist so that new or modified features do not disrupt ongoing operations. The development methodology should establish practices that ensure the resulting software is reliable, easily extensible, portable, maintainable, and well-documented.

1.3.3 Apply Appropriate Technology

The most appropriate technology should be used to solve the user's need or problem. Determination of the user's problem must not follow the development of the technology, but rather the user's need must be the driving reason for the introduction of the technology.

1.3.4 Use Existing Resources

Many parallel developments are occurring in information systems development and computer science. Techniques must be employed which ensure that available resources are utilized, and developers are aware of relevant work that has been completed or is ongoing. These awareness techniques include the use of consultants, colleagues, conferences/seminars, site visits, information publication and services, vendor packages, and publically-available software.

1.3.5 Gain Experiences

Direct experience provides valuable understanding and insights into user needs, the development processes, and the application of new technologies. It is desirable to take advantage of opportunities to gain experiences through the development of pilot applications addressing real user needs and problems.

1.3.6 Adhere to Standards

Architectural choices, which allow taking advantage of the new technologies as they develop, are extremely important. To this end, development and adherence to standards in such areas as operating systems, programming languages, networks, software architecture, data-base management systems, information representation, user-computer interface, application-foundation software interface are critical to the support of stepwise transitions.

1.3.7 Define the Information Representations

A central issue in an information-handling system is the representation and organization of the information it handles. The information collection accumulates over long periods of time, and it must be built consistently. In computer-based information systems, design attention must focus primarily on the data representations, data formats, file organizations and data management procedures, and secondarily upon the processes which operate on the information. Information must be recorded at a level of detail to support all the intended uses, and must be independent of any specific use, operating system, programming language, or input/output device.

1.3.8 Plan for the Long-Term

Planning and cost justification should be done with appropriate consideration for the long-term use. In information handling systems, it is not unusual for programmes to operate for 10-20 years with frequent and repeated use.

1.4 Communications Support and Networking

Communications and networking are fundamental components of any information system. Reliability and effectiveness of the information-delivery mechanisms are factors which can dramatically influence the distribution and the actual use of the information managed by a system. Therefore it is extremely important, in the design phase of an information system, to carefully consider the communications support to adopt and to select the most appropriate structure for information flow structure and the most suitable technology available. In general the solution is not represented by a single technology but by a combination of different inter-connected means. In the layered structure suggested for the information systems in China, for example, an integrated use of high technologies, along with conventional and even traditional ones could support the various layers as well as the exchange of information between different layers. Let's consider, layer by layer, the communications needs and propose possible solutions.

1.4.1 Communication Support for the Lower Layer

Communication from local information agencies to SMEs should take advantage, at least in the first phase of development of the information systems, of all the traditional means (Fig. 1.4-A).

Although the ideal solution for the SMEs would be the direct access of local data-bases, there are many objective constraints for the SMEs which presently do not make this solution feasible, namely:

- meagre financial resources;
- scarce availability of communication equipment and sometimes even non-availability of telephone;
- lack of expertise in developing and accessing data-bases.

In the first phase the local information agencies could create small-scale networks covering a well defined geographical area for an homogeneous group of SMEs. The information needs of the SMEs could be determined by directly interviewing the enterpreneurs. The dissemination of the information could be based on a variety of means according to the nature of the information. For instance, the telex or telefax systems, when available, are very effective for volatile information (see sec. 5.3). More static information could be distributed via paper using the postal service or even by visiting the users and directly passing on the information. The agencies might plan to have mobile offices installed in cars and periodically visit each of the SMEs served in order to deliver the information and at the same time study how to improve the service. Periodically updated public information panels could be created to satisfy specific information needs of groups of SMEs and dedicated mail-boxes could be used to collect requests from the users.

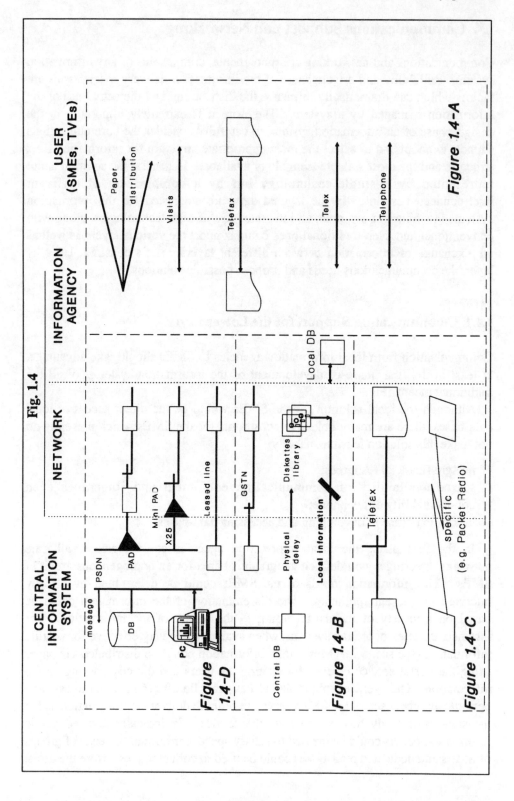

Fig. 1.4

In any case the central role played by the local information agencies in gathering, sorting and distributing the information, is important. The human intervention at least as far as this phase and this layer is concerned is fundamental.

1.4.2 Communication Support for the Intermediate Layer

The intermediate layer scenario consists of well developed information systems at regional level, managed by co-ordinating agencies, along with smaller, more specific information systems (basically subsets of the regional systems) run at the SMEs level. The flow of the information from the center towards the periphery and vice-versa (see Fig. 1.4-B) could be supported mainly by magnetic media (diskettes, tapes, etc.). Optical disks, when the optical readers are available, could be a good support for durable or slowly changing information.

The physical exchange of data sets is reliable and inexpensive and at the same time avoids telecommunications problems. Two major constraints for such exchanges could be:

i) the objective delays (such as overhead time for downloading, filing, transportation, gathering and management of the information) involved;
ii) the limited size of the files that could be exchanged.

In order to reach remote places (see Fig. 1.4-C) or when the exchange of information via magnetic media is not feasible, a valuable alternative could be the use of Packet Radio systems (see sec. 4.2). This system, which is easily affordable for the SMEs, could combine the benefits of tha data-transmission with low transmission costs and independence from the local telephone networks which are usually not reliable enough in most developing countries.

1.4.3 Communication Support for the Higher Layer

The higher layer includes large information systems (preferably DDBMS's), the use of nation-wide or world-wide networks and the availability of all the modern information services (see Fig. 1.4-D).

A very favourable supporting system for the information distribution in this layer is the Packet Switched Data Network. Its main features are the following:

- error protected transmission;
- standard procedures;
- lower cost than other on-line transmission means;
- no need for specific investments.

China already has a PSDN which serves only eleven cities. In future it is desirable that a larger number of entry points for the PSDN system be set up. At the present the General Switched Telephone Network (GSTN) has, even with MNP, low communication quality and often high costs especially for file transfer are involved.   Leased dedicated lines are rare and expensive.   It would be convenient to create, in collaboration with the telecommunications office, a structure where local information agencies could get access to the regional, national and international data-bases through the telephone network connected to the PSDN system.

The principal factors to consider are the following:

- which geographical areas to cover;
- which other areas should be covered by additional public or private small-size PAD's connected to existing nodes as X25 customers;
- which are the costs involved;
- which standard for PAD parameters management to adopt;
- the requirements of the error-protection procedures like MNP (CCITT V42) on the PAD entries;
- the use of X25/SDLC Frontal switches such as TRT's CP90 where a main processor does not have X25 software at its disposal.

The answers to these questions should be different according to the types of information transfer: short transactions, file transfers, requirement of transparency, etc.

1.5 From Pilot to National System

1.5.1 Basic Considerations

The direct use of information systems is the most effective way to draw SMEs and TVEs nearer to the modern information management technologies. User needs surveys provide valuable indicators of the expectations of the users but their outcomes cannot be considered as the best ground to build up new information systems. Only through the practical use of the services provided by information systems the actual information needs of the SMEs and TVEs can be arrived at and thus their fulfilment becomes the moving target of the information system development process.

In this framework the pilot system must be considered more as a market experience than a technical exercise and its main goal should be to develop a deeper knowledge of the needs and the potential benefits to the SMEs and TVEs.

In order to reach its target in a relatively short time, the pilot system must be designed avoiding any technical complexities, but paying extreme attention to the quality of the information provided. A dynamic and trial-and-error approach should be used to match the information produced to the expectations and new requirements of the users.

The pilot system should rely on available resources. Small computers and standard Chinese-adapted software should be the basic tools to use. The distribution of printed materials like catalogues or short reports could be the first information delivery mechanism to be adopted. Communication facilities such as telex or telefax and data communication services may be used as they become available.

Since SMEs and TVEs will not be able to directly deal with any information system in the near future, an information-brokers system, supported by a network of information agencies, should be the skeleton of the system. This approach will require careful recruitment and training of the information brokers who will act as interface between the information system and the users. They will provide the users with information and advices and they will gather feed-back and new requests in order to improve the service.

The performance of the information brokers will be crucial for the success of the pilot project and could even determine the growth of the system from pilot to national. The success of a local experience could represent a significant incentive for the replication of the experiment in other regions and could boost the whole SIPS programme.

A four-stage plan is proposed as follows:

1.5.2 Stage 1

A specific region should be selected for the pilot experience (possibly the Chong Ming County (see sec. 5.3)). The county information-agency (see Fig. 1.5.1) agency should be equipped wih a microcomputer configured with proper disk storage capacity and a good printer in order to manage the local data-bases and to produce good quality catalogues and printouts.

Standard software products should be preferred in order to avoid unnecessary delays caused by direct development of the software. The first data-bases, allowing collection, retrieval, and printing of information, could concern:

- lists of SMEs and TVEs;
- lists of qualified persons;
- TVEs products and technologies;
- raw material suppliers; etc.

A small group of information brokers should be trained and work on an homogeneous group of TVEs. Their main task should be the gathering of the information, the distribution of printed materials, the meeting of managers and technicians of the TVEs, etc.

When specific needs are detected the information brokers will contact the county information agency through any available communication channel. At the county center, the technical support personnel will process the requests of the information brokers. This support personnel will be trained to operate on microcomputer-based systems. They will be able to retrieve the required information from the local data-bases as well as update the data-bases with fresh data collected by the brokers. The questions-answers process as well as the data-bases and printed materials produced will be based on Chinese language.

When the system will be fine-tuned the county center will be able to answer around 90% of the questions submitted using its local data-bases. For more complex questions the county center will request the support of the regional or national centers using any available communication facility. The technical staff of the regional and national centers will be able to access regional, national or even international data-bases. The information retrieved, if necessary, will be translated in Chinese before being sent back to the county center.

1.5.3 Stage 2

Figure 1.5.2 shows the improvements foreseen in Stage 2. The communication between county and regional/national centers will be based on file-transferring systems. The preferable channel should be the Chinese Packet Switched Network CHINAPAC and the transmission modality should be the simple asynchronous connection through the PAD facilities. The technical staff of the county centers will

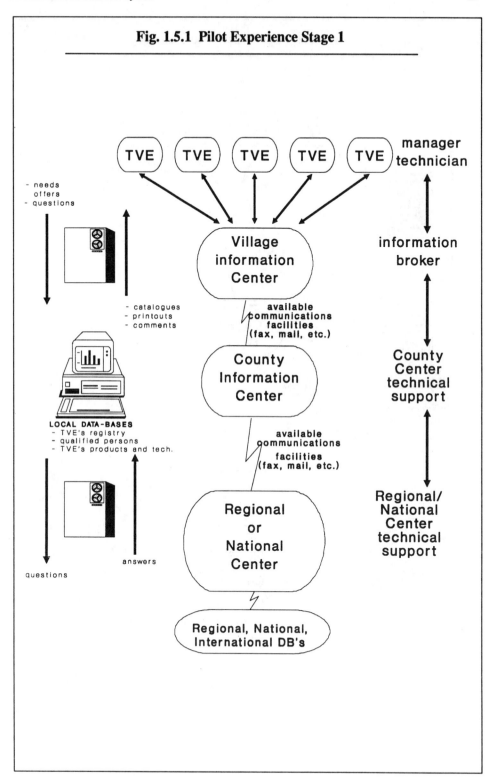

Fig. 1.5.1 Pilot Experience Stage 1

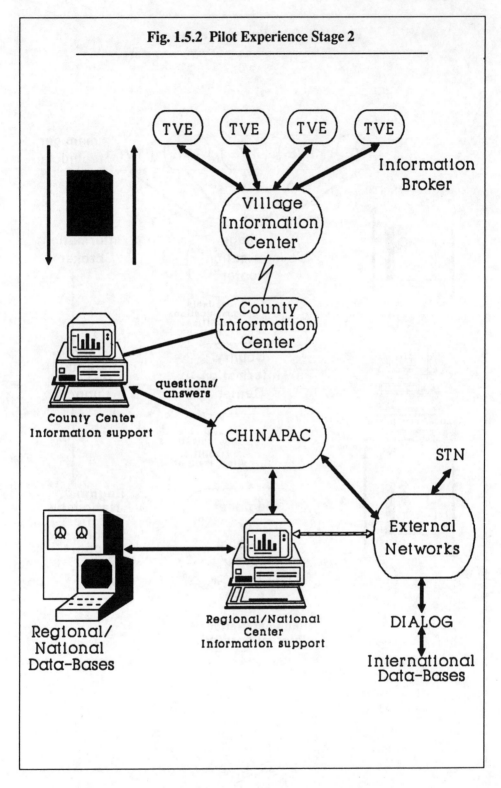

Fig. 1.5.2 Pilot Experience Stage 2

send the questions, in the form of message-files, to the regional or national centers. At this level the corresponding technical staff will receive the questions on their microcomputers and will try to retrieve the desired information referring to the available regional, national or international data-bases. The answers (translated in Chinese if necessary) will be forwarded to the requesting center as normal text-files. Once the pilot system has been properly fine-tuned, Stage 1 and 2 might be replicated in different counties in order to get further feed-back from different regions and types of enterprises.

1.5.4 Stage 3

In the third stage of the information systems development, some of the SMEs and TVEs will own microcomputers and therefore have the possibility of using these equipment to send/receive information to/from the county centers (see Fig. 1.5.3). Different county centers will be able to exchange information in electronic format using either a simple electronic mail system or maintaining a central data-base. If the second option is selected, it is preferable that the update procedures are made in batch mode instead of on-line in order not to complicate the system.

At this stage the county centers personnel will be trained to retrieve information directly from regional, national or international data-bases.

1.5.5 Stage 4

If the volume of information handled and the number of interactions among county centers become too big to be handled by the system described in Stage 3, a Distributed Data-Base System may be built, with sophisticated facilities like on-line updates and procedure-transparency (see Fig. 1.5.4). At that point user needs will be clearly known and the information brokers well trained; the users will be aware of the potentials of the information systems, and modern communication services will be widely available in China.

1.5.6 Final Remarks

In each stage of the information system development, TVEs and SMEs should be obliged, as normal users, to pay for the information services received. This is important because the users have to understand the value of the information they get and also it is desirable that the system should approach self-sufficiency. Moreover this idea would help the managers of TVEs and SMEs to become cost-conscious, to minimize the expenses and to maximize the efficiency in each stage of the development.

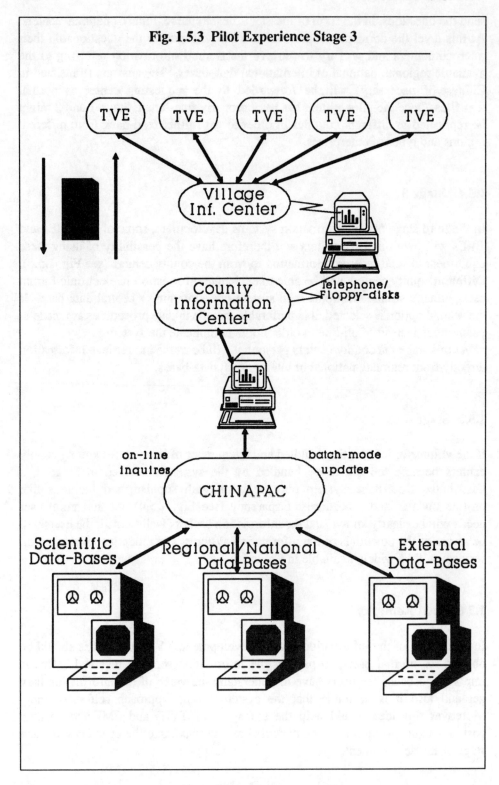

Fig. 1.5.3 Pilot Experience Stage 3

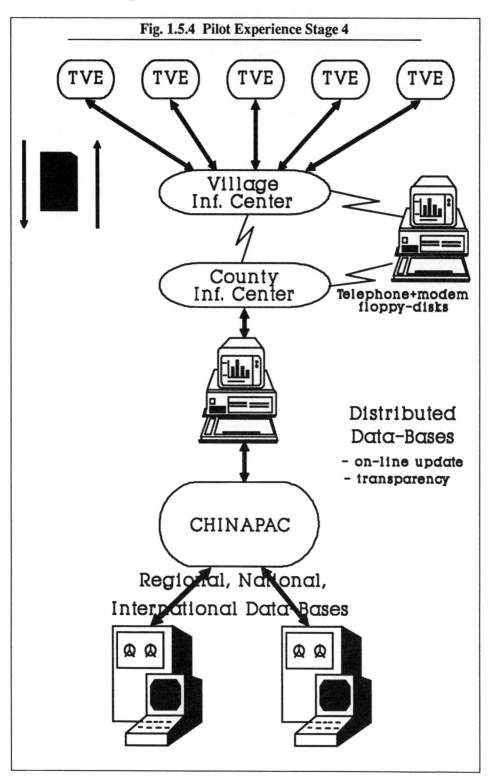

Fig. 1.5.4 Pilot Experience Stage 4

2 Determining the Needs

Summary

This section addresses the first phase of the development of the information systems for SMEs, namely, the analysis of the information needs and user cosiderations.

The papers, which form this section, provide:

- a general view of the needs of the SMEs;
- specific information-needs of the technical personnel of the SMEs;
- a comparative analysis of user expectations and actual benefits produced by information systems;
- an illustrative description of the use of information systems in Brazil and considerations about the evolution of user needs through the adoption of information systems.

2.1 Information Needs of Small and Medium Enterprises

Zhou Zhiyou

Personnel in an enterprise is the main user of the information system. Studying their information needs is a very important task for establishing an information system and information industry, as both system and industry serve the user. The user is the starting point as well as the destination of the system and industry. Enterprises can be divided into three categories: large, medium and small. This paper mainly discusses the information needs of small and medium-size enterprises.

At present, there are no clear-cut definitions in China for small and medium size enterprises (SMEs) and concepts of them vary with the developing of economy. In the 1950's, they were roughly divided in the light of their production capability of various trades, and in the 1960's, according to the number of people employed or the original value of fixed assets. In 1978, they were divided again according to their production capability; and in 1985, with respect to the original value of fixed assets and the amount of profits turned over to the state. For instance, enterprises which possess the original value of fixed assets of 3 million yuan and an annual profit of 0.3 million yuan belong to SMEs. However, the original value of fixed assets and production capability are the two criteria used in the 1988 "China Statistics Yearbook" for dividing enterprises. The present trend is that enterprises are divided with the two criteria combined. However foreign countries [9] consider SMEs to be generally enterprises with up to 100-200 workers.

According to the Yearbook, in China there are overall 493,573 industrial enterprises, of which 483,708 are small and 6957 are medium-size enterprises. These two represent 99,4% of the total, with an output accounting for 69.0% of China's total industrial output value and employees accounting for more than 78% of the total industrial labour force in China.

Furthermore, with a rural economy, township enterprises have grown very fast in recent years. According to statistics of the year 1987, there are 1.58 million township enterprises with 47 million workers, that is 12.38% of China's labour force in rural areas, its related output value is below the level mentioned above. Because township enterprises are such a high number, they are not statistically brought into line with SMEs.

2.1.1 Information Needs in SMEs

In the early 1970's, the British government began to take more interest in small business needs and set up a Committee of Enquiry under the chairmanship of John Bolton. This Committee presented its report in 1971 [10].

The Institute of Scientific and Technical Information of China (ISTIC) pays a great deal of attention to the information needs in SMEs and has made several sample investigations in 1981, 1982, 1984 and 1986. The survey results are described as follows: we think that "the information needs in SMEs" are a collective concept which may be expressed by following the requirements of two types of personnel.

2.1.1.1 The Information Needs of Management Personnel of SMEs.

Management personnel, comprising persons engaged in management and administration, in particular leaders at various levels in enterprises, are willing to have a clear understanding about the macro-information in areas of technology, economy and management, such as recent developments, trends, market supply and demand, new products, technology policies etc. As they are heavily engaged, they are not so interested in information with technical details, but they have an interest in concentrated information which is brief and to the point. For the decision-making requirements, they prefer that information can offer many alternatives to select and relate the marketing prospects of products and the superiorities and inferiorities in producing this data in line with the technological forecast. There is no need to give details of the technological specifications and requirements but to replace them with necessary data. The information should be reliable and systematic and technical terms which are too specialized and profound should be avoided. The form of "brief reports" is widely used to provide such information for leaders at all levels. Apart from brief reports, they are also interested in reviews, trends and popularized materials compiled by information organizations.

Surveys on the foreign language ability of management personnel in enterprises were made in 1981 [1], and it was found that those who have foreign language proficiency account for only 1.2%; those who can roughly read materials in foreign languages, 8.8%; and those who can hardly read, 90%. As large numbers of energetic young and middle-aged cadres with professional knowledge have been promoted to various leading posts in recent years, the situation may have slightly improved. But as this means no fundamental chance, the information provided should primarily be in the Chinese language.

It can be seen from the sample investigations made on 200 SMEs in 1986 [1] that 84% of them are in urgent need of information about new product development, which ranks first among all information needed. SMEs often introduce sample products from foreign manufacturers and hand them over to technicians for redrawing and analyzing in order to gain useful information on product development. The same survey shows that this kind of information ranks third among information sources needed, the first and second apply to standards and trade literature. It is expressed by 43% of the sample enterprises that this kind of information is in urgent need.

Moreover, leaders at all levels in enterprises often have chances to attend meetings. In the same survey, it is indicated by leaders of 32 enterprises that technical interchange meetings are ideal channels for collecting information, because from such meetings much vital and dynamic information can be gained from attending lectures, visiting and talking with participants.

In comparison with the results of a similar survey in Kyoto, Japan [6], it can be seen that they are above all interested in "professional information" which reflects the trends of respective trade and which accounts for 49.4% of all enterprises management information. However, in China this kind of information ranks second after the "new product development information".

It was reported by Silva (NOBIN) in Haque [11], that only 20% of SMI managers expected any significant contribution to their firms productivity from external information. In 1987, a survey [12] of technical managers in Australian firms enquired about unsatisfying information needs. The answers are summarized in the following table:

<table>
<tr><td colspan="2" align="center">**Table 2.1.1**</td></tr>
<tr><td>Unsatisfied information needs</td><td align="center">managers concerned</td></tr>
<tr><td>Corporate intelligence
(e.g. competition, markets, products)</td><td align="center">22</td></tr>
<tr><td>None</td><td align="center">20</td></tr>
<tr><td>Properly tailored information</td><td align="center">18</td></tr>
<tr><td>Data-Base access</td><td align="center">13</td></tr>
</table>

Thus so, they are desperate for information on competition, markets and products. Information from data-bases is the most satisfactory. The situation is similar in some respect to our own country.

2.1.1.2 Information Needs of Technical Personnel in Enterprises

Technical staff are mostly engaged in concrete technological work and the information they need differs from that management personnel. They prefer the information to be:

1) practicable so as to be applied to production technologies;
2) in greater detail;
3) related to technology development in respective trade areas;
4) used as background knowledge which is necessary sometimes to understand the interdisciplinary technologies;
5) of some search capability so as to allow proper use of secondary documents.

In comparison to scientific research and educational personnel, technical personnel in enterprises in China spend less time on collecting, processing and exploiting information (the respective time spent accounts for 14.52%, 16.63% and 12.8% of their overall working time). This is because our enterprises have a rather slow rate in upgrading and updating their technological products. New products are first developed by scientific research institutes, universities and colleges and then the results are transferred to enterprises. Thus, technical personnel in enterprises are not as eager to adapt to new technological advances as much as scientific research and educational workers are. Furthermore, the technical personnel in enterprises have less chance to engage in further education in foreign languages and in many enterprises there is no information department at all (the 1986 survey [4] indicates that 58% of SMEs do not have information departments). If there are any, they are generally inadequately equipped (the same survey reveals that the per capita copying of materials in enterprises is only 1.73 and information offices where conditions are somewhat better have only one or two copiers and typewriters).

According to one survey made in 1981 [1], the ranking of information sources which technical personnel use is:

1) trade literature;
2) books;
3) periodicals;
4) reports;
5) patents;
6) technical standards;
7) conference proceedings.

The corresponding order we found out in a 1986 survey [4] is:

1) standards;
2) trade literature;
3) sample products;
4) product data;
5) patents;
6) other documents.

According to American data presented in 1985, the information-seeking habits amongst scientists and engineers are the following: almost three-quarters of the

Table 2.1.2

Services supplied	increase %	stayed same %	decrease %
Current Awareness Service	53	30	18
Enquiry Service	55	37	7
System/Data-Base Advice	67	27	6
Literature Searching in Hard Copy	22	31	46
On-line Searching	29	7	3

respondents said they could not get the information they needed from their libraries. Two-thirds of the respondents wanted facts more often than just conceptual ideas, opinions and advice [12]. Table 2.1.2 summarizes how the services offered by British industrial information units changed over a period of six years from the late 1970's onwards.

Table 2.1.2 shows that: manual searching decreased significantly,on-line searching increased significantly during this period. According to an American survey in 1987, the factors which influence on-line searching are shown in table 2.1.3. We can see that most of American users (67.6-80.0%) are satisfied or very satisfied with on-line searching, dissatisfied users are more seldom (2.9-5.9%), but most of them are not willing to spend too much time on studying computerized searching techniques. The situation in our country is almost the same. Thus, the terminal operators in information organizations must continuously devote time for up-dating. Computerized searching must be simple and easy to practice and follow so as to facilitate users to operate on the terminal. A lot of work must still be done

Table 2.1.3

(Values in percentage)

Factors relating to	very dissatisfied	dissatisfied	neither satisfied nor dissatisfied	satisfied	very satisfied
on-line bibliographic searching	0	5.9	23.5	58.8	11.8
relevance of output to needs	0	5.9	26.4	58.8	8.8
time between request and receipt of output	0	2.9	17.1	51.4	28.6

in this respect.

The corresponding marks given to information sources by British Chemists in 1965 are shown in Table 2.1.4 (The highest mark is 9)

Table 2.1.4

	Reviews	Abstracts	Meetings	Periodicals	Personal contacts	Libraries	Patents	Reports	Hand-Books
CA	7	5	5	4	3	3	1	1	0
RS	3	6	1	6	4	4	1	0	3

With respect to Table 2.1.4 it is known that technical personnel in China's enterprises more often than not uses standards and trade literature as well as product data and sample products, whereas reviews and abstracts which are highly valued by foreign chemists are seldom used. In this connection, an analysis can be made as follows:

Why does the use of standards move from the sixth place to the first [4]? This is because our government has been practicing international technical standards for checking products in recent years, especially export products; and at the same time, the national standards are closing up to ISO and IEC standards. All this cannot but exert a tremendous influence on enterprises.

Patent literature is generally seldom used and the rank of its utilization is low both at home and abroad. It may be that it is low abroad because the object fields under survey are chemists engaged in basic research. In China, however, patent literature should be normally used regularly by technical personnel who are engaged in technology development. Besides, patent literature is in general novel, advanced and concrete as well as figures and tables. The reasons why it is seldom used may be:

1) the poor information handling capability of technical personnel. It is found that even in the industrially well-developed Shanghai municipality, from among 100,000 technical personnel of industrial and transport departments there are only 1,000 persons who are able to use abstract and index journals in foreign languages. According to our 1986 survey [4], among technical personnel in SMEs, 19.5% are poor-qualified; 74.5%, average-qualified and only 6%, well-qualified.
2) The foreign language ability of technical personnel is low. One survey made in 1981 [1] showed that among the engineers and technicians, 1.1% have an excellent foreign language ability, 5,2% good, and 68.8% have average foreign language ability, (they are capable of reading materials in foreign languages with some difficulties) while 24.9% have poor foreign language ability.
3) There are a few big cities which have patent literature collections.

According to our 1986 survey [4] , it is worthy to notice that books, periodicals, technical reports and conference papers all drop to the lower ranks, and reviews and abstracts are even more seldom used. This may be due to the fact that the documents are so excessively concentrated in a few big cities such as Beijing and Shanghai that the technical personnel of SMEs cannot have easy access to them. According to our 1984 survey [3] on 40 technical personnel from SMEs, 32% of them mentioned that it was very difficult to search for documents, 61% found it was difficult and only 7% thought it was easy. (see Fig. 2.1.1.1). As for the searching technique, 89.2% stated that it was not sufficient and only 10.8% said it was good. This situation has been improved recently, since document retrieval and utilization courses have been set up in many universities and colleges and, at the same time, the training of users has been strengthened by information organizations. Inter-library lending systems have proven to be an effective measure throughout the world. The british Library Lending Division is well known for successfully providing this service. However, this inter-lending service is not implemented yet in our S & T information organization. Our 1984 survey showed that the causes of poor results in searching for documents are:

1) lack of information materials in their organization (32%);
2) lack of search knowledge (26%);
3) impeded information channels and low information sharing (26%);
4) poor foreign language ability (11%);
5) disorganized materials and poor management (2%), see Fig. 2.1.1.2.

In our survey made in 1986 [4], it can be seen that the obstacles in information exchange in SMEs are:

1) inadequate information facilities;
2) lack of information personnel;
3) lack of information materials;

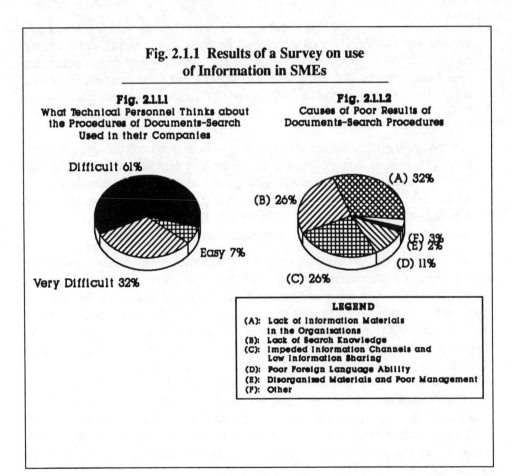

Fig. 2.1.1 Results of a Survey on use of Information in SMEs

Fig. 2.1.1.1
What Technical Personnel Thinks about the Procedures of Documents-Search Used in their Companies

Fig. 2.1.1.2
Causes of Poor Results of Documents-Search Procedures

Difficult 61%

Very Difficult 32%

Easy 7%

(A) 32%

(B) 26%

(F) 3%
(E) 2%
(D) 11%

(C) 26%

LEGEND
(A): Lack of Information Materials in the Organizations
(B): Lack of Search Knowledge
(C): Impeded Information Channels and Low Information Sharing
(D): Poor Foreign Language Ability
(E): Disorganized Materials and Poor Management
(F): Other

4) insufficient funds;
5) impeded information exchange channels;
6) weak information awareness;
7) low educational level;
8) strong information secrecy.

The survey reflects the current situation of a weak foundation and poor conditions of information services in China's SMEs.

SMEs exist in a social environment full of fierce competition. Especially export-oriented enterprises face competition from relevant foreign enterprises. Only by possessing an advanced information awareness and making good use of various information sources they can survive in competition. It is known that five big Japanese trade enterprises have information personnel of up to 14,000 persons residing abroad with annual expenses in telecommunication amounting to 260 million s$ (Singapore Dollar). They collect a vast amount of texts from all the parts of the world every day. The Tokyo Office of Marubeni Corporation alone receives texts equal to 800 newspaper pages each day. However, in our 1986 survey [4], product data and other materials only rank 4th and 6th; hence, if SMEs wish to hold their ground in world competition, mush work remains to be done in order to bridge the gap in this connection.

2.1.2 The Comparison of Information Needs of Urban SMEs and Rural Township Enterprises

Based on our 1986 sample investigation made for both groups of enterprises [4] [5], we can make comparisons with the following five aspects:

2.1.2.1 The Kind of Information Needed

Information on new product development holds the first place out of the information needed for both enterprises, while information on foreign trade and finance ranks last. The information needs of technology introduction, equipment updating and business management rank 2nd, 3rd and 4th respectively in TVEs, while the information needs of market quotations, production forecast and production technology rank 2nd, 3rd and 4th respectively in SMEs.

2.1.2.2 The Information Sources Used

The domestic standards and sample products rank 1st and 3rd in both enterprises, and domestic and foreign patent literature rank 5th, 7th in TVEs and 6th in SMEs;

Table 2.1.5

Information channel	Social intercourse	Radio & TV	Comanagement units	Information networks	Consultants	Specialized technical meetings
TVEs	1	5	11	19	13	20
SMEs	14	15	22	8	23	10

while product data and foreign standards rank 2nd and 6th in TVEs and 5th and 2nd in SMEs.

2.1.2.3 The Information Channels Used

The use of more than 20 information channels has been surveyed and the use of most of these is almost the same for both types of enterprises with the exception of 6 channels which are listed in Table 2.1.5. From Table 2.1.5 it can be seen that TVEs pay more attention to information channels, such as social intercourse, radio and T.V., co-management units and consultants, while SMEs lay particular emphasis on information networks and specialized technical meetings. Here, the information networks create an exchange links which is formed through meetings and journal exchanging etc. under the condition of backward telecommunication technology in China. The information networks have a history of development covering more than 20 years, they grew rapidly in the 1960's and early 1980's. At present, there are more than 600 comprehensive information networks in China. The specialized technical meetings are mainly organized by the Association for Science and Technology and professional societies. Owing to the weak technical force, TVEs have not made use of the two information channels as yet.

2.1.2.4 The Information Assimilation and Digestion Ability.

The ability to assimilate and digest information of SMEs is in a position slightly below the middle level. TVEs are thirsty for information (0.79 marks), fast in updating product (0.67 marks), because "the boat is small, so it is easy to turn around", middle rank in equipment adaptability (0.57 marks). But they are impeded in credit channel (-0.24 marks) and short of funds (0.4 marks), and these two factors are the key factors which affect their ability to assimilate and digest information.

2.1.2.5 The Barriers in Information Exchange

75% of SMEs have expressed that there are barriers varying in degrees which by rank are: information facilities, information personnel, information materials, information funds, information exchange channels, information awareness, the average educational level and information secrecy. In city enterprises, by rank: information materials, information funds, information facilities, information secrecy, information awareness, time and transport. So, it can be seen that TVEs have more obstacles than SMEs with materials, funds and secrecy. SMEs stress on the barriers in information facilities, while a few TVEs (18.1% and 21.72%) have specific problems with time and transport.

Conclusions

(1) The SMEs represent a comprehensive economic body which in itself calls for diverse information needs.
(2) SMEs face fierce competition. To survive and develop their organizations, they have to strive hard to acquire up-to date information through certain channels in short lengths of time.
(3)Leaders at all levels in SMEs have come to understand the importance of information for correct decision-making. However, a specific process is required to transform their recognition into action. They need to be clear about how to utilize information work for their own benefit, therefore, training efforts for them should be strengthened. The computerized searching procedures must be simple and easy to practice, so as to enable users to operate on the terminal directly.
(4)Technical personnel and information workers in SMEs are very small in number (the latter account for only 2.7%) and are low in quality. They are accustomed to collect information by means of social intercourse (e.g. business trips, meetings and visits, etc.). This is by far insufficient. The facilitation and dissemination of information knowledge (especially knowledge on looking up and using documents) should be enhanced and the work should be supported by society and the mass media.
(5)The existing conventional pattern of scientific and technical information work is largely unsuitable for the information needs of SMEs which become increasingly varied and comprehensive, hence, the system reform should be carried out from top to bottom.
(6)Attention should be paid in giving priority to the provision of and assistance with information materials, funds and facilities for SMEs in order to create the necessary working conditions for information centres.

References

[1] Liang Quianwen, Huo Shuniu, The Information Needs, "Practical Handbook of Scientific and Technical Information", 1982, Editor-in-chief: Zhou Zhiyou, Chapter 3, pp. 90-110, Information Science Journal Publisher, Harbin (In Chinese).

[2] Chen Binggang, Hu Shuniu, The Information Needs and Users Study, "A Brief Introduction to Scientific and Technical Information Work", 1984, pp. 499-531, Publishing House of Documentation for Science and Technology, Beijing (in Chinese).

[3] Zhou Zhiyou, Du Xiaojian, The Information Environment and Information Services for Small and Medium-Size Enterprises must be promptly improved, Journal of the "Information Science", 1984, Vol.5, No.6, pp. 93-96 (in Chinese).

[4] Chen Zhaonan, Zhou Zhiyou, Liu Dongwei, etc., " Case Study on Information Needs of Urban Medium and Small-Size Enterprises", The Institute of Scientific and Technical Information of China, Beijing, 1986, p. 40 (in Chinese).

[5] Huo Shuniu, Rui Guozhang, Zhao Dihua, etc., "Case Study on Information Needs of Township Enterprises", The Institute of Scientific and Technical Information of China, Beijing, 1986, p. 26 (in Chinese).

[6] "Information Practice" Edited by Human Institute of Scientific and Technical Information, 1983, Changsha, 1st volume (in Chinese).

[7] What kind of Information Enterprises Need? Japan "Measurement Instrument", 1982, No.4 (in Japanese).

[8] Vickery, B.C., Techniques of Information Retrieval, 1970, p. 53-57, Butterwork, London.

[9] Dr. L.V.Chico, Small and Medium-Size Industries in the Asia-Pacific Region: Their Information Needs and Technonet Asia's Response. The Use of Information in a Changing World, FID, 1984, pp. 365-371.

[10] D.Kennington, Use of Information in the Small Industrial Firm, ibid. 1984, pp. 373-380.

[11]R.H. de Silva, Document, Information and the Small Industrial Firm, ibid. 1984, pp. 381-384.

[12] J.Meadows. How Can the Information Industry Serve its Customers?, 44th FID Conference and Congress, Finland Aug. 26-Sept 1, 1988, Participants' Edition, part 3, edited by P. Hamalainen etc. IFID.FSIS 1988, pp. 5-12.

2.2 Better Information Service to Engineers in SMEs

Du Baorong, Zhang Baoming

With the deepening development of China's economic structure reform and the transformation of unitary planned economy to commodity economy with the guidance of planned economy, great changes are taking place in the constitution of information users. The law of commodity economy determines that, if an enterprise wants to exist, it has to manufacture the products based on market needs and renew the products according to market changes. In other words, if an enterprise wants to win in competition, it has to rely upon scientific, technical and economic information to unceasingly develop new products suited to the need of clients. Therefore, small-medium enterprises (including township enterprises) which occupy 99.6% of the total enterprises in China have become main users of information and major markets of information products. They not only require voluminous S & T information for their engineers to develop new products, but also need business information, such as product price, supply and demand, market forecasts, even activities of companies and factories, financial information, production and management information for administrators to make decisions. These new information needs, like a mighty torrent, vigorously pound the obsolete pattern of information services. Especially for ISTIC which mainly served the research institutes by providing scientific literature as the only means in the past, this is a severe challenge. It has forced us to ponder over and seek after a new pattern for information service.

In recent years, we have made experiments in the following aspects. At one hand, new information sources are looked for, service patterns improved and service items opened up to meet new demand of users. On the other, promotion work and user training is strengthened to increase information awareness of users, upgrade their diathesis and their ability of information digestion, utilization and absorption. Up to the present, these trials have reached initial results and they are appreciated by users from small-medium enterprises.

2.2.1 Developing and Utilizing New Information Sources

2.2.1.1 To Strengthen Collection of Various Product-Business Information

Domestic and foreign trade literature, business newspapers, directory of companies, list of products, all kinds of yearbooks and manuals are main information sources which we are collecting to provide information to

small-medium enterprises. In recent years, we have collected these materials
through all channels and by all occasions (such as by exhibitions or trade fairs).

2.2.1.2 To Fully Utilize Data-Bases of Business Information in International On-Line Retrieval Systems

Our division is connected to international on-line retrieval systems such as
DIALOG, ORBIT-INFOLINE, BRS, STN, ESA-IRS etc. In the past, we only
retrieved S&T bibliographical information, and paid no attention to the satisfactory
wide-ranging (DIALOG in particular) of data-bases of business information (such
as information on companies, commodities, finance, business activities and trade
marks). However, beginning last year, we have intentionally strengthened
utilization of these data-bases. Systematic analysis was made by persons specially
assigned on contents and searching methods of data-bases, and popularization
work was carried out among division staffs and users in a planned way. Starting
from this year, these data-bases have been successfully accessed to provide
small-medium enterprises with information on manufacturers and companies, price
of products and raw materials etc.

2.2.1.3 To Make Use of Outside Information Source

All kinds of exhibitions and trade fairs are important information sources for
collecting tangible samples, trade literature, marketing information and
information about price and manufacturers. If necessary, we also make use of
these outside information sources in accordance with the special demands of users.

Government agencies are reliable information sources for domestic commodity
production, conditions of importation and exportation etc. We once utilized this
material to analyze the output of production, quantity volume of importation and
exportation and nationalized level of certain products for small-medium
enterprises.

2.2.2 Changing Service Pattern and Improving Service Efficiency

2.2.2.1 Comprehensive Service Structure

In the past, we contacted our retrieval users mainly by visits, letters and telephones.
These patterns reflected not only slowness, but also ambiguity of user's real need.
In order to enhance the dissemination efficiency and accuracy of information, a
facsimile machine was installed last year. Now, users can send their queries and

we reply them (the result could be titles, texts, data and diagrams) through fax. It needs to specially mention here that the queries we receive through fax are not directly from small-medium enterprises, but via information agencies in some small or medium cities (such as Dandong, Yichang and Ningbo etc.). By doing so, the advantages of local information agencies familiar with their own user's needs can be brought into full play. At the same time, the advanced and complete retrieval means and qualified professionals of the national information centre can provide more and better services. Information agencies at different levels closely cooperate to serve small-medium enterprises with timely and accurate information. They characterize a comprehensive service structure which shows the combination of national and local information centres serving jointly small-medium enterprises.

2.2.2.2 To Provide Feasibility Reports for Importing Technologies and Equipment

To import technologies and equipment is a short-cut for small-medium enterprises to develop new products. In recent years, we have made contracts with certain factories in Anhui and Nanjing to undertake feasibility studies on their import projects. For each subject, a consultation report of several ten-thousand Chinese characters was written and submitted, and voluminous useful materials were provided such as patent documents, trade literature, periodicals, list of factories, quoted price of equipment, technical specifications and technical descriptions (some foreign materials were supplemented with Chinese translations). These reports and materials not only consisted of a comprehensive review of world development, trend, equipment manufacturers and quoted price, but also information on production process, technical specifications of equipment, technical descriptions, raw material components, physical and chemical properties. This information provided a reliable basis for enterprises to make decisions, as well as to solve specific problems. Therefore, enterprise administrators said that our report had saved their several hundred thousand Chinese RMB investment and enterprise engineers said that our report had helped them in solving specific technical problems.

2.2.2.3 To Serve the Application for Research Achievements and Patents

Novelty of research achievements and innovation must be testified by information agencies. Engineers in small-medium enterprises are usually not very clear whether their research achievement and innovation possessing the novelty, therefore, our retrieval service can help them to decide whether they can apply for patents or whether their research achievements are new.

2.2.3 Promoting Commercialization of S&T Achievements

Payment transfer of S&T achievements forms a technology market for sellers and buyers. Both sellers and buyers need an information agency as a "bridge" or an "intermediary". This is a new task entrusted to information workers by a new situation. As a S&T achievement, not only its advantages must be evaluated, but also its applications considered. It is necessary to decide whether their applications can create social or economic benefit, whether the applications are suitable to the present economic developments. In short, it depends on whether or not it is in accordance with social needs and whether or not it is able to improve productivity. We are not only help sellers to choose appropriate buyers who are acceptable to the conditions on investment, raw materials, market and technical assistance, but also help buyers to select sellers who can provide appropriate technologies. Only by doing so, we can play a role of "catalyst" to quickly transform the S&T achievements into productivity, so as to generate better social and economic benefits.

In the process of technology transfer, we can collect much reliable information and this can be considered as a "by product".

2.2.4 User Development

2.2.4.1 To Intensify Promotion Work to Users

At present, many engineers in small-medium enterprises in the country lack information awareness. Random surveys were carried out in 221 township enterprises in three cities of Shantou, Zhongqing and Huhehot. The results showed that only 2.7% to 3.6% of the total engineers asked information agencies or information networks to solve their problems. The rest did not, or not usually did so. They only acquired information through customer feedback, contract meetings, trade fairs, product appraisals and social activities. For these engineers, it is necessary to go further and to increase their information consciousness in order to lead them to be familiar with information source and information products we can provide with so to acknowledge the value of information and finally to become information users.

2.2.4.2 To Enhance User Training

Although some engineers in small-medium enterprises are aware of information sources, they are not familiar with the methodology of searching information. They are inclined to collect information by reading Chinese journals, newspapers,

Chinese and foreign trade literature, but seldom take advantage of retrieval tools to enhance the efficiency. For them, apart from continuously strengthening the information consciousness, it is more important to train them on information methodology, to increase their capability of searching, processing and utilizing information. Surveys were made in Wuxi city: 48% of small-medium enterprises demanded to hold training courses for their own information staff. This is quite understandable.

In recent years, we have held many different types of training courses. In some of them foreign experts were invited to extend lectures (e.g. experts from ESA-IRS, ORBIT, STN, ECHO, etc.). We were also invited by other agencies (including establishments outside of Beijing), academic societies (e.g. the Society of Engineers), conferences and specialized meetings to conduct manual and on-line retrieval courses. We ourselves also conducted several dozens training courses on manual retrieval and on-line retrieval respectively. These courses have trained many information service staff people for small-medium enterprises. In the future, concerning training programs, attention should be paid to information needs of small-medium enterprises. For instance, it is necessary to strengthen the training of searching business information such as information of national and international companies, product information, financial information and business trends etc. Patents, standards and trade literature are fitted in with the needs of small-medium enterprises because they contain a large amount of information. However, at present, many engineers are still not clear with retrieval methods for patents, to the effect that patent documents are not fully utilized. Therefore, the promotion and training work in this aspect also needs to be strengthened.

2.2.4.3 To Compile Training Materials

In recent years, we have compiled, in combination with our work, several dozen books on manual retrieval and on-line retrieval methods, user guides, data-base descriptions and retrieval tools, introductions etc. These publications have played a role both for ourselves and for user training in all parts of the country.

2.3 Factual Data-Base Structure and Development

Keith W. Reynard

2.3.1 Introduction

My main interest and concern over the last five years has been with the computerization of materials data and information. It is a subject more complex than many purely scientific areas with which I am also familiar, such as the physical properties of pure chemical compounds, and so provides an insight into the widest range of problems and pitfalls that are ready for the unwary.

I cannot in this paper provide all the answers but I intend to point to the questions that should be asked and to show where parallels and insights may be found. If in doing this I help in some small way to avoid repetitions of the errors of other workers then I shall have achieved something of value.

I also come to the subject from the point of view of an engineer. In this context that means from the point of view of a user for whom information is a tool to be used in the greater activities of design, analysis and synthesis. For an engineer the data is a necessary thing, some might say a necessary evil, when it is available in the right form at the right time he hardly notices it. When it is not in the right form or not readily available, then it becomes the most irritating obstruction to progress. This is the nub that is often forgotten by the information providers.

2.3.2 Terminology

When in this paper I refer to information I mean all kinds including numerical, descriptive, graphical and pictorial. I also use the term data-base to include what some would call data-banks. I would have preferred to make a distinction but fear that the battle to do so is lost.

2.3.3 The User is the Key to Success

If the information is in the form and of the quality that the user wants then the provider will be well on the road to success. If it is not then failure is inevitable.

Expert systems are not the panacea for all the ills of the information world. Their existence will not necessarily improve any situation. The audience for this paper is an expert system of distributed data-bases. On some topics it will know more and in certain situations individuals will react more quickly and more correctly than any computer. Its combined knowledge and interconnectivity is beyond anything that has yet been mounted on a hard or floppy disk. It also has the benefit of continuous updating and development.

So what can be and is gained by transferring knowledge and information to computers.

- Wider access
- Repeatability
- Long life
- New insights
- Connections

2.3.4 A Successful Data-Base

How does one judge success?

Perhaps the only necessary criterion is that the data-base will have users and that they will be satisfied with it.

Why will the data-base have users and why will it develop?

1) It contains information that is needed
2) The information is in a form that is useable
3) The information is of the quality that is needed
4) The data-base maintains contact with users and responds with changes to meet changing needs and a developing market
5) There is an expert human interface available when required as well as a computerized interface.

2.3.4.1 It Contains Information that is Needed

It is not sufficient for there to be a collection of information that someone thinks should be computerized solely because the collection exists. This road to ruin has been trodden by too many well meaning people in the past. To some extent all those involved in the information world suffer from a tendency to save scraps of information, fill filing cabinets with untraceable documents and extracts from journals and notes of meetings. Now with a computer on the desk the boxes of floppy discs grow in number, the need for a larger hard disk, 150, 300, 600 megabytes and upwards, seems to be always necessary. Why? and is it justified?

In some cases yes. But how often does a spring clean of out-of-date, redundant, useless information leave one with ample capacity to store the next months or years accumulation. We are however all fearful of the commonly observed fact that the piece of paper thrown into the waste paper basket last night had on it the vital bit of information needed today. Wonderful for the suppliers of filing cabinets and discs! However in this activity we are not always trying to 'sell' the collection of information to another person and there lies the great difference between storage for ones own use and storage for others to use. No one else wants most of the contents of our vital junk yard. No one else would pay much for it.

So as suppliers of information we must be selective and provide only what another user wants, and needs, and can use.

2.3.4.2 The Information Must Be in the Form that is Needed

The paperless office is not here yet. For many purposes a hard copy format has significant advantages over a computerized format, so frequently the latter is constructed so as to supply the former as well. But this paper is more concerned with the needs for computerized forms of information transfer.

The use of the word transfer should provoke the two clear lines of thought, the user will always want to take information out of the system, he will quite often want to put it in as well.

If in either of these actions there is difficulty through poor instructions, or through poor presentation of screen or print out or in connection to another program the system will fail. Fail not because the information may be poor, indeed it may be of the highest quality, but fail because it is not useable.

Frequently now computerized scientific and engineering data needs to be accessed by another computer to be used in another program. Typically in engineering, materials data is captured and used directly in a design program that leads on to a program that drives a machine tool. There could be no human interface anywhere in the sequence from data to the finished product. This is the ideal of some production engineers, it is being done in a few specialized cases with a large degree of human checking. But the point is again that if the information at each stage is not presented in the right form for acceptance by the next stage it cannot be used. If the next stage is a human then there is more flexibility and adaptability, if it is a computer program there could be total failure in either case there is the potential loss of a 'customer'.

2.3.4.3 The Information is of the Quality that is Needed

The quality of the information is a term that in isolation covers several aspects. The criteria is fitness for purpose. But fitness for purpose must also be visible to the user and not merely something declared by the provider of information. The labelling of consumer products to show contents and suitability for use is a growing feature of western life. In part this is a consequence of the increase in product liability legislation, in part a greater understanding by the customer of what is required and therefore greater discrimination.

Information may be satisfactory for a rough qualitative comparison or alternatively for the design of a critical component in an aircraft. That which will serve the second purpose will be very expensive to provide, typically costing as much as 1 to 2,000,000 Pounds to provide a designer with data on a single material. Clearly it may also be used for the first purpose but equally clearly data from a journal article may be adequate for the first purpose but an unreliable and even dangerous source for the critical design.

The methods of labelling data and data-bases are now the subject of one of the Sub-committees of ASTM E-49; the Committee on the computerization of materials data. This work is in an early stage as the problems of evaluation and validation of data are not sufficiently widely appreciated and so the difficulties of labelling the results of such labours in a manner that can be understood by users are considerable.

2.3.4.4 The Data-Base Maintains Contact with Users

In the design and preliminary building of a data-base potential users must be consulted at all stages. They will provide comment on the form, the content, the interfaces, the support and possible lines of development. Unless this is done it is very easy for data-base managers to provide aspects that are not required, to assign incorrect priorities to the stages of development or to fail to recognize important potential applications and needs.

In the early stage of running a data-base the data-base manager should contact all users soon after they have used the data-base. Only by this means will he learn of the setbacks, the difficulties and frustrations, as well as the successes and new insights that the user has experienced. Written questionnaires are never as rewarding as personal contact though they will have to be used later in the development of the data-base.

Once the system is running and available to users the contacts must be maintained not just in response to incoming comment and questions but by active research of the attitudes of those who use the data-base and do not comment. These users may well be very satisfied with what they get. Equally they may not or they may have useful and practical comment to make.

2.3.4.5 There is an Expert Human Interface

Hopefully userfriendliness is now the aim of all software writers. Increasingly it is the aim of those providing on-line or disc based services because they have seen how little used and ill-regarded are those systems that are difficult to use and provide meaningless messages in cases of failure. To get messages that do not tell the user what to do and leave him with no access to a real person to explain at a level any user can understand in the quickest way to the failure of a service.

All data-bases should be supported by trained and knowledgeable staff who can be contacted by users for help in case of difficulty and for advice and information related to the data-base. This is one of the parts of a good data-base service that can cost appreciable sums to maintain and yet will promote its use most effectively.

2.3.5 The Need for a Data-Base

Whilst the need for a computerized data-base may be obvious to some in an organization or seen as a marketable product by others, much time and money can be saved if some basic work is done before too many decisions are made. A data flow chart for the department or the company should be drawn. It is likely to be more complex than many would suspect. Figure 2.3.2 constructed by Rolls-Royce indicates some of the features.

This flow chart will show amongst other things where data comes from, what it costs, how much data is used, where it goes, who stores and maintains it - if anyone, how it is used, whether any transformations are made, who has responsibilities at various stages etc. From this a clearer picture will emerge not only of the advantages to be gained by creating a data-base but of the impact that it is likely to have on the work of many people.

The construction of a flow chart can be carried out, though with less precision, on the potential market if the data-base is for wider use in several organizations or is for sale.

This exercise will help to establish more firmly the need for a data-base, its benefits and costs.

2.3.6 Data-Base Construction

The construction of a data-base is a long and expensive task and it will always be sometime before the work is justified by the use that is made of it. Just as one cannot build a wall without the right kind of building blocks and suitable mortar so a data-base depends on the availability of agreed elements and interfaces.

Will the data-base be used only on-line or will it provide information also in the form of floppy disks or hardy copy, or perhaps CD-Rom? Must it be capable of use in more than one language or in more than one set of coherent units such as SI? Is the terminology defined and accessible and likely to be that used and understood by all users?

At the time of the Petten Workshop in 1985 the use of on-line services was given greater weight and had higher prospects than it would be given now. The two main reasons for this are firstly that the power of the PC has grown very rapidly and its availability to engineers has increased. Secondly management is still very reluctant to give the engineer unfettered access to on-line services. It believes that to do so would cause a loss of financial control in an area where the engineer has always been starved of funds, i.e. in the provision of information. This seems to be so even when the vendor is able to put limits on the use to assist management. It also has a fear of engineers using data and information over which it has no control. The use of discrete packages of data and information on a PC is felt to be more manageable. The extent to which either of these points accords with reality is open to question and debate. The fear exists and that is sufficient to provide problems.

Is the interface between the user and the system easy to understand and operate? These and many more questions with recommended approaches are set out in detail in Ref. [13]. This document was compiled by the CODATA Task Group on Materials Data-Base Management. As such it relates specifically to a materials data-base but only a small portion cannot easily be related to other scientific and engineering data-bases. It also contains a comprehensive bibliography on the subject.

A data-base under development should not be shown widely until it has been tested by a selected set of potential users. These should include some non-experts. Their comments and criticisms must be taken into account before the number of users is increased. An interesting instance arose in the recent testing of a new materials data-base dealing with ferrous alloys. A non-metallurgist asked the simple question 'what does it have on steel?' the answer came back 'nothing'. In fact all the data in the data-base was on steel but the constructor of the data-base had failed to consider the possibility of that simple question.

The quantity of information in the data-base should be large enough to ensure that there is a high chance of users finding what they want. A quick way to stop someone coming back is for him to fail to find anything in response to his first few enquiries.

2.3.7 Cost

In any country the question of cost must be considered in the setting up of a new data-base or in the running of an existing one and its maintenance. Someone has to pay for both of these, whether it is the taxpayer providing government with the means to fund the work and the operation, or whether it is the user or some mix of the two depends on the local situations and needs.

However the same factors should be considered in all cases:

- what does it cost to produce the raw data
- what does it cost to evaluate and validate it
- what is the value of the data input to the data-base

- what does it cost to put the data into the data-base
- what is the value of the output from the data-base
- what are the consequences of the data not being available
- what are the consequences of the data not being used

and finally one that is often forgotten

- what will it cost to maintain the data-base.

There is a habit in management or government bodies to overlook the fact that data goes out of date, needs adding to, expanding and developing. So the cost of maintaining a data-base must be taken into account from the start.

It should surprise no one that running a commercially viable numeric data-base is as yet difficult if not impossible and an enormous education programme is needed before data-bases, other than financial and bibliographic, are used more widely.

2.3.8 Data Forms and Reporting

Before computerized data-bases were envisaged many standards were produced on test methods, inspection procedures, naming of parts or materials, designation systems etc. These were written for use in hard copy formats.

Now the use of computers often requires that new formats are required either to take advantage of the possibilities opened up by the use of the computer, or to take into account the restrictions in use caused by the screen, the printout or the need for one machine to link with another.

The ASTM committee R-49 is devising a series of standards for the reporting of test data which could find their place as addenda to the existing test standards. They are not required in order to amend the test procedure but to ensure that all the information and metadata needed for a full and proper evaluation of the data may be available at some future date when those conducting the test are no longer present or their memories of facts not recorded become unreliable.

Figure 2.3.1 shows a typical checklist compiled by ASTM E-49 and at present in draft form. It lists the metadata for the recording of test information on plane strain fracture toughness. It should be noted that some of the items marked with an * are described as necessary and the rest are desirable.

Whilst this is again drawn from the material area it nevertheless shows the features and metadata essential if data that is put into a data-base are to be useable.

2.3.9 Acronyms and Labels

A great deal of use is made in computerized systems of acronyms as abbreviated identifiers of information. This is in many cases an aid to those inputting the data where the full title is too long to use and the acronym has some meaning and is clearly related to the full string. However as the number of acronyms grows the situation will eventually be reached that a sufficient number of meaningful acronyms cannot be found. It is probably better to consider starting with a meaningless numeric string and a related help facility to relate the number to the full title for ease of use and for checking on the data input. This is a feature of the Chemical Registry System used not only in Chemical Abstracts but also by many other workers in that subject.

2.3.10 Data-Bases, Expert Systems and Knowledge Based Systems

The use of data-bases leads inevitability in many cases to the use of an expert system for the application or selection of the data. What is often forgotten is that an expert system may be used to check the data input. This is especially useful if large amounts of data are being handled when keyboard errors may arise or when the person entering the data may not understand its significance and so fail to observe erroneous data. Thus the system could be arranged to accept densities of steel that lay between 7.5 and 8.0 g/cm^3, question anything in a band 0.5 on either side of that range and reject anything outside that. Equally the system can be arranged to check the value of one property against another for example, if the material is a metal and the strength, sigma y, is 200MPa then the fracture toughness Kc will be between 5 and 200MPa ml/2 and if it is a cast iron then it will be between 5 and 20.

Figure 2.3.3 is an example of a 'map' produced by Ashby [15]. This is a particularly interesting and successful approach to materials selection by an engineer. To appreciate it fully one should ready a forthcoming paper in Acta Metallurgica showing a new development and the engineering background to the combination of properties. For the purpose here the figure shows limits of possibility to the values of certain properties and relations between properties. This can be done with all kinds of data and it will prove helpful in defining the error catching routines if nothing more.

Some software exists in the UK that will provide these types of error catching facilities and it can be applied to all types of numerical data-bases.

Engineering differs from science in that a solution however far from ideal has to be found to a practical problem. So often the best solution has to be found, not necessarily the perfect one. Frequently the solution is needed to meet an immovable deadline.

Expert systems are based on rules and many software shells exist that enable very useful systems to be set up quite easily, some also have inbuilt connections to draw off and use data sets from particular data-bases. However one important area of information is non-rule based knowledge. The relationships are not rigid rules like the second law of thermodynamics. Knowledge is full of if's and but's and maybe's and statements such as "if you are in this situation then try so and so".

So far this area has not been well developed to provide useable systems. Yet potentially it is as valuable as either of the others and possibly more so if useable systems can be devised. How else can we store the accumulated experience of experts in any subject. When they retire or move to other occupations then a great deal of knowledge goes with them that they are unable to pass on to their successors.

2.3.11 Where is all this leading?

In science and engineering there is an exceptional degree of collaboration and exchange of knowledge and experience on these topics. In part this is because of the activities of CODATA, VAMAS and the CEC, in part because of the need for standards for formats and the exchange of data and information and the resulting activities of the national standards bodies and ISO.

There seems little doubt that the exchanges will continue, helping many to avoid the pitfalls and problems that others before them have experienced. This seminar and workshop will add to that exchange and by bringing together new ideas from different viewpoints lead to enhanced facilities not only in the small and medium enterprises but also in the international exchange of data and information that helps even the smallest unit.

References

[1] VAMAS Bulletin No.'s 1 to 9 No. 1 January 1985 and in January and June each year up to the most recent, No. 9 January 1989, National Physical Laboratory, Teddington, UK.

[2] Westbrook, J.H. and Rumble, J.R. Editors, "Computerized Materials Data Systems", Proceedings of a CODATA Workshop devoted to discussion of problems confronting their development, held at Fairfield Glade TN USA November 7-11 1982, published by NBS, Gaithersburg MD, USA, pp.133.

[3] Krockel H., Reynard K.W. and Steven G. Editors, "Factual Material Data-Banks", Proceedings of a CEC workshop held at JRC Petten November 14-16 1984, publishing by CEC, Luxembourg, pp.178,ISBN 92-825-5322-1.

[4] Westbrook, J.H., Behrens, H., Dathe, G and Iwata, S. Editors, "Materials Data Systems for Engineering", Proceedings of a CODATA workshop held at

Schluchsee, The Black Forest, Federal Republic of Germany, September 22-27 1985, published by FIZ, Karlsruhe, FRG, pp.189, ISBN 3-88127-100-7.

[5] Krockel H., Reynard K.W. and Rumble J.R. Editors, "Factual Materials Data-Banks, the Need for Standards", the Report of a VAMAS Task Group, National Bureau of Standards, Gaithersburg, MD, USA, July 1987.

.[6] "ISO 31/0 to 31/13", TC 12 Quantities, units, symbols, conversion factors and conversion tables, International Standards Organization, Geneva, Switzerland, some parts in 2nd Edition, 1978-1981, pp.various.

[7] "ISO 2955 Information processing - representation of SI and other units in systems with limited character sets", TC 97 information processing systems, International Standards Organization, Geneva, Switzerland, 2nd Edition, 1983, p.5.

[8] "Code of Practice for Use in the Material Data-Banks Demonstrator Programme", Ed N.Swindells for the Commission of the European Communities. Document No. XIII/MDP (MAT-02)-OS-03, CEC, Luxembourg, November 1986, pp.12.

[9] "ISO 7498 Information processing system - Open Systems Interconnection - Basic Reference Model", TC 97 Information processing systems, International Standards Organization, Geneva, Switzerland 1984, pp.40.

[10] J.G. Kaufman "Sources and Standards for Computerized Materials Property Data and Intelligent Knowledge Systems", Engineering with Computers 4, pp.75-85, 1988.

[11] A.J.Barrett "On the Evaluation and Validation of Engineering Data", 10th International CODATA Conference July 1986, Ottawa Canada, published in "Computer Handling and Dissemination of Data" North Holland: Elsevier Science Publishers.

[12] K.W.Reynard, "VAMAS Activities on Materials Data-Banks, 1st International Symposium on Computerization and Networking of materials Property Data-Bases, November 1987, full proceedings published by ASTM as STP 1017.

[13]J.G. Kaufman Ed "Guide to Materials Data-Base Management", pp.50, published as CODATA Bulletin No. 69 by Hemisphere Publishing 1988.

[14]K.W. Reynard "Standards for the Presentation and Use of Materials Data. A Review of the Activities of ASTM, CEC, CODATA and VAMAS with Proposals for the Future", 11th International CODATA Conference September 1988 to be published.

[15] M.F. Ashby forthcoming paper in Acta Metallurgica.

Fig. 2.3.1 Recommended Standard Data Format for
Computerization of Plane Strain Fracture Toughness Data
per ASTM Method E 39949E02 04R3

Field No.	Field Name and Description	Category Sets or Units
1*	Material identification	This information will
2*	Lot identification	be supplemented by mat.1
3*	Data source identification	description data.
4*	Type of test	Fracture toughness
5*	ASTM,ISO or other applicable test standard	c.g. ASTM E 399
5*	Material yield strength	MPa(psi)
6*	Material elastic modulus	GPa(psi*10**6)
7*	Specimen identification	
8	Specimen location	
9*	Specimen orientation	e.g. L-T,T-S
10*	Specimen type	e.g. CT,NB,C
11*	Specimen width (depth),W	mm. (in.)
12*	Loading hole offset (Arc-shape specimen)	mm.(in.)
13*	Inner radius(arc-shape specimen)	mm.(in.)
14*	Outer radius(arc-shape specimen)	mm.(in.)
15*	Specimen thickness, B	mm.(in.)
16	Specimen span length, S	mm.(in.)
17	Fatigue crack. maximum load, Pfmax	N(lbs)
18	Fatigue max. stress intensity, Kfmax	MPa(sqrt m.) (psi(qrt in.))
19	Fatigue cracking load ratio, R	
20	Cycles to complete fatigue cracking	**10**3
21	Fatigue crack length, edge, fce1	mm.(in.)
22	center, fcc	mm.(in.)
23	edge, fce2	mm.(in.)

./..

Fig. 2.3.1 (cont.)

Field No.	Field Name and Description	Category Sets or Units
24	KQ loading rate	N/min(lbs/min)
25	KQ test chart slope	\
26	KQ candidate load, PQ	N(lbs)
27*	Candidate plane strain stress intensity factor, KQ	MPa(sqrt m)(psi(sqrt in.))
28	Maximum load, Pmax	N(lbs)
29	Maximum stress intensity factor Kmax	MPa(sqrt m)(psi(sqrt in.))
30	Total crack length, edge, a1	mm.(in.)
31	quarter, a2	mm.(in.)
32	center, a3	mm.(in.)
33	quarter, a4	mm.(in.)
34	edge, a5	mm.(in.)
35*	Average crack length, a,	mm.(in.)
36	Fracture appearance	\ Oblique
37	Fatigue crack plane angle to crack plane	\
38	$2.5(KQ/TYS)**2$	mm.(in.)
39	Pmax/PQ	
40	a/W	
41	Kfmax/KQ	
42	Kfmax/E	sqrt m(sqrt in.)
43	Minimum fatigue precrack length	mm.(in.)
44	Maximum difference Between a2,a3,a4	mm.(in.)
45	Difference between a1 and a5	mm.(in.)
46	Kq stressing rate	MPa(sqrt m)(psi(sqrt in))
47	Is B=/2.5>(KQ/TYS)**2?	Y-yes, N-no
48	Is a=/2.5>(KQ/TYS)**2?	Y-yes, N-no

.\.

Fig. 2.3.1 (cont.)

Field No.	Field Name and Description	Category Sets or Units
49	Is a/W=0.45-0.55?	Y-yes, N-no
50	Is Pmax/PQ</=1.10?	Y-yes, N-no
51	Is Kfmax/KQ</=0.6?	Y-yes, N-no
52	Is Kfmax/E</=0.02?	Y-yes, N-no
53	Is max diff between a2, a3, a4</0.10 a?	Y-yes, N-no
54	Is diff between a1 and a5</=0.10 a?	Y-yes, N-no
55	Is min.fatigue precrack >/=0.050 in.?	Y-yes, N-no
56	Is fatigue crack plane angle </=10 deg?	Y-yes, N-no
57	Is loading rate=30000-150000 psi(sqrt in)?	Y-yes, N-no
58	Is KQ test chart slope=0.7-1.5?	Y-yes, N-no
59*	Is KQ valid measure of KIc? (all criteria met?)	Y,N
60	Specimen strength ratio	ratio
61*	Test temperature	degC
62	Test environment	
63	Test humidity	\
64	Test date	MMDDYY
65	Special notes	

* - Essential information for computerization of test results.

** - Field numbers are for reference only: they do not imply a necessity to include all of these fields in any specific data-base, or a requirement that fields utilized are in this particular order.

|| - Units listed first are SI: those in parentheses are English.

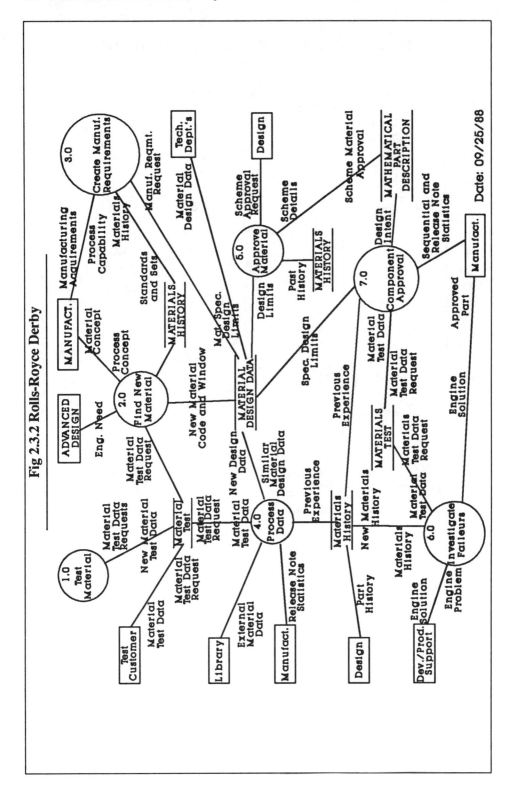

Fig 2.3.2 Rolls-Royce Derby

Date: 09/25/88

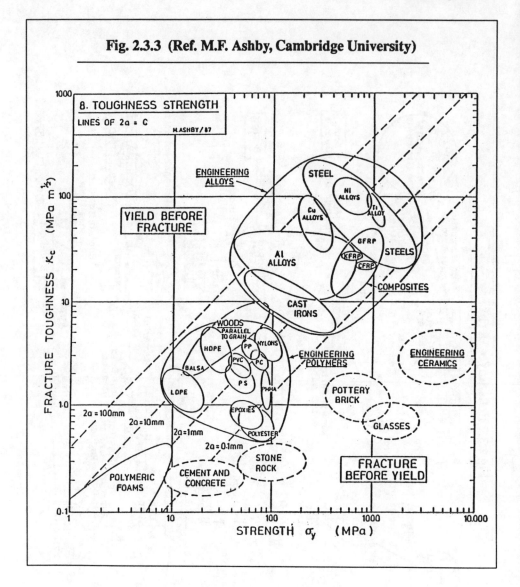

Fig. 2.3.3 (Ref. M.F. Ashby, Cambridge University)

2.4 Information and Data-Base Systems in Brazil

Renato Cerqueira Lima Brea

2.4.1 Introduction

Brazil is a big country with a great potential but very serious economic and social problems. In some areas, like Informatics, it chose to follow its own way by trying to maximize local manufacturing of equipment and local developing of technology. In other areas, like Communication, it decided to modernize very fast its networks and offer very sophisticated services.

In order to understand how information systems and data-bases are used in Brazil it is important to know a bit about the country, the communication facilities available and its particular informatics policy. This is done in sec. 2.4.2, 3 and 4.

In sec. 2.4.5, we discuss basically the use of public information systems and data-bases in Brazil and try to analyze the factors that restrict this use.

Even if we don't know the similarities between Brazil and China with respect to information systems and data-bases, we think that the best contribution we can give to ISTIC is to show our problems in this area and the reasons of these problems.

2.4.2 An Overview of the Country

Brazil is the largest country in South America both in terms of area (8,511,965 kmnd population (147,000,000 people). A major part of Brazil lies on the tropical region between the Equator and the Tropic of Capricorn with average temperatures normally above 20° C.

The country spans 4 time zones, but GMT-3 is considered the official time. Distances from North to South and also from East to West are over 4,000 km. Brazilian coast on the Atlantic Ocean has more than 7,000 km and concentrates the most important and oldest cities (Fig. 2.4.1).

The country was colonized by Portugal from 1500 to 1822 when it finally became independent. As a consequence, Portuguese is the country's official language and Roman Christianism, its main religion. In 1960, Brasilia, today with 1,200,000 people, was built to be the federal capital - an old idea from the time of the first rebellions before independence.

Almost 80% of the population now lives in urban areas, the southeast region concentrating 44% of the country's population. In the metropolitan regions of São Paulo and Rio de Janeiro live more than 28 million people, many of them in poor conditions.

Since 1889 the country has been a Republic. There is a federal government and 26 states with a total of 8,543 municipal districts. The largest is Amazon state in the north region and the richest and most populated is São Paulo state.

Both federal government and local governments are based on the traditional 3-power model: Executive, Legislative and Judiciary. A new constitution was approved in 1988, ending a period of more than 20 years of military ruling.

Brazilian GNP was around 300 billion US dollars in 1987, with services representing 54%, industry 36% and agriculture + stock raising 10%. The country's economy is quite dependent on the success of its exports: soya, coffee, cacao, sugar, iron, steel, shoes and automobiles. In 1987, Brazil exported 26 billion US dollars and imported 16 billion US dollars (oil being the most important imported item), but this positive balance (repeated in 1988) was totally spent to roll over an enormous external debt of 110 billion US dollars.

After a period of fast economic growth during the 70's, Brazilian economy has been facing a serious crisis in the 80's. A high rate of inflation (900% during 1988) forced the government to use non-traditional economic procedures (like price and salary freezing, for example) generating uncertainty and recession.

The most important problem is an unfair distribution of wealth that forces the major part of the population to live at the level of poverty or even starvation.

2.4.3 Telecommunications in Brazil

2.4.3.1 Structure

Brazilian Government has the monopoly of operating the communication services such as telephone (local and long distance), telex and data communication services and also the postal service, in the tradition of European PTTs.

The Ministry of Communications has under it a governmental company, TELEBRAS, which is a holding company for the operation of the communication services. Under TELEBRAS, EMBRATEL is the company responsible for the international and long distance lines, telex and data services. Also controlled by TELEBRAS, there is one company per state, responsible for operating local telephone and data services. Finally, TELEBRAS controls CPqD, a research center located in the city of Campinas, state of São Paulo.

2.4.3.2 Historical Perspective

In 1963, Brazil had very incipient communication facilities, with only 1 million telephones and 1,000 telex terminals installed, low quality service and telephone operating companies (more than 1,000) scattered throughout the country.

In 1964, the government decided to give high priority to the creation of extensive and reliable communication services. EMBRATEL was created and, soon, three microwave links were built interconnecting the most important Brazilian cities. The telephone companies were consolidated to just one per state, all of them controlled by the holding company TELEBRAS.

From 1 million telephones installed in 1963, Brazil jumped to 9.8 million in 1983 (Fig. 2.4.2), with more than 1,000 cities able to make long distance and international direct dialing. The telex network experienced a similar growth. In the late 70's, in order to extend to the Amazon region the facilities already available in the rest of the country, Brazil began to make extensive use of the INTELSAT satellite also for domestic communications. Afterwards, two domestic satellites were contracted and put into operation, providing a total of 48 transponders, used mainly for voice, TV and new data services. Figure 2.4.3 gives a complete view of the present basic transmission network.

With the economic crisis of the 80's, telecommunications have lost their high priority and government expenses with new equipments and people have been restricted, putting to risk the quality of the services provided, since the demand has never ceased to grow (Fig. 2.4.4).

2.4.3.3 Data Communication Domestic Services

Specialized data communication services began to be offered in the late 70's by EMBRATEL. The TRANSDATA service provides urban and long distance leased (non-switched) data circuits with speeds going from 1,200 to 9,600 bits per second. There is a fixed monthly cost, depending only on speed and distance, including the rental of lines, modems, multiplexers and maintenance. As a general idea, a 2,400 bps data circuit linking Rio de Janeiro to São Paulo (or any two cities distant more than 300 km.) costs 2,500 US dollars per month. The TRANSDATA service has been steadily growing at a rate of almost 50% a year, comprising now over 21,000 installed circuits and covering more than 800 cities. Because of government restrictions on investment and people, around 12,000 circuits are still awaiting installation.

In 1985, EMBRATEL started the RENPAC service, a packet-switching X.25 public network, with nodes or concentrators in 25 cities. Computers, control units or terminals can be connected to RENPAC over dedicated leased circuits, with speeds going from 1,200 to 9,600 bps, in more than 60 cities (to stimulate the new service, EMBRATEL offers the same rates in all these cities, as if there were already installed a node or concentrator).

Terminals can also access RENPAC from any telephone within the country, with connection rates that are completely distance independent. The same happens with terminals connected to the telex network. RENPAC is also connected to other packet-switching networks, allowing access, at present, to 38 countries.

Costs are basically traffic dependent, which favors small users and interactive applications. As a general idea, connection time is charged at a rate of 0.06 US dollars per minute and volume transmitted is charged at a rate of 0.05 US dollars per 1,024 characters. An average interactive session using RENPAC will cost 80% less than a long distance telephone call of the same duration. Even with all these advantages, only recently RENPAC became better known and used (Fig. 2.4.5). The present network has around 2,700 terminations (all of them already sold), a number that will be duplicated at the end of this year and duplicated again in 1990.

With the availability of domestic satellites, EMBRATEL began to offer new data services like high speed (19.2 kbps to 2 Mbps) circuits for interconnection of Data Processing Centers and low speed (1,200 to 9,600 bps) broadcast or interactive services, specially attractive for users with very large private networks or needing to reach very remote places. A new commercial approach has been taken, allowing the user himself to buy the equipment needed, but optionally using EMBRATEL to operate and maintain it. These services, which are quite new, are attracting the heavy users of TRANSDATA service, most of them unsatisfied with the long delays to get new circuits installed or repaired. Last year, TELEBRAS authorized its local companies to begin providing data services in their areas. The situation is still confusing but companies of the southeast and south regions are getting ready to take over a big part of EMBRATEL's present urban and intra-state leased circuits.

2.4.3.4 Data Communication International Services

EMBRATEL provides the following data communication international services:

- non-switched leased lines or data circuits from 1,200 to 9,600 bps;
- a packet-switching service, called INTERDATA, connecting RENPAC to 81 networks in 38 countries;
- special purpose services like AIRDATA (access from air-line companies to the SITA network), INTERBANK (access from banks to the SWIFT network), and FINDATA (access from financial institutions to the REUTERS network);
- satellite digital service (access to INTELSAT Business Service).

The INTERDATA service was introduced in 1983 (before the RENPAC network), after claims from multinational companies and Brazilian research centers for access to public data-bases in the US and Europe. In the beginning, users could access the INTERDATA node only through the telephone network, at 1,200 bps; since 1985, any terminal or computer connected to RENPAC can also make or receive an international call, using the INTERDATA service. INTERDATA costs are based on connection time (US$ 0.42 per minute) and volume transmitted/received (US$ 0.52 per 1,024 characters). An interactive session using INTERDATA costs roughly 50% the cost of a similar session using an international telephone call.

The service has been growing at very high rates (Fig. 2.4.6), multinational companies and the Brazilian Ministry of Foreign Affairs being its biggest users.

2.4.4 Informatics in Brazil

2.4.4.1 Structure

In the beginning of the 70's, in an unusual alliance between the Brazilian intellectual establishment and the military, the government decided to create special policies for this sector to help the development of technology within the country. In 1984, the Congress approved the Informatics Law, structuring the present model and giving protection to the infant informatics industry. So today big computers are sold in Brazil by foreign companies like IBM and Unisys and joint ventures like ABC-Bull, which also assemble some of their computer models in the country, and by other companies like Fujitsu, DEC, Control Data, without any local manufacturing capabilities.

National companies produce PC's, supermicros, terminals, serial printers, small winchester drives, floppy disk drives, etc... with their own know-how. They also produce superminis, medium capacity winchester drives, line printers, ATM's, distributed process control equipment, etc... with acquired know-how. Government action is co-ordinated by a committee - CONIN - and by the Special Secretary of Informatics (SEI).

2.4.4.2 Market

In 1986 the Brazilian market for informatics and related digital equipment was 3.0 billion US dollars, 43% of the total Brazilian electronic market (Table 2.4.1). This market grew quite fast - almost 30% per year - from 1983 to 1986 (Fig. 2.4.7), a period of very little growth for the Brazilian economy as a whole.

Since 1985 national companies have been responsible for more than 50% of the total annual sales. In 1986 they sold 86 superminis, 1,370 minis, 1,240 supermicros, 56 thousand PC's and 49 thousand 8-bit micros. They also produced 18 thousand banking terminals, 32 thousand video terminals, 60 thousand serial printers, 12 thousand 5" 1/4 floppies and 17 thousand winchester disk drivers. The number of general purpose computers installed up to 1987 is shown in Fig. 2.4.8, divided by class. National companies are heavily concentrated in classes 1 to 3 while foreign companies dominate classes 4 to 7. Figure 2.4.9 shows that, according to the value of the installed base, foreign companies still retain more than 50% of this market. Table 2.4.2 shows that IBM is by far the leader in classes 5 to

7, being behind Unisys in class 4. Cobra, the only informatics company owned by Brazilian government, is losing its market share very fast but still leads classes 2 and 3. Class 1 is shared by several companies if we divide it in professional 16-bit (class 1A) and non-professional 8-bit (class 1B) microcomputers.

2.4.4.3 Users

Big companies of the financial, industrial and governmental sectors are the heavy users of informatics equipment in Brazil. They acquire a great number of equipment and have sophisticated needs. They have always an enormous back-log of new applications awaiting to be developed. Only in recent years with the availability in the country of PC's and departmental computers, they did begin to decentralize processing and sometimes development.

Small and medium enterprises in Brazil are still starting using computers. Although Brazilian equipment are still quite expensive (an entry level 16-bit PC costs 3,000 US dollars), SMEs are buying PC's and even larger computers but have great difficulties in hiring experienced people and getting their most critical applications to work. Lack of well trained people in programming or even in computer use is one of the most serious problems in Brazil and this affects specially SMEs, since big companies are already used to investing intensively in internal training. Lack of good software packages adapted to the Brazilian conditions (specially legislation) makes things even more difficult. But it is clear that, even with these problems, the use of informatics is penetrating very fast in SMEs. Also the educational system is beginning to pop into the labour market thousands of young programmers and system analysts with a formal background in informatics. And finally a software law protecting the intellectual rights was approved in 1987 and this will certainly promote a better offer of software packages in Brazil.

2.4.5 Information and Data-Base Systems in Brazil

2.4.5.1 Overview

In 1984, SEI published the results of a research work where 1,029 data-bases were catalogued in Brazil, with 225 more in the process of development. Most of them were restricted-access data-bases related to administrative, financial and business information of private and state companies; only 8% were or could be of public access. In 1986, SEI continued its research work, this time covering only government institutions. A directory with 390 data-bases, 150 of them available for public access, was published. In 1987, a joint research of EMBRATEL and

INFO magazine estimated the existence of around 300 data-bases of general interest and public access. A catalogue with detailed information on 226 public access data-bases divided in 32 subject areas was published based on this research work.

From this total, 25% were in the area of Economy and Finance (where the activities of private companies are concentrated), 12% about Science and Technology and 12% about Agriculture and Stock raising.

From the 50 data bases found in the area of Science and Technology, 30 were of foreign origin, although distributed by institutions like IBICT - Brazilian Institute of Information on Science and Technology.

The access to most of the 226 data-bases listed can be done only by personal contact, letter and sometimes by telephone, but several Brazilian institutions are beginning to offer on-line access to its data-bases through the telex, telephone and RENPAC networks. Also, since 1983, Brazil has gained access to several foreign data-bases through the INTERDATA service.

In the next sections we will concentrate only on the information and data-base systems already available for on-line public access.

2.4.5.2 Domestic Public Information Systems Available

Most of present domestic public information systems began a long time ago as private or restricted-access information systems, having only local terminals or using leased lines to connect remote terminals accessed by their most important users. This has been, for example, the case of IBGE - the Brazilian Census Bureau - an official institution with an ancient tradition of gathering and structuring data. IBGE has been offering on-line access to its data-bases for more than ten years but only for users of the Ministry of Planning. A few years ago they began to offer very limited public access to some data-bases through the telex network and only now that they are connected to the RENPAC network are they beginning to offer some less-limited information service.

FGV - Getulio Vargas Foundation - is another example. FGV is the most respected private Brazilian institution in the area of Economy and Finance. For more than 40 years they have been producing economic indicators, some of them used by companies to adjust the prices of their goods or services. These indicators are published in their monthly magazine and also distributed on magnetic tape. Last year they began to offer interactive access to their data-bases through the telex, telephone and RENPAC networks. Alternatively, FGV's computer can call registered telex terminals and send them a fixed list of economic indicators (chosen by the user at subscription time). 2,300 telex terminals are already registered.

Another type of economic indicator - construction costs - is made available by Control Data do Brazil, also through the RENPAC and telex networks.

The area of Economy and Finance concentrated most of the use of public information systems today in Brazil. Rio de Janeiro Stock Exchange - BVRJ - allows you to have information on stocks and even to negotiate from any Brazilian large city through the RENPAC or telephone network. CMA, a former software-house and computer bureau, provides up-to-the-minute information on commodities, stocks, money, rates, precious metals, etc..., with on-line connections to Brazilian, American and European commodities and stocks markets. SCI/Protector and other companies offer some kind of credit verification services which are becoming popular because of the great number of check and credit card holders on the "black list".

Bibliographic references about several topics on the areas of Science and Technology are provided by IBICT - Brazilian Information Institute for Science and Technology - and CNEN/CIN - Nuclear Energy Commission Information Center. Some of their data-bases are of foreign origin (like INSPEC from the Institution of Electrical Engineers of England) while others are of their own responsibility structuring information from several Brazilian government documentation centers.

BIREME - Caribbean and Latin American Information Center for Health - has a most important domestic information system on Medicine already with on-line public access. It is basically composed of international and latin-american texts on health. They are also beginning an experience of distributing information in CD-ROM to selected libraries.

SERPRO - Ministry of Finance's Data Processing Company - was the first Brazilian company to invest seriously in the public information business. In 1977, as there were no reliable data communication services available, they built their own network getting ready to provide easy access to their data-bases in São Paulo, Rio de Janeiro and Brasilia from any part of the country. They carefully prepared all the infrastructure to distribute both bibliographic and numeric data-bases. But frequent changes in the company's priorities and difficulties with their information providers (several government institutions) have turned their ambitious project into a failure. SERPRO still provides some public information services through the telex, telephone and RENPAC networks, the access to the INPI (National Institute of Industrial Property) data-base of trade marks and patents being the most interesting one.

Three important institutions do not allow on-line access to their data-bases yet, but will probably do it in the next years:
- EMBRAPA - a government institution with the objective of doing research work in the area of agriculture and stock raising;
- FIOCRUZ (Oswaldo Cruz Foundation) - the most important Brazilian research center in the areas of Biology and Public Health;
- DATAPREV - the Social Security Ministry's Data Processing Company.

2.4.5.3 International Public Information Systems Available

In 1983, EMBRATEL began to offer its INTERDATA service allowing access to international public information systems in the United States and Europe. In order to free the users from the cumbersome burocracy for payments in foreign currency, EMBRATEL has been authorized by the government to charge the users in local currency and to pay the foreign information services. EMBRATEL makes the necessary agreements with the foreign information services and also promotes them, but sales, training and technical support are done directly by the foreign companies' representatives in Brazil.

Table 2.4.3 shows the international public information systems accessible from Brazil at present. They are well known services with millions of bibliographic references on every possible area of human knowledge, but specially on the area of Science and Technology.

DIALOG with its 230 different data-bases and over 100 million references was one of the first systems available and is still one of the most used. The use of EMIS has been growing mainly because of PETROBRAS - the Brazilian Oil Company - who is its heaviest user. STN is the third service in volume of use, after EMIS and DIALOG.

2.4.5.4 The Use of Public Information Systems in Brazil

The numbers showing the effective use of public information systems in Brazil are still disappointing. Table 2.4.4 shows that the most used international service had less than 4,000 minutes of connection time last December and the second had less than 2,000 minutes. the INTERDATA service, whose original purpose was to provide access to international public information services, has today only 3% of its total traffic related to that. If we skip financial services where companies like CMA and others had 32 million dollars of revenue in 1987, the performance of domestic public information systems is not brilliant. IBICT, one of the most used non-financial domestic services has around 6,000 inquires per month, most of them generated by a small number of users.

What are the reasons for that? First, let's consider the problem of telecommunication facilities to access public information systems. As it has been shown previously, the opening of RENPAC service on 1985 brought to an end the technical problems for accessing domestic or even international information services from anywhere within the country (Fig. 2.4.10). One problem could be the unavailability of adequate terminals or workstations but, with the increasing use of PC's in most Brazilian companies, this is not the point. Also there are software products available in Brazil that can change a normal PC into an IBM 3270 or DEC VT100 terminal and inexpensive modems to connect them to the telephone and RENPAC networks.

There are no technical problems in making a standard PC access any public information system but most of the potential end-users of these services are not yet able to do that. First of all, it is not so common to use a PC like a terminal in most Brazilian companies; as a consequence, the modem is not yet a standard PC peripheral. Second, most companies which in fact use PC's as terminals have them directly connected to their computer centers, since the popularity of the RENPAC network only began in 1988; as a consequence these PC's are not able to access other systems. Third, even end-users with basic knowledge of computers do not have any knowledge of data communications. So, we see that one reason for the low use of public information systems in Brazil is not lack of telecommunication facilities or workstations but lack of end-user experience in using data communication switched services and PC's as general purpose terminals. Time will certainly solve that, but meanwhile why don't people working in the data processing departments help end-users to access public information systems?

The first reason is that most of their energy is still devoted to building basic private information systems critical to company's business (specially in the financial, marketing and manufacturing areas). Even a traditional heavy user of computers like PETROBRAS - the Brazilian oil company - with tenths of large and very large mainframes and thousands of terminals installed, is only now extending automation to its refineries and offices scattered throughout the country, by building a large distributed private information system shown in Fig. 2.4.11. The second reason is that technical people only very recently learnt how to use a switched network and a PC as a general purpose terminal. But why don't end-users put pressure on them to have access to public information system?

First because these services are not known by most of its potential users. With the exception of financial services, the greatest part of domestic information services is operated by academic or government institutions, which do not have enough money and people to promote their services, since there is no government priority to that. Even international systems representatives are not very active in promoting their services, perhaps because they are disappointed with their results in Brazil. In fact the only promotional efforts have been done by EMBRATEL, but with modest results. The second and most important reason is that there is a general lack of what we would call "information culture" in Brazil. From the elementary school up to the university, Brazilian educational system does not favor research work; students are not used to spending time searching for information in libraries; good public libraries are quite rare. As a consequence, the same happens within the companies: most of them do not have a good library service and, even if some of them do, few people are used to consulting it systematically. If people are not used to looking for information in their own libraries why would they fight for access to public information systems?

Probably time will help to solve this cultural problem as end-users get more and more involved in using private information systems and as public information systems begin to be known. But let's consider another point: are present user interfaces in public information systems appropriate for the average Brazilian end-user? We don't think so. First of all, most end-users still have difficulties in using command-oriented query languages, specially because they are never given extensive training. They are fond of menu-driven or form-driven applications with extensive on-line help facilities that need almost no training or manuals to read. Second, as far as international systems are concerned, the use of commands and keywords in a foreign language will certainly be a problem to several of them. Third, since they are not used to searching for information in libraries, they need to be guided to find what they want.

The last question is: will the cost of using information systems and telecommunication facilities be a serious restrictive factor? Well, today in Brazil, except in the financial area, most of domestic information systems available charge very little or even nothing for their services and the RENPAC costs are quite reasonable. The situation with international systems is different, mainly because an international call can cost 10 times as much as a domestic one. However, we don't think cost will be a big problem for companies who have already learnt the value of information, but this is the real problem since most Brazilian small and medium enterprises have not.

2.4.5.5 The Role of the Government

There has been no integrated action from the part of the government in order to promote the use of public information systems. If we sum up investments made by several governmental institutions in this area, we will come to an impressive amount of money, but with poor results. The lack of a plan didn't allow the government to concentrate the available money to develop one or two very good public information systems, instead of having several official institutions developing separate systems and none of them offering a good service.

Telecommunication companies have also wasted a lot of money buying computers and trying themselves to build public information systems, instead of concentrating only in the communication business. EMBRATEL, for example, lost 5 years with an ambitious project called CIRANDÃO, promising universal access to data-bases. The project was finally redefined to concentrate only on electronic mail services.

TELESP - the local telephone company of the São Paulo state has been trying since 1982 to sell, without success, its Public Videotex service (Fig. 2.4.16). TELESP insisted for several years in approaching the non-business user, offering low-cost terminals and decoders to be used with domestic TV sets. Finally they decided to turn their efforts to business applications.

Other local telephone companies like TELEMIG (of Minas Gerais state) are also offering Public Videotex services. TELEMIG decided to have no local data-bases in its Videotex server, acting only as a gateway to external data-bases. They also decided to work mainly with closed groups of business users with common interest to specific applications like credit authorization, sales support or banking services. With only 1,000 users they achieved 19,000 hours per month of traffic, while TELESP with 15,000 users has only 60,000 hours. An average TELEMIG users makes 52 inquires per day, while a TELESP user makes only 3.

2.4.6 Conclusions

The use of public information systems in Brazil will certainly grow in the near future. Very soon end-users will learn how to use their PC's as general purpose terminals to access different services through the telephone and RENPAC networks. Then today will be interested in trying to access public information systems and, at that moment, promotion, training and guiding facilities for beginners will be important. As it has already happened in the financial area, SMEs will find out the value of information in the area of Science and Technology and will accept to pay for the use of information and communication services.

This will certainly stimulate present information providers to improve their services and new public information systems to show up. The weakest link of the chain will continues to be education. The solution will not come from teaching people how to use computers, but from teaching them how to use information.

2.4.7 Information sources

The main information sources used for this paper were:

- IBGE - Fundação Instituto Brasileiro de Geografia e Estatística
  Av. Franklin Roosvelt 166
  20021 - Rio de Janeiro - RJ
- TELEBRAS - Telecomunicações Brasileiras S.A.
  SAS - quadra 6 - bloco E
  70313 - Brasília - DF
- EMBRATEL - Empresa Brasileira de Telecomunicações S.A.
  Av. Presidente Vargas 1012
  20071 - Rio de Janeiro - RJ
- SEI - Secretaria Especial de Informática
  SAS - quadra 5, lote 6, bloco H, 2º andar
  70070 - Brasília - DF
- Revista INFO
  Av. Brasil 500 sala 620
  20949 - Rio de Janeiro - RJ
- IBICT – Instituto Brasileiro de Informção em Ciência e Tecnologia
  SCN - quadra 5, bloco K
  70710 - Brasília - DF
- FGV - Fundação Getúlio Vargas
  Praia de Botafogo, 184
  22253 - Rio de Janeiro - RJ

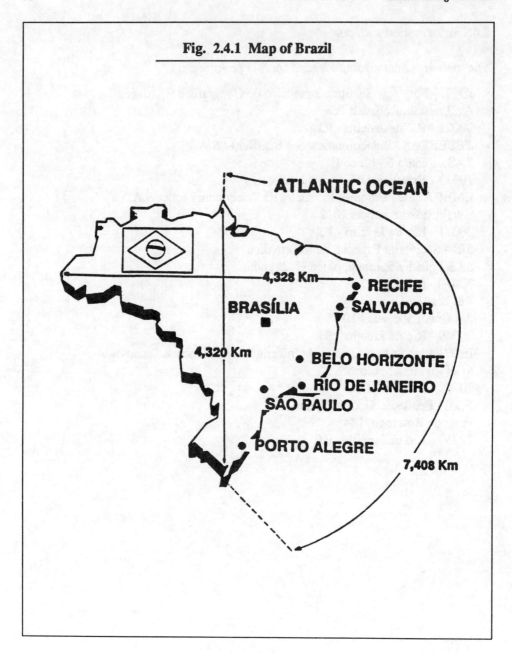

Fig. 2.4.1 Map of Brazil

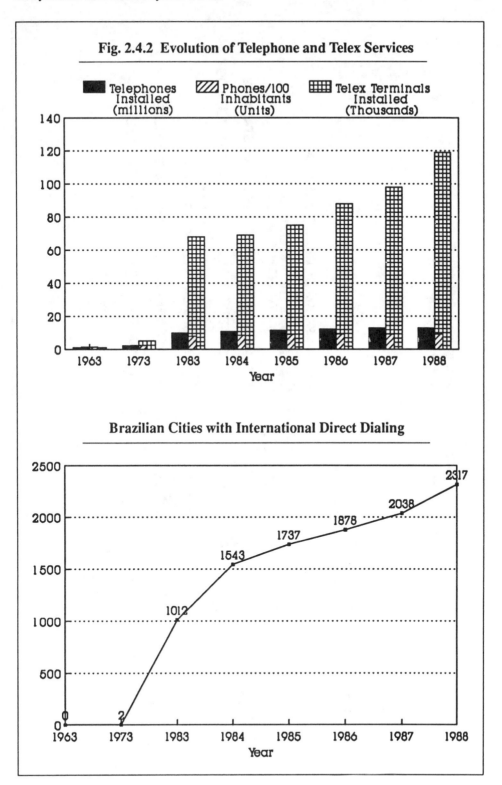

Fig. 2.4.2 Evolution of Telephone and Telex Services

Brazilian Cities with International Direct Dialing

Fig. 2.4.3 Basic Transmission Network

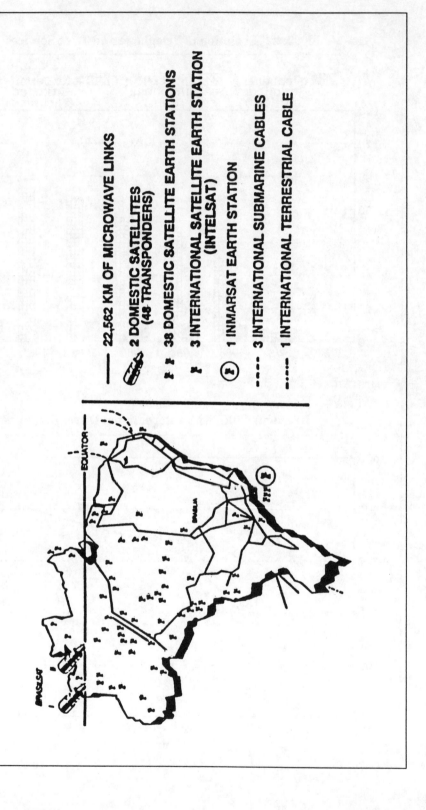

22,562 KM OF MICROWAVE LINKS

2 DOMESTIC SATELLITES
(48 TRANSPONDERS)

38 DOMESTIC SATELLITE EARTH STATIONS

3 INTERNATIONAL SATELLITE EARTH STATION
(INTELSAT)

1 INMARSAT EARTH STATION

3 INTERNATIONAL SUBMARINE CABLES

1 INTERNATIONAL TERRESTRIAL CABLE

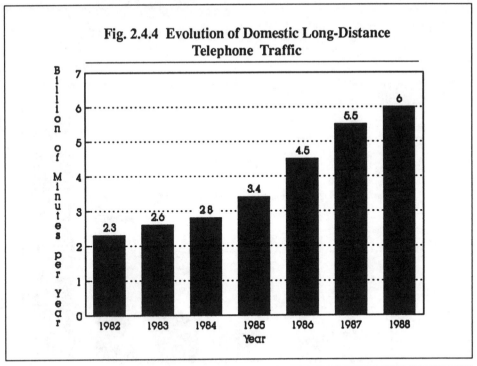

Fig. 2.4.4 Evolution of Domestic Long-Distance Telephone Traffic

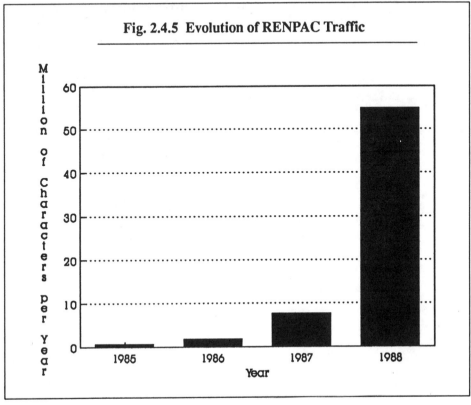

Fig. 2.4.5 Evolution of RENPAC Traffic

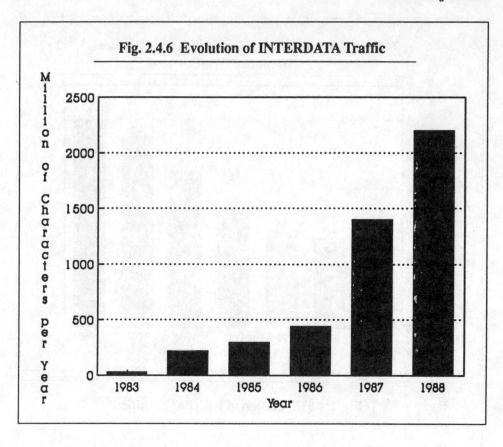

Fig. 2.4.6 Evolution of INTERDATA Traffic

Table 2.4.1 Brazilian Electronic Market (1986)

	Value	US$ %	Million Imports	Exports
Consumer	2620	37	138	315
Communications	1050	15	65	43
Informatics	3035	43	315	203
Other	380	5	116	17
Components	-	-	606	190
Total	7085	100	1240	768

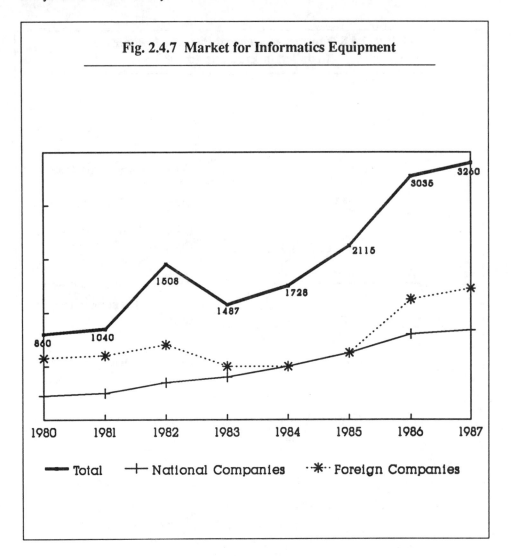

Fig. 2.4.7 Market for Informatics Equipment

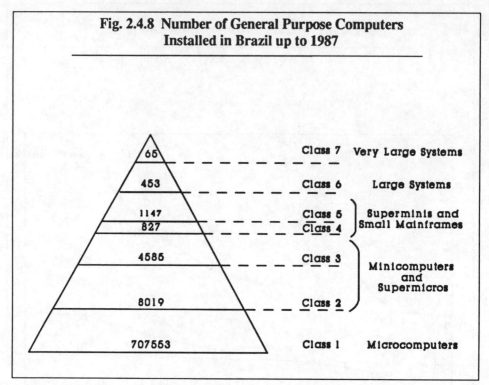

Fig. 2.4.8 Number of General Purpose Computers Installed in Brazil up to 1987

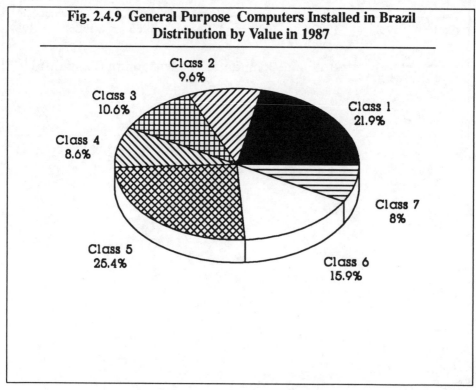

Fig. 2.4.9 General Purpose Computers Installed in Brazil Distribution by Value in 1987

Table 2.4.2 General Purpose Computers
Market Leaders

Company	% of Total Equipment Installed per Class							
	Class 7	Class 6	Class 5	Class 4	Class 3	Class 2	Class 1-A	Class 1-B
IMB	88	77	62	29	12	-	-	-
FUJITSU	9	3	1	2	-	-	-	-
UNISYS	3	9	18	37	4	1	-	-
ABC-BULL	-	6	8	3	-	-	-	-
DEC	-	4	5	5	13	-	-	-
ELEBRA	-	-	-	10	-	-	-	-
COBRA	-	-	1	2	25	41	1	-
SISCO	-	-	-	-	21	11	-	-
LABO	-	-	-	1	6	15	-	-
EDISA	-	-	-	-	4	13	-	-
MICROTEC	-	-	-	-	-	-	18	-
ITAUTEC	-	-	-	-	-	-	16	-
SCOPUS	-	-	-	-	-	-	16	-
MICRODIGITAL	-	-	-	-	-	-	-	38
PROLOGICA	-	-	-	-	-	-	-	20
GRADIENTE	-	-	-	-	-	-	-	13

Table 2.4.3 International Public Information Services Accessible from Brazil

Name of the Service	Country
BRS - Bibliographic Retrieval Services	USA
DRI - Data Resources Inc.	USA
DIALOG Information Services	USA
EMIS	USA
MDC - Mead Data Central	USA
OCEANROUTES Inc.	USA
PERGAMON Orbit Infoline Ltd.	ENGLAND
PERGAMON Infoline	ENGLAND
QUESTEL Telesystemes	FRANCE
REUTERS	ENGLAND
STN International	FRG

Table 2.4.4 Use of International Public Information Services in Brazil

Values per Month in December '88	Name of the Service				
	EMIS	DIALOG	STN	QUESTEL	MDC
Calls	274	75	95	33	17
Minutes	3610	1592	1109	412	412
10^3 Characters	6450	2454	2408	683	654

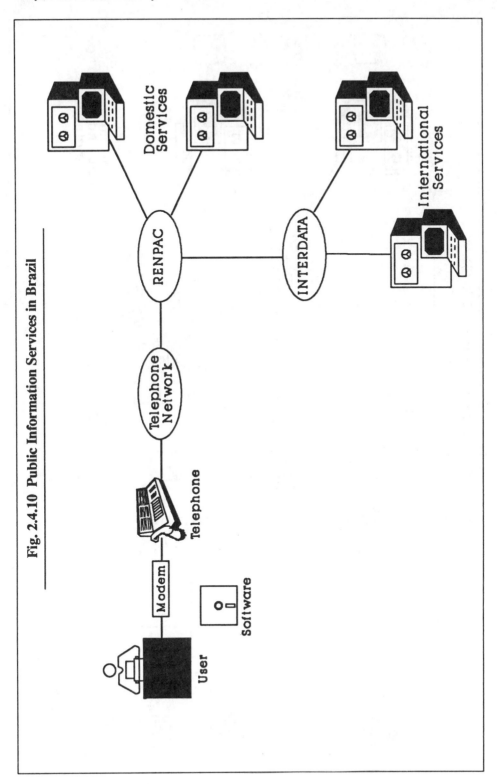

Fig. 2.4.10 Public Information Services in Brazil

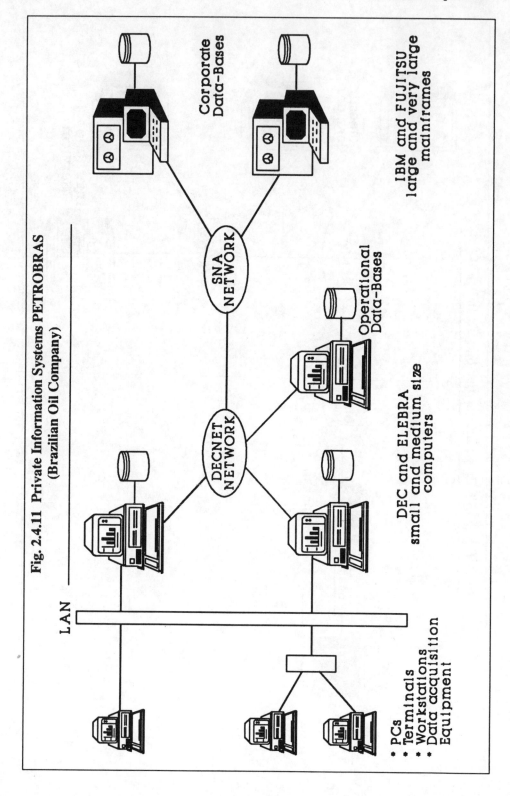

Fig. 2.4.11 Private Information Systems PETROBRAS
(Brazilian Oil Company)

Corporate
Data-Bases

IBM and FUJITSU
large and very large
mainframes

SNA
NETWORK

DECNET
NETWORK

Operational
Data-Bases

DEC and ELEBRA
small and medium size
computers

LAN

* PCs
* Terminals
* Workstations
* Data acquisition
  Equipment

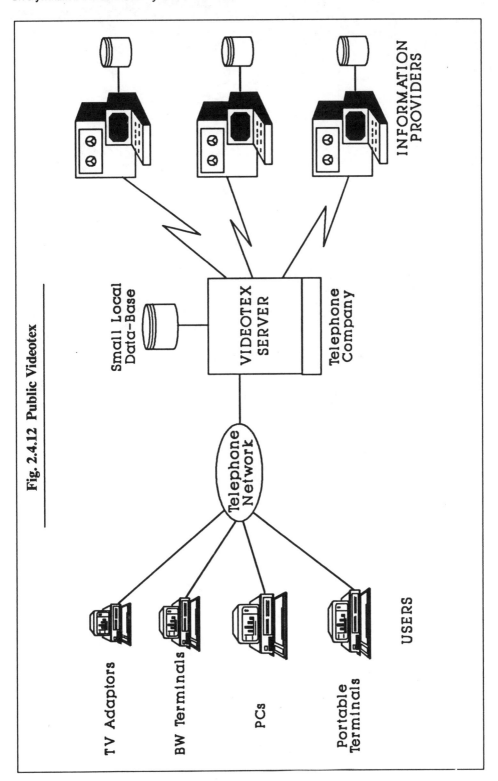

Fig. 2.4.12 Public Videotex

3 Designing the System

Summary

This section deals with principles and design of information systems for SMEs. The various issues which must be considered in the design and maintenance phases of an information system are listed and explained, and a development methodology is suggested.

Technical aspects of distributed architectures of data-bases together with questions related to the use of thesaurus-based data-bases and development of thesauri in chinese are also addressed. A proposal for a global information system to support the "SPARK" Information Pilot System concludes the section.

3.1 Information Systems and Abstract Services

Louis J. O'Korn

3.1.1 Summary

The experiences of Chemical Abstracts Service(CAS) with the development and operation of a high-volume, integrated, computer-based data-base-building and information service-delivery system are described. Brief background information on the CAS organization, its processing, and its products is provided. The problems addressed and some major milestones achieved during the transition from a manual to a computer-based production operation are discussed. Some of the critical underlying system design principles are identified. The application of these system design principles in developing an integrated data-base building, publishing, and online information service delivery system are illustrated. Finally, some views and considerations on future environments and technology are put forth.

3.1.2 Background

Some background on the activities of CAS and the nature of the information it handles will provide insight into the size and environment of its information systems, data-base building, and information service delivery activities.

CAS is a financially self-supporting division of the American Chemical Society, a not-for-profit scientific and educational association chartered by the United States Congress. The mission of CAS is to provide scientists and other users of chemical information with a means of accessing published research findings in chemistry, chemical engineering and related sciences from the massive outpouring of published scientific and technical information worldwide. CAS is located in Columbus, Ohio, and currently employs more than 1,400 people. CAS staff monitor some 14,000 scientific and technical periodicals from more than 150 nations, patent documents issued by twenty-six nations, conference and symposium proceedings, dissertations, government reports, and books from around the world. More than seventy-five percent of the material CAS abstracts comes from outside the United States and is published in more than fifty different languages. Over 309 journals from the People's Republic of China are covered by CAS.

Since the American Chemical Society first published Chemical Abstracts (CA) in 1907, CAS has had as its purpose to guide scientists and engineers to the chemical information they need. Toward this end, CA has carried more than eleven million abstracts of reports of chemical research and development since 1907, all thoroughly and precisely indexed.

For much of his history, CAS produced a single publication, CA. Today, delivering information means delivering it in a variety of ways, including printed, microform, computer-readable, and on-line electronically. In the 1960's and 1970's, CAS pioneered many of the methods now used to process and store scientific and technical information by computer. Production of all CAS services is highly automated, and CAS provides worldwide online access to the full content of CA and the CAS Chemical Registry System from Columbus. CAS information systems staff continue to work at the forefront of computer and information-processing technology, seeking still more effective approaches to processing, searching, and disseminating chemical and chemical engineering information. The CAS Report [1982] provides additional details on the history of Chemical Abstracts Service.

3.1.3 The Transition

With the rapid expansion of the scientific and technical activity in the 1950's and 1960's, it was obvious that traditional methods of abstracting, indexing, and publishing would not keep up with the rapidly growing volume of chemical and chemical engineering literature. In 1907, CA covered a total of 12,000 documents. By 1940, CA was publishing 65,000 abstracts a year. The growth accelerated even more rapidly in the 1950's and 1960's. The number of documents covered annually rose to 100,000 in 1957, 200,000 in 1966, 300,000 in 1971, and 400,000 in 1977. Approximately 485,000 documents will be covered in CA in 1989. Approximately 14,000 abstracts were generated and appeared in CA in 1988 from the 280 journals from the People's Republic of China.

With this large volume of literature to be handled, CAS found that manual processing techniques were causing unacceptable delays in the publication of the abstracts and indexes. Also, the cost of the labor-intensive approaches of the manual system were becoming prohibitive, and the customers were asking for additional, and more sophisticated, information services. In the 1960's, CAS began to experiment with the application of computer technology to the processes of handling chemical information. This early experimentation lead to the automation of the CAS information handling system. The automation effort has resulted in improved staff productivity, significantly improved currency of publication, an expanded range of CAS services and products, and a foundation for future products and services.

Some of the major milestones during the automation are described in the following paragraphs:

- In 1961, CAS introduced Chemical Titles, the first periodical to be built, organized, indexed, and composed almost totally by computer.
- In the mid 1960's, CAS developed techniques for translating chemical structure diagrams into a form that can be stored and manipulated by computer. These techniques provided the basis for the CAS Chemical Registry System, a computer-based system that uniquely identifies and encodes chemical substances and organizes information about them. During this time, CAS developed an initial batch-mode substructure search system.
- In the late 1960's, CAS developed several specialized computer-based services in biosciences and polymers that were issued simultaneously in printed form and in computer-readable form for searching.
- In the early 1970's, the production of CA was converted to computer-based production. A result of the automation of the CA processing was the creation of computer-searchable products based on the full CAS data-base. Many organizations were licensed to provide public services from the CAS computer-readable files.

- In the 1970's, some organizations began offering on-line public access to the CAS data-base content. The development of the highly computer-based information-handling system also made it possible to produce a diversity of products. In addition, custom products to meet the specialized needs of small groups of subscribers, individual companies, and organizations became possible during this time.
- In the early 1980's, CAS introduced a service that permitted online worldwide access to the substance information in the CAS Chemical Registry System by structure, substructure, chemical name, and molecular formula.
- In the mid-1980's, this initial on-line service expanded into the STN International network. STN International is a cooperative undertaking in which organizations in several nations are sharing electronically linked computer systems and other resources to reduce costly duplication of effort, and to provide integrated on-line access to data-bases in science and technology. CAS now provides direct on-line access to major portions of its data-base through the STN International network.

Wigington [1985] described the evolution of Chemical Abstracts Service with special emphasis on the changes brought about since the early 1960's due to advantages in computer technology. Weisgerber [1984] described the impact and importance of applying computer technology at CAS.

3.1.4 Design Approaches

Computers are used extensively in the preparation and delivery of the products and services that CAS offers. This application of computers involves large-scale information processing where the computer is a critical component of the production process. Because of the rapidly developing technological environment and the need to respond to increasingly demanding user requirements, much design attention has been given to positioning for the deployment of new technology as it becomes available. Several of the design approaches that are critical to the stepwise development of the CAS computer-based information processing system are described on the following pages.

3.1.5 Information Representation

A central issue in an information system is the representation and organization of the information it handles. The CAS information collection accumulates over long periods of time, and it must be built consistently. In computer-based information systems, design attention must focus primarily on the data representation, data formats, file organizations and data management procedures, and secondarily upon the processes which operate on the information. Information must be recorded at a level of detail to support all the intended uses, and must be independent of any specific use, operating system, programming language, or input/output device.

This early attention given to information representation and organization has been critical to the stepwise development of CAS information systems and to the external interface with CAS. This design attention has allowed CAS to build very large data-bases, over a number of years, with a variety of input devices. This information is stored in a device-independent form, and can be retrieved for output on a variety of devices. The information representation has provided a consistent format for the delivery of CAS electronic information products worldwide. Anselmo [1971] described a file format that has been used at CAS since the late 1960's. Blake et al. [1977] described the information representation used for chemical structure diagrams. The extension of the CAS information processing system to handle the publication of the American Chemical Society's primary journals was discussed by Schermer [1978].

3.1.6 Modularity

The general design of a computer-based information system such as that operated by CAS includes three major segments: Input, Data-base, and Output. The Input segment includes the functions to acquire, select, input, edit, certify, and convert the information to the form for storage in the data-base. The Data-Base segment includes the functions to store, update, provide access, enforce access privileges and limitations, and provide backup and recovery. The Output segment includes the functions to select, organize, format, and package products. This modularity has been extended into the subsegments of these major segments so that the operation can be continuous while technological advances in the subsegments can be introduced as they are available. By grouping functions in this way and by appropriately constructing the interfaces between segments, it is possible to upgrade and extend portions of the system while minimizing the disruptions to other portions of the system.

3.1.7 Authority Functions/Files

To simplify input processing, reduce the editing load, and ensure consistency, authority functions and files are used wherever possible. For example, each year CAS abstracts and indexes over 200 papers from the Chinese journal, Gaodeng Xuexiao Huaxue Xuebao. To avoid having to derive the abbreviated title for this journal, transcribe it, and edit it over 200 times, the journal is identified during input and processing by its computer-checkable ASTM CODEN, KTHPDM. The CODEN is substituted for the title until final preparation for output, at which time the CODEN is used as an access key to extract the correct abbreviated title from a carefully controlled authority file that contains CODEN and abbreviated journal titles for all journals regularly covered by CAS. Besides saving effort, this practice helps ensure both accuracy and consistency. The CAS Chemical Registry System performs a similar authority function in identifying chemical substances in the index-processing system. The Chemical Registry System is an integral component of CAS index-processing flow. It is based on an algorithm for generating a unique and unambiguous computer description from a two dimensional drawing representing the chemical substance, plus other information relating to stereochemistry. The Registry System provides for the unique identification of a chemical substance based on the input of the substance name or diagram. When each substance first enters the CAS Registry Data-base, it is assigned a unique identifying number - the CAS Registry Number. This CAS Registry Number is used as a key to automatically retrieve the systematic chemical name from the appropriate file. The CAS Chemical Registry System is one of the most powerful information processing tools utilized at CAS. Dittmar et al. [1976] described the general design of this system.

3.1.8 Data-Base Management Software

CAS was an early practitioner of and leader in the central control and administration of large computer data-bases. During the 1960's CAS conducted several in-depth reviews of commercially available data-base software, and CAS has found that commercial data-base software did not provide adequate capability and efficiency to process very large files of chemical information. CAS built a data-base management system with capabilities to handle the large character sets needed for a high quality editorial operation, to handle graphics and chemical structure representations, to handle large files with a large number of variable length data items, to provide highly optimized access to large fully inverted files, and to retrieve chemical information in a parallel computing environment. Because of the size, complexity, and responsiveness required, CAS has developed a wide variety of tools and techniques for backup and recovery from system failures. Today, some of the data-base requirements are satisfied through acquired data-base management software, but several major applications still use the CAS developed system. Huffenberger and Wigington [1975] described the overall CAS approach to data-base management.

3.1.9 Standards and Common Practice

CAS is committed to using national and international standards whenever possible. Development of several major components of the CAS information handling

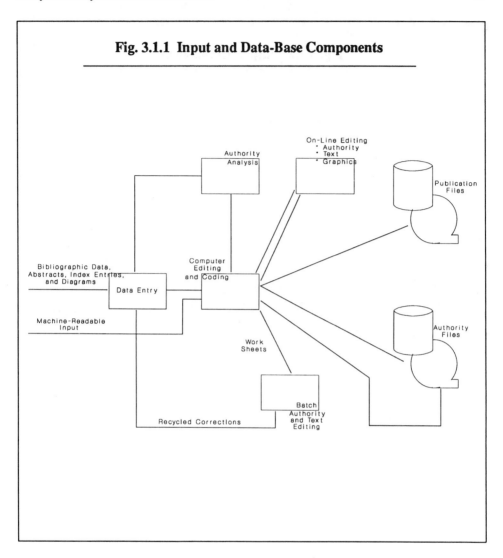

Fig. 3.1.1 Input and Data-Base Components

system predated the development of applicable standards. For any application area developed prior to the definition of the standards, CAS has established internal standards and common practices. These standards and practices address such issues as information content, information representation, information structure, character sets, file formats, user-computer interaction, application-foundation software interface, programming languages, and operating systems. The adherence to these standards and practices at interfaces between components has allowed the various system components to evolve without causing a sequence of changes to other components of the information system. Adherence to these standards and practices has made system more readily extensible to meet future needs while continuing to meet the ongoing operational commitments. Over the years, CAS has made significant changes to input and output equipment and to processing

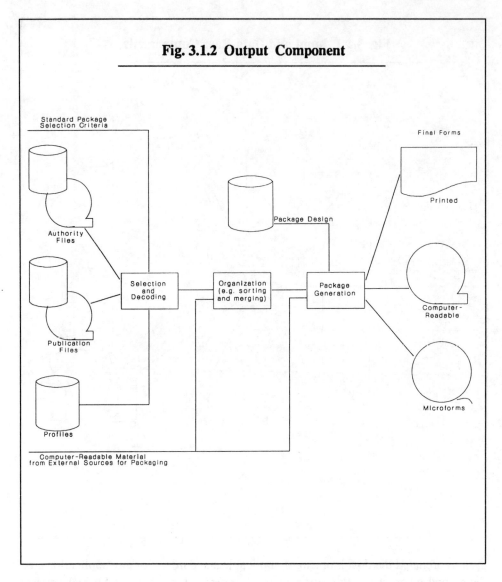

Fig. 3.1.2 Output Component

algorithms without requiring large-scale changes to the overall information handling system.

3.1.10 Consistent User Interface

The CAS internal processing system and STN International involve on-line human/computer interaction. A simple, consistent command language to an integrated set of files and functions is needed to ensure full and effective use of the automated capabilities, and to enhance the overall user productivity. In

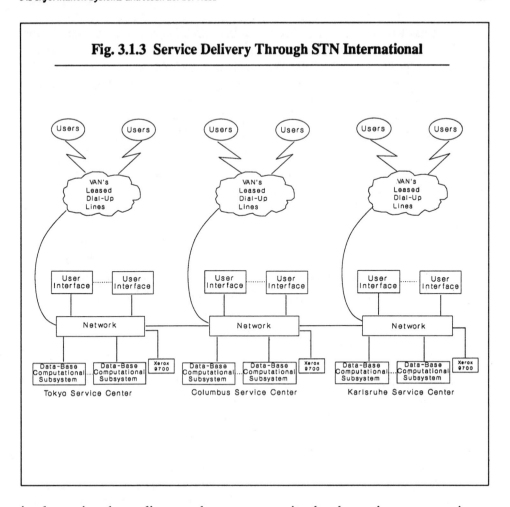

Fig. 3.1.3 Service Delivery Through STN International

implementing the on-line search system, attention has been given to a consistent command language and a consistent data-base definition. An expert/novice mode of user interaction has been developed so that the user is guided until the function is understood by the user, and then a more efficient interaction occurs. All of the system functions are supported in a consistent manner. All files loaded on STN International are handled in a homogeneous manner in order to achieve a unified user view. Integrity groups have been established to ensure adherence to these principles of user interaction and file design.

3.1.11 Automated Editing

Automated edits have contributed to the overall effectiveness of the computer-based information handling system at CAS. The ability to avoid redundant human effort and to transfer functions from human to computer execution has led to a significant reduction in editorial costs. It is recognized that an intellectual review by a human cannot be eliminated totally, but automated support can provide routine checks, validation, preservation of integrity, and elimination of redundant processes. This permits the human intellectual affort to focus on likely sources of errors. These human and machine processes provide early and sufficient validation of the information so that the remaining components of the computer system can operate without human intervention. Many simple characteristics of data can be handled completely by programmed algorithms. Check digits are normally used to verify identifiers. In addition to this artificial redundancy, natural redundancy of data provides the basis for further computer checking. For example, when both a structure diagram and molecular formula are entered for a chemical substance, the molecular formula can be generated from the diagram and compared to the input molecular formula. Consistency with previously captured information may also be the basis for additional checks. Vander Stouw [1975] and Dayton and Zamora [1976] provided details of the CAS approach to text and chemical substance editing.

3.1.12 Automated Packaging

The output segment of the CAS information-handling system includes the functions of selection, ordering, formatting, and composition. These totally automated processes produce printed or computer-readable data-base subsets corresponding to specific product package requirements. Selection criteria can be of varying complexity as long as essential information is included in the data-base. In some cases these are standard criteria and in others cases these are search profiles for custom services. The incorporation of the specific product style and the specific output device are incorporated at a late stage in the flow of the information system. This automated packaging principle has been extended and applied to the preparation of the American Chemical Society's primary journals in addition to CAS' secondary products. Aspects of the CAS output capabilities are described by Bammel [1975] and Couvreur et al. [1977].

3.1.13 The System

The system supporting the information processes at CAS replaced a traditional manual publishing operation. Rather than automate the typesetting process, a data-base production operation was built, with printed products as one of several possible outputs.

Wigington [1979] has described the system used for input and data-base management and output packaging. Figure 3.1.1 describes the Input and Data-base Management Components of the system. The information handled by the CAS information processing system consists of bibliographic data, abstracts, keyword phrases, index entries, and chemical substance diagrams. The data entry processes operate in a distributed on-line environment, and support the processing of text, chemical structure diagrams, and graphics. After all types of information are captured, extensive computer edits are applied, and material is encoded based on authority files. As new authority entries are identified, the analysis, data entry, editing, and maintenance of authority files are conducted. Virtually all information is edited on-line; some limited material still uses batch edits and correction cycles. A capability exists for accepting some information in computer-readable form.

Figure 3.1.2 describes the Output Component. These processes are almost totally automated. On the basis of standard selection criteria 'either standard issue criteria or specialized search criteria', material is selected from the appropriate publication data-base and decoded using authority files. The information is organized and generated for the appropriate output form. During the package generation processes, the style characteristics of a specific product are incorporated into the product package. Formatting for final output occurs late in the flow. Package design rules which define the type of information and its intended use are applied to determine the format. Output device characteristics are also added at this stage.

In the early 1980's, CAS made portions of its data-base available through a CAS-developed on-line service delivery system. This on-line search and retrieval system has expanded into STN International. STN International is a joint service offered by CAS located in Columbus, Ohio, USA; by FIZ-Karlsruhe, a scientific and educational organization located in Karlsruhe, the Federal Republic of Germany; and by the Japan Information Center of Science and Technology, an information organization located in Tokyo, Japan. STN International is a resource sharing endeavor that provides a broad range of integrated scientific and technical information services.

Figure 3.1.3 illustrates the on-line service delivery mechanism provided by STN International. Many of the design principles discussed earlier have been applied to the development and operation of STN International. Messenger is the name of the CAS developed software used to support STN International. It is a powerful software package designed to satisfy a broad range of user needs including search and retrieval from a variety of scientific and technical data-bases, data-base loading, computationally-oriented packages, document ordering, electronic mail, and bulletin boards. It provides the computer-to-computer interaction and single command language for consistent access to all STN data-bases regardless of searcher and data-base location. The Messenger software operates at STN Service Centers in Columbus, Ohio; Tokyo, Japan; and Karlsruhe, West Germany. The three Service Centers are electronically connected through a dedicated communications facility. Currently, over seventy-five data-bases are available through STN International. Each data-base is loaded at only one STN Service Center. This same software has also been installed at the United States Patent and

Trademark Office for use in searching the full-text files of United States Patents, as well as abstracts of Chinese patents.

All STN International data-bases are located with a consistent information format, representation, and structure. For each data-base available through STN International, a Data-base/Computational Subsystem handles all search and retrieval functions. Users of STN International can use a variety of terminals or personal computers to access STN International. Access to the nearest STN Service Center is accomplished through value-added networks (e.g. Venus-P in Japan, Datex-P in West Germany, and Telenet in USA), leased line, or dial-up connection. For each user connected to the system, a User Interface Subsystem is initiated. This User Interface Subsystem manages all the query formulation functions, verifies that the user is permitted access to the requested file, and connects the User Interface Subsystem to the Data-base/Computational Subsystem for the requested data-base or computational function. Once the search or computational function is complete, the User Interface Subsystem handles the interaction for answer display. A distributed software product called STN Express, which runs on IBM compatible personal computers, is available to perform some of the user interface functions. High-speed laser printers operate at each STN Service Center to provide any requested hard-copy output. Farmer [1984] described the design principles used in building this large-scale distributed on-line search and retrieval system. Particular emphasis was given to descriptions of the chemical substructure system developed to search the CAS Chemical Registry Data-Base.

3.1.14 Conclusions and Outlook

Approximately twenty-five years ago, CAS was faced with enormous information processing problems:

- the volume of material was great and increasing,
- processing delays were long and increasing,
- staff demands for intellectual review were great,
- processing costs were becoming prohibitive.

A long term automation program has been conducted and is continuing. This program has resulted in greatly increased staff productivity, significantly improved timeliness of processing and publication, improved accuracy and consistency of data-bases and products, a strong entry in the electronic information environment, and a foundation for future products, change, and growth.

In building the CAS information-handling system, attention has been given to designing for change. The system needed to be extensible for future purposes, but also had to handle past and current needs. For the stepwise migration to occur, attention had to be given to development of an open system architecture to incorporate existing application needs as well as future plans.

Architectural choices which allow taking advantage of new technology as it develops are extremely important. To this end, development and adherence to standards in such areas as operating systems, programming languages, networks, software architecture, data-base management systems, information representation, and user-computer interactions will support stepwise transitions. In addition, the use of standard interfaces to underlying data-base management , networking, and user interface software simplifies development and increases the flexibility of resulting systems.

In reviewing CAS' accomplishments and some technological trends, a few observations are appropriate:

- Software is a critical component of an overall information handling system. A rigorous software development methodology that results in highly reliable, easily extensible, portable, maintainable, and well documented programs must be employed. Disciplined testing and strict software management procedures must exist so that new or modified features do not disrupt ongoing operations. The environment must foster continuous and orderly system evolution.
- Cost justification and planning should be done with appropriate consideration for this long-term use environment. CAS has found that many of its programs operate for 10-20 years with frequent and repeated use.
- Early in the CAS automation program, CAS staff developed most of the application software. More recently, CAS has found opportunities to purchase software packages. Potential difficulties must be recognized with integration into the internal environment, dependence on an external organization, and adherence to internal standards.
- With the development of more powerful workstations that can provide highly responsive interactions, the trend is to automate more complex human intellectual functions. To his end, CAS has ongoing research thrusts in the areas of natural language processing, improved human-computer interactions, knowledge-based systems, automatic language translation, and enhanced document analysis. These workstations are also heavily employed in support of the software developmentprocesses as well, and emphasis has been given to the development of capabilities to support these processes.
- Costs of CAS staff significantly outweigh hardware costs, and the difference is increasing. A large portion on the data-base building costs are associated with the human effort. Great leverage is obtained from the reduction of human effort through the elimination of redundant processes or the transferring of functions from human to computer processing.
- Costs of staff for software development represent a significant and rising component of the overall system life cycle costs. Great leverage in reducing

costs can be obtained from software reuse. To this end, increasing attention has been paid to software portability and general purpose software.

- The CAS information handling system has evolved from a centralized, batch-oriented, and sequential environment to a distributed, on-line, and direct access environment. The attention given to internal standards for computer-to-computer communications, well-defined information representation, explicit procedures for use and update of authority information, and software components available on multiple computers has been extremely important. Bringing internal standards and common practices up to national and international standards is a challenge that needs continued attention.

Baker [1985] speculated on the future of scientific secondary services. He identified a variety of barriers to the development of scientific secondary services in the areas of intellectual property rights and legal mechanisms; economic matters; political, social, and cultural concerns; and technical issues. Wingington [1987] reviewed the evolution of information technology, and identified some lessons from history to be applied to the future. Although much has been accomplished at CAS during the automation of its information-handling system, there is much yet to be done.

References

[1] Anzelmo, F.D., 1971. "A Data-Storage Format for Information System Files", IEEE Transactions on Computers, Vol. C-20, No.1, pp. 39-43.

[2] Baker, D.B., 1985. "Chemical Abstracts Service's Secondary Chemical Information Services, "Journal of Chemical Information and Computer Sciences, Vol. 25, pp. 186-191.

[3] Bammel, S.E., 1975. "Automatic Full Page Formatting of Technical Journals", Proceeding of the National Computer Conference, pp. 825-829.

[4] Blake, J.E., Farmer, N.A., and Haines, R.C., 1977. "An Interactive Computer Graphics System for Processing Chemical Structure Diagrams, "Journal of Chemical Information and Computer Sciences, Vol. 17, No. 4, pp. 223-228.

[5] CAS Report, 1982. "The First 75 Years of Chemical Abstracts Service", CAS Report, No. 12, pp. 3-9.

[6] Covreur, K.M., Dittmar, P.G., and Mockus, J., 1977. "An Algorithmic Computer Graphics Program for Generating Chemical Structure Diagrams", Journal of Chemical Information and Computer Sciences, Vol. 17, No. 3, pp. 186-192.

[7] Dayton, D.L., and Zamora, A., 1976. "The CAS registry System. V. Structure Input and Editing", Journal of Chemical Information and Computer Sciences, Vo. 16, No. 4, pp. 219-222.

[8] Dittmar, P.G., Stobaugh, R.E., and Watson, C.E., 1976. "The CAS Chemical Registry System.I.General Design", Journal of Chemical Information and Computer Science, Vol.16, pp. 111-121.

[9] Farmer, N.A., 1984. "Searching Large Files of Scientific and Technical Information", Proceedings of the CompCon '84 Twenty-eighth IEEE Computer Society International Conference, pp. 156-159.

[10]Huffenberger, M.A., and Wigington, R.L., 1975. "Chemical Abstracts Service Approach to Management of Large Data-Bases", Journal of Chemical Information and Computer Sciences, Vol. 15, No. 1, pp. 43-47.

[11]Schermer, C.A., 1978. "The Primary Journal System - A Case Study", GCCA Journal, Vol. 11, No. 1, pp. 19-24.

[12]Vander Stouw, G.G., 1975. "Computer Programs for Editing and Validation of Chemical Names", Journal of Chemical Information and Computer Sciences, Vol. 16, No. 4, pp. 232-236.

[13]Weisgerber, D.W., 1984. "Application of Technology to CAS Data-Base Production", Information Services and Use, Vol. 4, pp. 317-325.

[14]Wingington, R.L., 1979. "Computer Architecture for Editorial Processing Within an Integrated Publishing Organization", Journal of Research Communications Studies, No. 2, pp. 25-38.

[15]Wingington, R.L., 1985. "Applications of Computer Technology to Science Information Services", The Role of Data in Scientific Progress, P.S. Glasses (ed.), CODATA, pp. 505-509.

[16]Wingington, R.L., 1987. "Evolution of Information Technology and Its Impact on Chemical Information", Journal of Chemical Information and Computer Sciences, Vol. 27, No. 2, pp. 51-55.

3.2 Structural Principles of Distributed Data-Base Management Systems

Chou Longhsiang

3.2.1 Background and Status Quo

There is a lot of research and development work in the field of Distributed Data-Base Management Systems (DDBMS) since the middle of the seventies. The reason of this trend comes from two sources. One is that the application requirements, the distributed data processing requirements are growing rapidly in recent years. Distributed data processing has entered into the life of the people, for example airline and train reservations, banking, management of geographically distributed companies, factories, schools, hospitals, stores and organizations, collection and processing of economical information, working out economical plans, collection and application of military information, etc. The other one is the miraculous progress of computers, especially the microcomputers, the workstations, the communication networks, particularly the local area networks (LAN). In the past ten years much has been reported on DDBMS, and a few pioneer systems have been established.

After more than ten year efforts, DDBMS has arrived at decisive achievements: many elementary questions have been suggested and solved, new technology has been proposed and used, several prototypes have been established and more comprehensive experiences have been provided. Some marketable DDBMS are supplied or will be supplied. So we are able to say that DDBMS is now a mature technology, the next step is to apply it and develop more market products.

3.2.2 Two-Level Views of DDBMS

Generally, in Distributed Data-Base Systems (DDBS) we have two level views that are described through a global level scheme and a local level scheme and controlled by DDBMS and Local Data-Base Management System (LDBMS) (Fig. 3.2.1).

For the global users they know and access all data stored on each site through the global scheme. The local users only know and access the data stored on their own sites through the local scheme, and they do not know the existence of DDBS. The control of DDBMS has two strategies, centralized and distributed. The former has a central site to control the whole DDBMS. Its merits are easy to keep the consistency when updating data, but the demerits are easy to form bottle necks and weaken the system stability. The distributed strategy is more stable and balancing. Crashes on some sites will not destroy the whole DDBMS. For distributed control

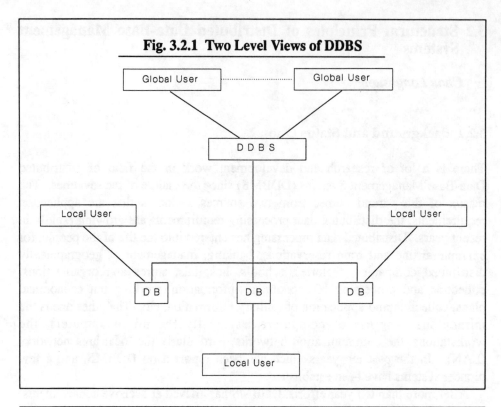

Fig. 3.2.1 Two Level Views of DDBS

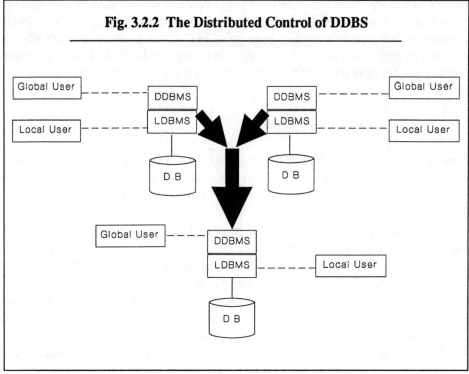

Fig. 3.2.2 The Distributed Control of DDBS

the catalog architecture is a key question. Figure 3.2.2 gives the distributed control DDBS.

There are different transparent views for different DDBS. We have total transparent view, half transparent view and nontransparent view. For the first one, the global users face a single unified DDBS, they need not to know where the data are stored and where their transactions are executed. For the third one, the global users have to know at which sites the data they accessed are stored and what are the languages that can access that data. The middle situation is the second one, the global users use a single language to write their transactions but they need to specify where the data they accessed are stored. The transparency spectrum of DDBS is shown in Fig. 3.2.3.

Of course, the first one is the most advantageous for the user but this type of DDBMS also is the most complicated one. The third one imposes more tasks to the user and the DDBMS is relative simple. The second one is in the middle situation between the first and the third.

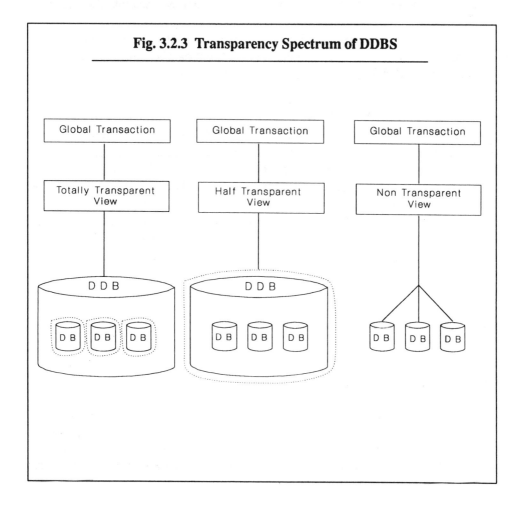

Fig. 3.2.3 Transparency Spectrum of DDBS

3.2.3 Architecture of DDBMS

There are two modes to establish DDBMS. One is to set up DDBMS from beginning. The LDBMS are parts of DDBMS, both of them form together a single unified system. The DDBMS can control each site totally and no transformation is needed. The other one is to integrate the different existing LDBMS on different sites to form a whole DDBMS. The problems of transformation and consistency make the design of this kind of DDBMS rather difficult.

Here we list some problems that must be solved:

1) The transformations of data models. For example the relational codasyl or hierarchical models have to be transformed into a common global model and vice versa or transformed mutually. The overhead of transformations is rather high, and to keep the transformation consistency is not easy because the structure correspondence among these data models is not simple.

2) The assertion transformations. Each data model has its own privacy and integrity assertions. To transform them into a global recognizable form is not a easy task.

3) Command transformations. The difference of DML is very large among different data-models. The statements of different data models have no one by one correspondence, the transformations are rather complicated.

Considering the above difficulties most of the existing pioneer prototypes took the first mode to establish DDBMS such as SDD-1, Distributed INGRES, R*, SIRIUS-DELTA, POREL, C-POREL, ADA-DDM, VDN, etc. Relating to data transformation, DDBMS is divided into two kinds, homogeneous and heterogeneous. The former only allow the same data model in each site. If the operating systems and computers are also the same, then they are called totally homogeneous. The latter allow different data models on different sites. They are called heterogeneous. The data transformation has several levels, the data model transformation, the representation transformation (ASCII or EBCDIC, word length, scale,...), the unit transformation (kilo meter or mile, net salary or total salary) and so on.

3.2.4 Several Pioneer Prototype Systems

3.2.4.1 SDD-1

SDD-1 is one of the easiest DDBMS in the world. It is designed and developed by Computer Corporation of America (CCA). This is a relational system supporting single statement transactions. SDD-1 uses Datalanguage as its query language which will be translated into QUEL and optimized. Concurrence control strategy is timestamp and conflict graph analysis. The catalog management idea is to settle catalog data as normal relations just like the user data, then they can be accessed through the unified interface. For managing catalog itself a catalog locator is used. SDD-1 supports relation horizontal and vertical fragment and data replica. Semi-join is an optimization method suggested by SDD-1. The prototype system of SDD-1 is implemented on a DEC machine with Datacomputer as its local DBMS. The communication system is the Mail system of ARPANET. SDD-1 has a great influence in the field of DDBMS.

3.2.4.2 Distributed INGRES

Distributed INGRES is the successor project of INGRES. It is also designed and developed in California University in Berkeley. Like SDD-1, Distributed INGRES is a relational system and supports single statement transactions. The user language is QUEL, concurrence control strategy uses locking technique. It supports relation horizontal fragment but does not support data replica. The catalog strategy is different from SDD-1. It distinguishes the local data (can only be accessed from one site) from the global data (can be accessed from the whole network) and sets up the local catalog and the global catalog correspondingly. The prototype is implemented on a VAX machine using UNIX, the market product is named INGRES/STAR.

3.2.4.3 R*

R* is the successor project of System R designed and developed by IBM San Jose Laboratory. In the field of relation systems, System R got the position of a milestone, its market products are SQL/DS and DB2. R* is also a relational system using SQL as its user language. Each program running in System R can also run in R*. R* means arbitrarily many Systems R. Site autonomy is the peculiar feature of R*. Each site in R* controls its own data. There is no centralized control in the network. The objects in R* have a special naming mechanism which allows different user on different sites using different external names to access the same object or using the same external name to access different objects. R* uses a distributed catalog management strategy which is user-oriented distinguishing itself from the data-oriented catalog used in SDD-1, Distributed INGRES, POREL and C-POREL. In R*, the concurrence control is locking and using a distributed dead lock testing method. R* does not support relation fragment and data replica, it provides good authorization and authentication facilities. The running environment is MVS, site communication is performed by using IBM SNA through CICS.

3.2.4.4 POREL

POREL is a relational DDBMS designed and implemented by the research group in Stuttgart University led by Prof. E.J.Neuhold. The user language is Relational Data-Base Language (RDBL) which is SQL-like and the host language is PASCAL. It supports relation horizontal fragment and data replica. POREL is a half homogeneous DDBMS using Relation Base Machine (RBM) as an interface to unify the different operating systems and computers. The concurrence control strategy is locking and adopts prevention techniques to prevent dead lock. POREL distinguishes two kinds of catalogs, short catalog and long catalog. The former stays on every site and contains global information which is changed slowly such as relation schemes. The latter stays only on the sites that the corresponding data stored. It contains the information that is changed frequently such as the cardinalities of relations. The catalog data are arranged like the user relations and the same concurrence control and recovery facilities are used. POREL has three kinds of user interface, namely, the RDBL transactions, the RDBL+PASCAL transactions and the application supporting interface. A unified communication system (CS) is provided to perform communications among system modules as well as network sites. The network communication obeys Reliable State Control (RSC) protocol. The prototype of POREL is built on a VAX machine using simulant network.

3.2.4.5 SIRIUS

SIRIUS is a French nationwide DDBMS project sponsored by the French government through INRIA. This project concerns a lot of universities and institutes and has got many results and prototypes such as SIRIUS-DELTA, POLYPHEME, MICROBE etc. The networks used in these systems are EURONET and TRANSPAC. SIRIUS-DELTA is a relational DDBMS supporting horizontal and vertical fragment and data replica. The computers and operating systems in the SIRIUS-DELTA may be different. The concurrence control is locking, adopting dead lock prevention strategy. The recovery facilities are relatively good. SIRIUS-DELTA has been running. It is called the preindustrial prototype.

3.2.4.6 DDM

Distributed Data Manager (DDM) is designed and developed by CCA. Its user language is Adaplex which is an integrating data-base programming language through embedding the data-base sub-language Daplex into Ada. The centralized DBMS supporting Adaplex is called LDM (Local Data Manager) also developed by CCA. DDM supports dynamically joining of new sites, data replica and a function data model which has more powerful modelling ability than hierarchy, network and relation data models. It uses semi-join technique to optimize. The concurrence control is locking and doing check periodically for solving dead lock. DDM uses a multiversion mechanism to make read-only transactions never be rollbacked. It suggested some efficient methods to renovate old versions and to do recovery. About site communication it implemented an enhanced network which uses RSC protocol. The implementation language of DDM is Ada to guarantee portability. A DDM prototype is set up on VAX 11/780 with VMS.

3.2.4.7 C-POREL

C-POREL is designed by the Institute of Mathematics, Academia Sinica and implemented by the same institute cooperating with the Shanghai University of Science and Technology and Normal University of East China. The design of C-POREL is based on the pioneer DDBMS such as SDD-1, Distributed INGRES, R*, DDM, SIRIUS-DELTA, particularly POREL. The main goals of C-POREL are practicability, advancement and limited portability. C-POREL is a relational DDBMS, its user language is RDBL, host language is PASCAL and implemented by PASCAL and C. The compiler of RDBL is generated by Compiler Generator Tool (CGT) which is developed by the C-POREL Group. C-POREL supports relation horizontal fragment and implements refined algorithms to optimize distributed queries. The concurrence control is built through integrating locking and time-stamping. Local and global recoveries are supported by using local and global system logs. The catalog management of C-POREL has peculiar features. The separate catalog manager is set up and uses copy mechanisms to upgrade the system efficiency. The communication system distinguishes intersites from local communications. The intermodules local communications are performed through OS., and the intersites communications are committed to CS. A broadcasting layer and a global clock system are developed in the bottom level of Ethernet. In C-POREL, the RSC protocol is used and implemented totally. Its efficiency is better than the one of the original papers. The user interface of C-POREL has several functions including pull down menu, whole screen windows, report writer, spreadsheet, various graphics and complex table generators. A natural language (Chinese) intelligent interface is just being developed. The developing environment is 32 bits microcomputers Universe 68 with 4MB memories, they are connected through the Universe net which is Ethernet like. The operating system is UNOS which is compatible with UNIX. The architecture of C-POREL is shown in Fig. 3.2.4.

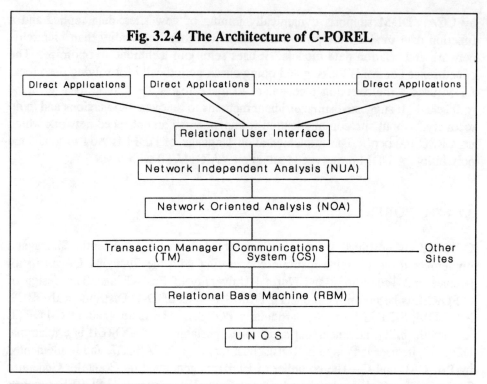

Fig. 3.2.4 The Architecture of C-POREL

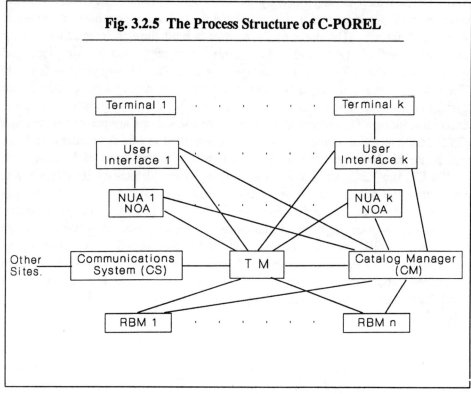

Fig. 3.2.5 The Process Structure of C-POREL

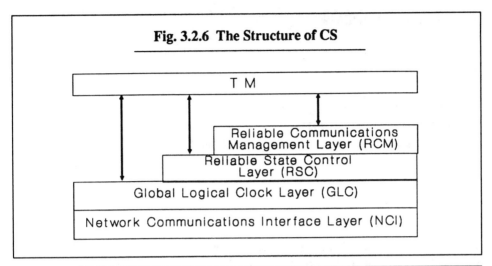

Fig. 3.2.6 The Structure of CS

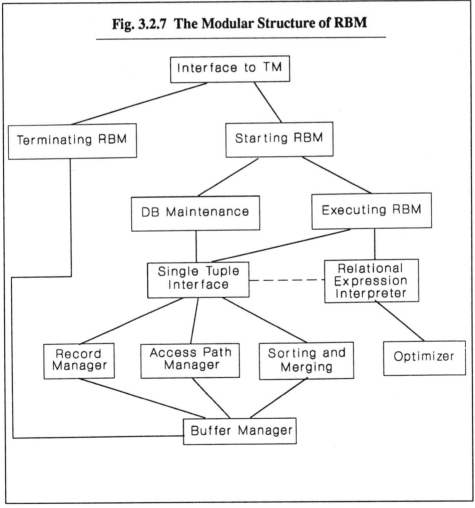

Fig. 3.2.7 The Modular Structure of RBM

3.2.5 Features of DDBMS

3.2.5.1 Transparency of Sites

In DDBMS the users normally face a logical unified data-base. The distribution of data and distributed data processing are transparent to users. The users feel that their data are stored in their site and their transactions are processed on the same site.

3.2.5.2 Two Architectures

DDBMS has two architectures, homogeneous and heterogeneous. The former means that there are the same data models on each site. If the computers, the operating systems and the LDBMS are the same on each site, this DDBMS is called totally homogeneous. Otherwise it is called partially homogeneous. The latter means that there are different data models. POREL is an example of half homogeneous DDBMS. It has the same relational data models but can be set up on sites which possess different computers and different OS's. POREL uses the same structure RBM and CS to unify the different OS's and computers. Most of the DDBMS are set up from the beginning, but some DDBMS are built through integrating the different existing local data-base systems. The practical requirement of this DDBMS structure is no doubt necessary, but the transformation difficulties including data model transformations, integrity assertions transformations, language transformations, data representation transformations and data model transformations have to be overcome correctly and efficiently.

3.2.5.3 Site Autonomy

There are two control levels, local and global. In some architectures the sites are not autonomous. This only allows the global transactions. Transactions processed only in the single site are processed as special global transactions. For example POREL, C-POREL are this kind of control. Some DDBMS's allow site autonomy. There are pure local transactions, they are only processed on the local site and the users even do not know the existence of DDB. The local sites can decide which data belong to the local site and which data may be shared by the whole system. For example R* has a high degree of site autonomy.

3.2.5.4 Catalog Structure

Most of DDBMS's are supporting global catalog such as SDD-1, Distributed INGRES, POREL and C-POREL. This data-oriented catalog structure controls globally the whole DDB. The distributed catalog structure supports site autonomy such as R*, it is an user-oriented catalog structure. In this kind of DDBMS, each site announces to other sites its local data that are provided to whole DDB. The users of other sites have to record these data into their own catalog for using.

3.2.5.5 Data Fragment

The relations are normally too large and not flexible. It is necessary to divide them. There are two types of fragments, horizontal and vertical. The horizontal fragment is performed through restriction operations which cut the relations into sub-relations. The vertical fragment is performed through projection operations which have to guarantee the loseless join. The sub-relations in most DDBMS are not overlapped but VDN allows overlap. POREL, C-POREL, Distributed INGRES and DDM support horizontal fragment, SDD-1, SIRIUS-DELTA and VDN support horizontal as well as vertical fragment.

3.2.5.6 Replica

The goals of the replica are efficiency and safety. A data object has several copies which are transparent to the users. Replica raises difficulties when updating date. A lot of papers discussed the algorithms of these questions but only few of them are implemented.

3.2.5.7 Optimization

Optimization is a very important issue in DDBMS because of the extreme complexity of distributed systems. For providing acceptable system efficiency we have to use optimization to reduce the system overhead. The optimization is generally divided into two parts, local and global. It contains the costs of data processing (cpu), disk access, I/O, process exchange and network communications (including message length and message number). For wide area network the dominating factor is communication cost, but for local are network the cpu, I/O and the communications costs all have to be considered. SDD-1, POREL and POLYPHEME only considered the communication overhead, but DDM and C-POREL considered data processing cost as well. As the optimal criterion the optimal goal function has two modes: one considers total time and the other considers response time. Considering response time has the merit of parallel execution on the network. For doing optimization we have two choices, the static optimization (compiling time optimization) or the dynamic optimization (executing time optimization). During optimization the sizes of intermediate relations are very important factors. For static optimization the estimation error will propagate and accumulate in successive estimations. The merits of static optimization are simple, with less system overhead and having the advantage of parallel execution on the network. The demerits are difficult to estimate the size of intermediate relations and to design the optimal execution plan. POREL and C-POREL use the static optimization and use the statistic and dynamic programming method to improve the algorithms. The dynamic optimization estimates the sizes of intermediate relations during execution process and then decides which sites the data have to be sent to. This will reduce the propagation and accumulation of estimative errors, but the demerits are enlarging the system overhead and loosing the advantage of parallel execution. Some systems adopt a mixed strategy. The dynamic estimation is used only when the sizes of intermediate relations are much different from the static estimation. After doing the optimization a query plan is designed. One possibility is making it centralized on the site where the transaction is submitted. The other one is doing it distributedly on all of the sites of participating partners. The optimization scope can be one simple query statement or several query statements.

3.2.5.8 Data Model

Most of the DDBMS are relational models. As mentioned by E.F. Codd the relational model is most suitable for distribution. DDM is an exception, it uses function data model Daplex which has more powerful modelling ability.

3.2.5.9 Concurrence Control

Three concurrence control techniques have been suggested, namely, the locking, the timestamping and the optimizing. Most of the DDBMS adopt the locking method. SDD-1 uses timestamping. C-POREL uses the mixed technique of locking and timestamping. No systems have adopted optimizing technique.

3.2.5.10 Deadlock

Several techniques have been suggested for solving deadlock. They are deadlock prevention, deadlock checking, deadlock avoiding and time out. Deadlock checking can be made centralized or distributed. R* implemented a distributed deadlock checking technique.

3.2.5.11 Interpretation and Compilation

Binding time is an important factor for system efficiency. The early binding in compiling time may improve the execution efficiency. However it has to recompile if the system state between compiling time and executing time is changed. The interpretation is more flexible for dealing with the changing of the system state. SDD-1 and Distributed INGRES used interpretation. R*, POREL, C-POREL and DDM adopted compilation.

3.2.5.12 Network Topology

It is assumed that there are the same communication rates in the link level of the network. In the algorithms the different network topologies have to be considered. SDD-1 considers ARPANET. POREL obeys X.25 protocol. R* is SNA and C-POREL is Ethernet. For DDBMS the broadcasting network is very reasonable.

3.2.5.13 Relational Operations

There are a few systems supporting complete relational operations. R* does not support UNION, DIVISION, INTERSECTION and DIFFERENCE, but it supports aggregate functions AVG, MAX, MIN etc. and nested sub-queries. SDD-1 supports semi-join but R* and Distributed INGRES do not. C-POREL supports nested sub-queries and aggregate functions.

3.2.5.14 Recovery and Reliability

The principle of recovery is very simply that of redundancy. Relatively speaking the investigation of recovery is not so deep. The main problem is the huge system overhead. Recovery is used for enhancing the system robustness and tolerance for dealing with the exceptions. However it consumes a lot of space and time. The question is that for dealing with very rare exceptions we have to pay very large cost which reduces the efficiency of normal major situations. Is it reasonable? Can the users tolerate these expenses? Of course the ideal technique is that we can deal with various exceptions and pay only small cost. R* developed a variant protocol of two phase commitment which has relatively good performance in normal situations. Many papers have suggested a lot of complicated protocols and techniques, their overhead in normal cases is very large. This defect is not yet revealed clearly because most of them are not implemented at all. Recovery normally is divided into two parts, local and global. C-POREL implemented these two level recoveries. R* supports dual logging.

3.2.6 Comparison of Some Pioneer Prototype Systems

We list two tables as Table 3.2.1 and Table 3.2.2.

3.2.7 Conclusions

As mentioned above we are now in a position of harvest. The elementary problems of DDBMS are solved and several market products are just productive. For deepening the existing results further we have to investigate the following problems:

- Collection and analytic comparison of implementation experiences: although there are a lot of DDBMS papers and research projects, only a few deal with the integration of whole DDBMS, the testing and debugging of the system, the comparison of different algorithms, the system performance analysis and the summary and analysis of implementation experiences. In C-POREL we are just investigating its testing and debugging environment and trying to set up this environment. We are also studying the problem of the system performance analysis. Some comparative analysis of different catalog structures is being carried out.
- Load balancing, distributed data-base design and user access pattern analysis.
- User interface.
- Large amount of sites (for example more than 5000 sites) in DDBMS.
- Totally heterogeneous DDBMS.
- Relations with the work stations.

Table 3.2.1 Some Pioneer Prototype Systems

Name of System	Data Model	Fragment	Replica	Interpretation or Compilation	Query Plan	Optimal Factor	Concurrency Control	Deadlock
SDD-1	relational model	horizontal vertical	yes	interpretation	centralized	communication	timestampling	
Distributed INGRES	relational model	horizontal	no	interpretation	centralized	communication,	locking CPU	
R*	relational model	no	no	compilation	half centralized	communication CPU, I/O	locking	distributed testing
POREL	relational model	horizontal	yes	compilation	centralized	communication	locking	prevention
C-POREL	relational model	horizontal	no	compilation	centralized	communication, CPU	locking, timestamping	prevention
SIRIUS-DELTA	relational model	horizontal vertical	yes	compilation	centralized	communication	locking	prevention
POLYPHEME	relational model	no	no	interpretation	centralized	communication	no	
ENCOMPASS	relational model	horizontal	no	interpretation	centralized		communication	locking	timeout
DDM	functional model	horizontal	yes	compilation	centralized	communication, CPU	locking	centralized testing
VDN	relational model	horizontal (overlap)	yes		centralized		lock by user	

Table 3.2.2 Some Distributed Query Algorithms

Papers or Systems	Optimization Mode	Goal Function	Optimization Factors	Network Topology	Semi-Join	Fragment	Replica	Complexity of Algorithm
P.M.G. Apers, A.R. Hevner, S.B. Tao	static	response total time	number of messages length of messages	general	yes	no	no	polynomial
SDD-1	static	total time	length of messages	general	yes	yes	yes	polynomial local optimal
W.W. Chu, P. Hurley	static	total time	length of messages, CPU	general	no	no	yes	exponential (global optimal)
Distributed INGRES	dynamic	response time or total time	length of messages, CPU	general or broadcast	no	yes	no	polynomial (local optimal)
UNITY	static	response time	length of messages, I/O	star	yes	no	no	
R*	static	total time	number of messages, length of messages, CPU, I/O	general	no	no	no	dynamic programming
POLYPHEME	dynamic	total time	length of message	broadcast	no	no	no	dynamic programming
POREL	static	total time	length of messages	general	no	yes	yes	dynamic programming
C-POREL	static	total time	length of messages, number of messages, CPU, I/O	Ethernet broadcast	yes	yes	no	dynamic programming

3.3 Thesauri Management for On-Line Information Systems

Yu Yongyuan

3.3.1 Introduction

In the fields of information and documentation, in particular, in information retrieval systems (IRS) the use of terminological tools which are called thesaurus is very important.

The word "thesaurus" comes from Greek, meaning "treasury". Since the Middle Ages it has been used as "language treasury" or "dictionary". The forerunner of the thesaurus is a synonym dictionary named "Thesaurus of English Words and Phrases" (1852, Peter Mark Roget). But it is not a documentation thesaurus. Therefore it is necessary to distinguish between the two types of thesauri: a synonym dictionary and a documentation thesaurus; both of them can be used to find the exact expression for a group of synonyms, but their aims are different. The purpose of a documentation thesaurus is not to show all variants of synonyms, but instead, it selects one of them as the preferred term which is called descriptor for the use in an information system.[1]-[5].

The development of Thesauri began in the 50's, as the electronic data processing has been used in information and documentation. In the meantime a lot of topics concerning this have been discussed, e.g.:

- the ideal structure of thesauri and their presentation;
- establishment of multilingual thesauri;
- combination of different thesauri (e.g. superordinated thesaurus and some special thesauri in the same field);
- advantage and disadvantage of thesauri-aided retrieval versus free-text word retrieval.

The development of full-text data-base and free-text word retrieval is a great challenge to the thesaurus retrieval principle, because thesauri are very expensive. Sometimes the free-text word retrieval is very useful, especially for some new topics which have not yet been taken into the thesaurus; but a terminological control with the help of the thesaurus principle is still necessary for an efficient information retrieval system.

Comparative studies have shown that the combination of the retrieval based on descriptors with free-text terms gives the best results. Factors which influence the search results are as follows [2], [6], [7].

- Volume of the data-base
- Quality of the thesaurus
- Topics of the retrieval

- Special knowledge of the searcher

During past years a lot of people believed that the thesauri principle would soon be replaced by the free-text term retrieval and that the thesaurus method would be out of date. But recently there has been a new boom in thesauri work.

The decisive reason for the rejection of the thesaurus principle is the great effort and the high cost of the manual preparation and management of thesauri. Therefore computer-aided thesauri preparation and management is an important factor for the new upward trend. In addition the acceptance of the thesaurus method in fields other than traditional documentation (e.g. expert systems) and comparable development in artificial intelligence research (e.g. knowledge representation, semantic network) have also made their contributions [8], [9].

3.3.2 Some Basic Aspects for Thesauri Management

3.3.2.1 Topics Regarding Thesaurus Work

3.3.2.1.1 Definition of Thesaurus

There are many versions for defining this concept. A very simple and clear definition given by the West German Society of Documentation is as follow: A thesaurus as an aid for documentation is a collection of words in natural languages (common and special language) with representation of their conceptual relationships.

According to the West German Standard DIN 1463 (1987) a thesaurus has the following characteristics:

- concepts and relationships are exactly referred to each other;
- synonyms should be included as completely as possible;
- homonyms and polysomies should be marked clearly;
- every concept must have its own features (preferred term, concept number, classification) which clearly characterize this concept;
- relationships between concepts (represented by some common features) should be described.

3.3.2.1.2 Conceptual Relationships in Thesauri

There are three types of relations which are in the center of thesaurus development, that is:

- equivalent relations, i.e. terms are considered as equal or similar in their meaning (synonyms and quasi-synonyms) and can be classified in the same group. In an information retrieval system, if one is selected from such a group as a descriptor, then the others would be seen as non-descriptors. In the thesauri users are referred from the non-descriptors to descriptors.
Example:

Non-descriptor:	Motion Pictures	
	USE	Films
Descriptor: Films		
	USED FOR	Motion Pictures

- hierarchic relations which represent super and sub-ordinate relations. Among the two concepts in such a relation, the more general one is called broader term (BT), the other one narrower term (NT)
Example:
   BT: Aircraft
   NT: Fixed-Wing Aircraft
- associative relations, which represent the horizontal or diagonal relations (neither hierarchic nor equivalent) between the two concepts. They are called related terms (RT).
Example:
   Aircraft
   RT: Flight

3.3.2.1.3 Thesaurus Words

All words which stay in a thesaurus are called thesaurus words, they include:

- Descriptors as preferred concepts representatives;
- Non-descriptors as forbidden terms to a certain information system;
- Dependent thesaurus words which would be used only in combination with other words.

3.3.2.1.4 Terminological Control

This is an indispensable function for a thesaurus to prevent any misunderstandings between communication partners due to non-uniform use of terms, especially synonyms and homonyms. This aim can be achieved in two ways:

- reference from non-descriptors to the corresponding descriptors;
- leading from a forbidden term over some common features in the system (e.g. classification number) to other corresponding terms.

3.3.2.2 Available Guidelines for Thesaurus Work

In order to support thesaurus work, many efforts have been made all over the world. There are a lot of international and national standard and nonstandard guidelines for thesaurus and indexing which are listed in the annex 3.3.1. Among them, there are two guidelines from the ISO:

- Guideline for the establishment and development of monolingual thesauri;
- Guideline for the establishment and development of multilingual thesauri.

Many countries have made their own guidelines, e.g. the above mentioned DIN 1463 of West Germany. The symbols for thesaurus terms according to the ISO guidelines are shown in annex 2.

3.3.2.3 Structure of the Thesaurus

According to the ISO guidelines a thesaurus may have the following parts:

- contents list
- introduction .
- alphabetical display
- systematic display
- graphic display

Thesauri items can be constructed in various ways. They should, however, comprise the following basic data elements:

For descriptors:

- descriptors
- scope note (narrowing or broadening of the concept)
- "USED FOR" references
- broader term (BT)
- narrower term (NT)
- other broader terms (of various levels)
- other narrower terms (of various levels)
- related terms (RT)

For non-descriptors

- non-descriptors
- "USE" reference

3.3.2.4 Card Files for Thesaurus Purposes

The card files are very useful for the preparation and management of thesauri. A detailed description for the establishment of a card file is given in ISO/R 1149. Annex 3.3.3 contains an example [1].

3.3.2.5 Scope for Thesauri Management Work

It is difficult to give a definition of thesauri management, but its main tasks could be listed as follows:

- collecting and extracting terminological data for the preparation and modification of thesauri;
- establishing and updating thesauri files;
- checking and correcting thesauri entries;
- control of the relationships between concepts;
- statistics study of utility frequency of terms;
- preparation of subject or alphabetic index of terms for printing and layout for publication;
- display of the relationships between concepts;
- using the thesauri to support indexing and retrieval in information systems.

3.3.3 Thesauri Management System (TMS)

Recently the thesauri is usually managed by computer. The latest literature about thesauri work has mainly dealt with topics on software development or experience in using it. Today there is hardly any information retrieval system which is not supported by thesauri programs. On the computer market, there are a lot of TMS software programs available [2], [10], [22].

3.3.3.1 The Main Functions of Thesauri Software

According to Rohou, C. [10] the following functions are important for the development and evaluation of various thesauri software program:

For preparing descriptors and managing relationships:

- maximum character number for a descriptor;
- type of relationship-management (system-predetermined or user-determined relationships);
- number of relations;
- possibility for management of reverse relations (automatic build up or erase);

- number of hierarchical levels;
- possibility for poly-hierarchical structure (to manage BT's in more than one hierarchical level);
- distinguishing of preferred and forbidden terms in equivalent relations;
- linguistic equivalence for multilingual thesauri (selection of preferred terms in each language for corresponding descriptors).

For input and updating of entries:

- interactive modus is preferred;
- simplicity and convenience for updating work.
  Checking functions:
- automatic eliminating of doublets of descriptors or relations for prevention of non-logical entries (the same term to be entered as both the descriptors and non-descriptors);
- warning for incorrect relations, e.g. two descriptors are taken in an equivalent relation, a non-descriptor would be taken into a hierarchic relationship.

Functions to produce and print term indexes and layout; a good program should be able to produce and print the following indexes or word lists:

- alphabetic index;
- hierarchic index;
- subject index;
- permuted index;
- micro thesauri;
- multilingual index;

Display functions:

- display of terms in subject list;
- display of terms in alphabetic list;
- browse in the thesaurus.

Functions facilitating indexing work:

- free indexing;
- controlled indexing with TMS programs (refusion of non-descriptors and automatic replacement with appropriate descriptors);
- proposing a similar term in the alphabetic list for a missing term;
- possibility for making statistics of utility frequency;
- updating during the indexing for e.g. new topics.

Functions to facilitate information retrieval by connecting TMS and IRS:

- implicit consideration of term equivalence (automatic replacing of the non-descriptor entered by the user, with the corresponding descriptor);

- extending the searching field to super and sub-ordinate terms or related terms, if the user wishes (autopoastage).

It is difficult to have all these functions in one TMS software, especially for microcomputer systems, but this should be considered while developing or evaluating TMS programs.

Some new TMS Software display the relationships in graphic modus (e.g. via semantic network) and in windows for various term environments. This trend should also be taken into account [19], [20].

3.3.3.2 A Survey of Some Available TMS Software

Rohou [10] has compared the following ten TMS Software which are used in France (see Tab. 1 [10]):

(1) ASTUTE
   Author: Commission of European Community (CEC)/DG XIII (Luxembourg) 1973-74
   Hardware: IBM 360-370, Siemens 7700
   Programming Language: COBOL and PL1

(2) A LEXIS
   Author: ERLI (Etude et Recherche en Linguistique et Informatique), Charenton 1984
   Hardware: IBM MSV/TSO or VM/CMS, Bull DPS 8
   Programming Language: PL1

(3) BASIS
   Author: Batelle Columbus Labs, Columbus (Ohio) 1970
   Hardware: IBM 370, 30XX and 43XX, Digital Equipment DEC 10, DEC 20, VAX 11/7XX, DOC Cyber and series 6000, Univac series 110, Prime X50, Wang-V-XX
   Programming Language: Fortran and Assembler

(4) MISTRAL (V4)
   Author: CII Honeywell-Bull, 1973
   Hardware: Iris 42760, Siris 2/3; Iris 80 - 100 70, Siris 7/8 - DPS 7; Unidata series 7000, BS 1000
   Programming Language: CPA

(5) MINISIS
   Author: Centre de Recherches pour le Developement International (CRDI), Ottawa
   Hardware: HP 3000 MPE III

(6) JLB-DOC
   Author: JLB Informatique, Paris 1982

Hardware: Mini 6 (CII-HB), Model 6/33 E BCOS 6
Programming Language: COBOL
(7) MICRO-CAIRS
Author: Leatherhead Food Research Association 1982
Hardware: IBM PC, ACT Sirius, FTS, Wang PC; Multi-User-System: DEC PDP RSTS or RS X 11 M
(8) SACADO
Author: SYSECA 1985
Hardware: B 20, B 25 of Burroughs, B 4000, Questear 400 of Bull, IBM PC, SP 57 of Bull
Programming Language: PASCAL
(9) LIBER
Author: Top System LTD and Triple D Software LTD
Hardware: IBM PC and Compatible, M24 of Olivetti, Bull Micral 30, 60
(10) CAMPUS-DOC (MINIDOC)
Author: University of Nice 1985
Hardware: IBM PC XT, Macintosh
Programming Language: PASCAL

Besides, there are some other TMS Software to mention [10]-[20]:

- For Mainframe: TMS (FIDAS), SABIR (Cancernet), PROHTE (IFP), STATUS, ISIS, TLS (IBM), GOLEM.
- For Minicomputer: TINAS, MILOR, DOMESTIC.
- For Microcomputer: PROTERM, INDEX, CICERO, MICRO-STATUS IDA, SIDERAL.

As an example we could take some Software which are widely used in West Germany to show how such a system works.

3.3.3.2.1 TMS (The Thesaurus Maintenance System) von Berlin [14]

This software has been developed by the Berliner Arbeitskreis Information (BAK) in the technical university of Berlin and has been serving several information centers in Berlin since 1982. The system can be used for maintaining and updating thesauri with any structure and contents. TMS is based on the data-bank system FIDAS and the operating system BS2000 on the Siemens Mainframe. It is a modular system which has the following parts:

- an input-interface for extracting term data from an available thesaurus or data-bank;
- an interface for interactive input of entries;
- a program for sorting term data and references;
- a program for producing term lists with various layout-formats;

- plausibility checking;
- an output interface for retrieval systems or other data-bank systems;
- additional help, e.g., statistic evaluation, complete transformation of reference types.

The maximum term number is 999999 (in practice the record is 22000). The maximum number of references per descriptors is 127 (18 of them can be updated). The maximum length of the descriptor is 256 characters, for scope note it is 965.

The system can be used for system conception, composing term data, evaluation and control of data, establishment of relation structures, system testing, expending and updating. With this system, ten thesauri have been recently created and maintained. The disadvantage of this system is that there is no possibility of connecting it directly to IRS software or any other data-bank system. In addition, its performance is restricted by its basic software FIDAS.

3.3.3.2.2 TINAS [12]

TINAS is an integrated information and thesauri management system based on a minicomputer (50-120 KB, 16 Bit) which is used at Fraunhofer Institut fuer Betriebsfestigkeit. It consists of three parts:

- basic system
- thesauri management
- lending and reminder

The program has several modules. TINAS 1 is for data input, including thesaurus entries; a procedure named Editor can be used for the modification and correction of data elements. TINAS 2 is for finding the data which is stored in the data bank based on the integrated thesaurus. The thesauri management system is a bilingual system. Two thesauri have been produced and are now maintained by this system. It can combine the dictionary and inverted files of documents together with the alphabetic and subject index of the thesauri and their foreign language codes to create a complete data-bank, so that the thesauri can be well used in the searching process.

3.3.3.2.3 PROTERM [13]

PROTERM is a typical and rather popular software in West Germany for construction, updating and output of thesauri and other vocabularies on a PC. There exist three versions:

- PROTERM-T is for development and maintenance of the thesauri, subject headings and classification systems;

- PROTERM-K comprises the basic program of PROTERM-T and allows communication with external data-banks via an individual search vocabulary;
- PROTERM-G serves for the development of other kinds of terminologies and glossaries and supports the organization of scientific work.

The software consists of two levels: the first one is an universal tool including all necessary functions for terminological work. The second level is a user specific tool. Both of them build up an organic unit. This software can be used on all PC's based on the MS-DOS operating system, but the preferred hardware is AT with 512 KB memory for version T and G, 640 KB for version K.

PROTERM comprises three function levels:

- dialogue function
- batch function
- management function

All the work of input, update, modification including checking, correction, editing, erasing can be done in dialogue modus. The batch function serves for printing term lists in various formats, especially hierarchic lists and KWIC lists. The management function enables the user to change or to reorganize the vocabulary structure and the format of input, display and printing. The field length is variable, from a standard version the term length is 60 char., the scope note is 150 char.

In version K a special communication software INFOLOG is inserted. Via it one can send the selected descriptor to the external target data-bank in order to search for information. With the function "m" (mark) one can label the selected descriptor. With the function "r" (Retrieval) a menu for selecting a target data-bank is available.

PROTERN has been developed by PROGRIS Co. in Berlin. The price in ca. DM 1000 (version T or G), DM 1800 for version K.

3.3.3.2.4 INDEX [17], [18]

The program INDEX is a new type of thesaurus software with innovative features and a new structure. It is similar to expert systems. It contains:

- term data-bank with basic term data (words and classification);
- semantic network which represents the relationships between the basic term data;
- knowledge base with rule system for creating relations.

The user can define the relation structure in the knowledge base in any way. 15 relation types are fixed in advance. A dialogue component which enables the user to handle the data in a rather natural way is available. INDEX is based on a basic software for data-base management, the DATAFLEX of DATA ACCESS Co. This system can handle files of virtually unlimited size. Entries of up to three million can be handled as fast as a very small file. For 10000 words with an average of 10 relations, only 2 MB storage space is needed. INDEX is capable of performing true multi-user operations and is independent of hardware.

This software is now being used by "Frankfurt Allgemeine" in the newspaper editorial department for the preparation and maintenance of thesaurus and as a comfortable aid for searching archive files. Thoessen, B. in the teaching institute of documentation in Frankfurt has reported that the software INDEX and PRIMUS-IDX, developed by SOFTEX Co., connected via an external interface, could be used to make automatic indexing.

3.3.3.2.5 The Development Trend

In the last ten years the development of thesauri has changed very much. The following trend is to mention:

- the thesauri work is more based on data processing, especially on PC based software;
- the thesauri concept is tended to extend from the terminology field to knowledge engineering; in the centre is relation representation:
- the classification component is more emphasized,
- developing of multilingual thesauri,
- application of knowledge based retrieval system.

Besides, the application of thesauri in distributed information retrieval systems is an interesting topic, too. A model of distributed IRS based on thesauri and the organization of inverted files in such a system is discussed in the literature [21], [22].

3.3.4 Thesauri Management for a Chinese Language Information System

3.3.4.1 Problems Concerning the Thesauri Using Chinese Characters

A very difficult problem in the creation and use of Chinese language thesauri or term banks is the assortment and arrangement of Chinese entries. In the modern Chinese it is common, to assort the words according to the Chinese phonetic symbol system Pinyin in order to produce an alphabetic index.

Most of the available input systems for Chinese characters use the unsortable GB-code as internal code, thus it is very difficult to produce a usual alphabetical index. The GB-code is a standard code for information exchange between different computer systems, introduced by the Chinese national standard office (GB is an abbreviation of the Chinese word "national standard").

A font of Chinese characters for the GB-code consists of two parts. The first part is arranged according to the phonetic characteristics, while the other part is done according to the radicals. Therefore, there is no uniform criterion for the assortment of Chinese words in this code system. By the way, it does not consider the situation that, even in the first part, the same character may have several different pronunciations, for example:

行 can be pronounced either as "hang" meaning "a line" and as "xing" meaning "to go".

This character is assigned in the first part in GB-code system only to the group of "xing", not "hang". For this reason, we need a sortable data-base-internal code for Chinese characters. Another difficulty in constructing a Chinese language term base is the laborious work for the input. It is very important to develop a convenient input system for Chinese characters.

The Chinese phonetic symbol system Pinyin is really a very good aid for input of Chinese characters, because it is a natural tool and not an artificial code which the user needs to learn outside the schools especially. The problem of this method is that there are too much characters of identical pronunciation (homophone). For example, the syllable "yi" has more than 126 characters. This ambiguity makes it very difficult to differentiate the homophones during the input. But if we input the text word by word, then the ambiguity would be greatly reduced. We need also an automatic character transformation system with a knowledge base to change the Pinyin-letters to the Chinese characters for the often used terms.

The solution to these problems (to make a sortable code for Chinese characters to develop a comfortable input system etc.), would provide a solid basis for a convenient and effective workstation for processing Chinese term data.

3.3.4.2 Software for Computerized Chinese Language Thesauri

In order to solve the above-mentioned problems, a special Software MAP-DACS (Microcomputer workstation for Creation Data-Base with Chinese Characters) has been developed with joint Efforts of Chinese and German scientists in Gesellschaft fuer Mathematik und Datenverarbeitung (GMD) in West Germany [23]-[24]. As hardware an IBM personal computer PC-XT with an additional font for Chinese characters is used. For printing Chinese characters, a 24 needle matrix-printer is needed.

A sortable code called Indexcode is designed which consists of phonetic symbol, intonation and identification of the characters. The input and output of Chinese data are based on the Indexcode. The software consists of several layers. In the centre of the Program package the Chinese characters are processed with the help of an adaptive vocabulary knowledge base for Chinese.

The knowledge base includes three parts: character list of 6763 Chinese characters with the phonetic information, word list and list of word groups. It is arranged according to the Pinyin and provides a basis for the automatic transformation of Pinyin to Chinese characters of a word or a phrase. All the lists are based on the indexcode, so that the assortment of the Chinese data is very easy. Around the kernel of the software we can put many more shells for application software, for example, a shell for input, a shell for retrieval and so on. The kernel-shell-structure of the system is shown in Fig. 3.3.1.

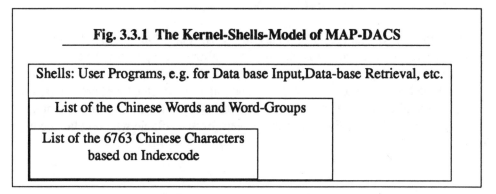

Fig. 3.3.1 The Kernel-Shells-Model of MAP-DACS

Shells: User Programs, e.g. for Data base Input,Data-base Retrieval, etc.

List of the Chinese Words and Word-Groups

List of the 6763 Chinese Characters based on Indexcode

MAP-DACS contains two parts:

- DBINPUT: a software for off-line input work of term entries, especially for translating thesaurus entries from an European language to Chinese;
- RETRIEVAL: a software for on-line retrieval in a term bank

In addition there are some programs for printing alphabetic and systematic index of the terms. The MAP-DACS has the following basic functions which are very important for a Chinese term bank:

3.3.4.2.1 Automatic Assortment of Chinese Entries for Index Production

The sortable Indexcode enables the assortment to be done according not only to the alphabet, but also according to the Chinese Pinyin-letters for producing an alphabetical index. The Indexcode makes also the differentiation of the homophones in the Chinese language possible.

3.3.4.2.2 Automatic Transformation of Chinese Words from Pinyin-Letters to Chinese Characters

The system has a "Character-transformer" of phonograph to semograph with an internal vocabulary data-base for Chinese words as a knowledge base which enables the user to store all frequently used words in his domain. Using this system, the user can input the Chinese words in Pinyin-letters. The system transforms them automatically to Chinese characters. This character transformer is an adaptive system which allows the user to put in new words or to erase the old words which are no longer useful, so that it can always be adapted to the individual user needs.

3.3.4.2.3 Comfortable Input Facility

As mentioned above, a user inputs his Chinese data not character by character, but word by word with a normal keyboard which allows to type both the Latin letters and the Chinese Pinyin. The Chinese words which are not often used and therefore not included in the knowledge base can be put in character by character (s. Fig. 3.3.2). It is also possible to compose from the simple words composite words or word-groups (s. Fig. 3.3.3). There is a screen mask available which helps the user during the input.

3.3.4.2.4 Convenient Searching with Chinese Terms

There are two possibilities to find information in Chinese:

Fig. 3.3.2 Character by Character Input

```
| Please type the Pinyin of a Chinese character,       |
|                                                      |
|   zhong       1.  中 zhong(-)                         |
|               2.  中 zhong(\)                         |
|               3.  盅 zhong(-)                         |
|               4.  忠 zhong(-)                         |
|               5.  钟 zhong(-)                         |
|               6.  衷 zhong(-)                         |
|               7.  终 zhong(-)                         |
|               8.  种 zhong(∨)                         |
|               9.  种 zhong(\)                         |
|               10. 肿 zhong(∨)                        |
|               11. 重 zhong(\)                        |
|               12. 仲 zhong(\)                        |
|               13. 众 zhong(\)                        |
```

Fig. 3.3.3 Composition of a Composite Word

```
Please type the Pinyin of a word:


zhongguo
         1. 中国 zhong(-)guo(╱)




Please type the Pinyin of a word:
the input word is: 中国
zhong(-)guo(╱)
kexueyuan
         1. 科学院 ke(-)xue(╱)yuan(╲)




Please type the Pinyin of a word:
the input word is: 中国科学院
zhong(-)guo(╱)ke(-)xue(╱)yuan(╲)
```

- to use Pinyin: The retrieval in Pinyin is in principle identical to that for English or German, e.g.

  00003
  AQUARIUM SEARCH QUERY 00003
  JIANZHUFENGGE   2 OCCURRENCES   2 DOCUMENTS
  RESULT   2 OCCURRENCES   2 DOCUMENTS
  (The retrieval result is shown in Fig. 3.3.5)

  The search with Pinyin is very convenient, but it produces sometimes ballast,
  e.g.

  方法 fang fa (method)
  民防法 min fang fa (civil defence law),
  排放阀 pai fang fa (outlet valve).

  in order to avoid this, the MAP-DACS provides the possibility of formulating the questions in Chinese characters.

- to use Chinese characters: This method is called "controlled input". A user types Chinese descriptors at first in Pinyin, then MAP-DACS transforms them into Chinese characters and prompts the user for confirmation before sending

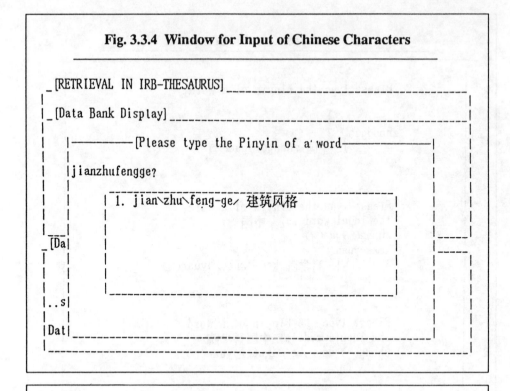

Fig. 3.3.4 Window for Input of Chinese Characters

Fig. 3.3.5 Controlled Input for Retrieval of Chinese

```
_[RETRIEVAL IN IRB-THESAURUS]_____
| [Data Bank Display]_____|
|..b a                                                        |
|I0405 * WORDLIST-CREATION IS IN PROGRESS.                    |
|SYSTNR    13.010.070.4                                       |
|DESKDT    ARCHITEKTURSTIL                                    |
|DESKEN    architectural style                                |
|CODECH jian\zhu\feng-ge/ 建筑风格                            |
|PINYIN1    jian zhu feng ge                                  |
|PINYIN2    jianzhufengge                                     |
|                                                             |
|           END OF DOCUMENT                                   |
|                                                             |
|_____|
                                                              
_[Data Bank Input]_____
|                                                             |
|                                                             |
| ..b a                                                       |
| ..sea jian\zhu\feng-ge/建筑风格                             |
|                                                             |
```

Fig. 3.3.6 An Alphabetic Index of the Search Result
According to Chinese Pinyin

IRBT86000801 DOCUMENT=   1 OF 7   NUMBER OF LINES= 4
DESKDT   AUTOBAHN
DESKEN   motorway
CODECH   gao-su\gong-lu\   高速公路

IRBT86000802 DOCUMENT=   2 OF 7   NUMBER OF LINES= 4
DESKDT   AUTOBAHNBAU
DESKEN   motorway construction
CODECH   gao-su\gong-lu\jian\she\   高速公路建设

IRBT86000803 DOCUMENT=   3 OF 7   NUMBER OF LINES= 4
DESKDT   AUTOBAHNBRUECKE
DESKEN   motorway bridge
CODECH   gao-su\gong-lu\   高速公路桥梁

IRBT86000804 DOCUMENT=   4 OF 7   NUMBER OF LINES= 4

IRBT86000805 DOCUMENT=   5 OF 7   NUMBER OF LINES= 4
DESKDT   AUTOBAHNTUNNEL
DESKEN   motorway tunnel
CODECH   gao-su\gong-lu\sui\dao\   高速公路隧道

them to the data-bank. The system provides a variety of windows to support the user (s. Fig. 3.3.4/5).

3.3.4.2.5 Output and Index Production of Results

There is a buffer in the workstation to store the result. A user can display all the entries which were found on the screen with the browse command. It is possible to sort these data according to Chinese Pinyin with the sort command in order to produce a Chinese alphabetic index. A 24 needle printer prints a hard copy of the search result. Fig. 3.3.6 shows an index of some words found in the data-bank.

3.3.4.3 Experience in Construction of Computerized Thesaurus

A German-English-Chinese on-line term data-bank on architecture and construction has been created using MAP-DACS. There are more than 10,000 entries in the term bank. It is installed on an IBM mainframe in Frankfurt. The STAIRS system has been chosen as the basic data-base software.

The German and English data of the data-bank is based on the thesaurus of the international information data-bank ICONDA (International Construction Data-Bank) set up by the Information Centre for Regional Planning and Construction (IRB) of FRG in Stuttgart. The IRB thesaurus is a facet-oriented indexing system for ICONDA. It consists of two parts: a systematic part and an alphabetic part. The systematic part has a hierarchical structure of four levels. All these properties are considered in building up the terminology data-bank. The German and English data was provided in machine readable form which we could copy into the personal computer and display via a screen mask. Our contribution is mainly to the Chinese component. The needed Chinese equivalents were put in with the help of MAP-DACS. The completed data was sent to the computer centre and converted to the STAIRS system.

For this data-bank, the following fields are defined:

SYSTNR: classification number
DESKDT: German descriptor
DESKEN: English descriptors
CODECH: Chinese character
PINYIN1: Chinese phonetic symbol, separated
PINYIN2: Chinese phonetic symbol, together.

The software RETRIEVAL serves as a communication interface and can make the PC to an intelligent terminal for on-line searching of terms via post network.

With the help of MAP-DACS Print program an alphabetic index and a systematic index of Chinese descriptors are produced.

The term-bank and MAP-DACS had shown their success at both the international industry exhibition, Hannover, and the INGOBASE International Fair, Frankfurt, in 1987.

The result shows that MAP-DACS can be well used for Chinese thesauri work. If we take a descriptor list in Pinyin-character relation as a knowledge base in the word file of MAP-DACS, then we can also use MAP-DACS retrieval program for on-line searching in other Chinese language information systems. If we take a multilingual descriptor list as a knowledge base, then the software can be used as an interface between Chinese and other data-banks, too. Thus a Chinese user can search foreign information with Chinese terms, and a foreign user can search Chinese information with terms in his or her own language.

In order to realize this idea we are going now to translate the descriptor list of the data-bank INFODATA into Chinese to build up a multilingual term list for the new knowledge base and test it as an interface [23]-[31].

3.3.4.4 Some Considerations and Proposals

The thesaurus principle is very important for Chinese language IRS, because the Chinese texts are written continuously without space between the words. It is difficult to use the free text terms for retrieval, if an automatic word separation software is not used. Such a software is naturally very expensive and takes large memory space. Furthermore, the results can not be hundred percent right. Therefore, it has better to separate the important words at least in the titles or abstracts during the entry input, if a free text term principle should be used. By using "word by word" or "word group" input method we can transform every CR key to a space per program, so that the words can be separated. It is very useful to take a thesaurus as the above mentioned knowledge base in an IRS software for

畸变 = 失真 = distortion   情报 = 信息 = information

通信 = 通讯 =communication   信号 = 讯号 = signal

Chinese language. Then one can input the descriptors only in Pinyin without intonation, then the system knows what is the corresponding term and will send it to the target data-bank. In this way we can save much valuable on-line time.

In addition there are very many synonyms in Chinese, e.g.

With the help of a term list as a knowledge base it is very easy to go from one synonym to the preferred term and to have it sent for searching in a data-bank.

References

[1] Felber, H.: Terminology Manual, UNESCO and Infoterm, Paris 1984, p. 426.

[2] Hitzeroth, Ch.: Bibliographie zur Thesaurus-Literatur. Nachr. Dok 39 (1988), pp. 266-268.

[3] Wersig, G.: Thesaurus-Leitfaden, 2 erg. Auflage, K.G.Saur Verlag, München, DE 1985, p. 394.

[4] Laisiepen, K. etc.: Grundlagen der praktischen Information und Dokumentation. pp. 276-326, Verlag Dokumentation, München, DE 1972, p. 651.

[5] Robels, N.: Historical studies in documentation. Journal of documentation, London, GB 40(1984) 4, pp. 271-285.

[6] Antopol'skii, A.B. etc: Analysis of the use of controlled and free vocabularies in dialogue searching in foreign data-bases. Automatic documentation and mathematical linguistics, New York, US 21(1987) 1, pp. 22-36.

[7] Dubois, C.P.R.: Free text vs. controlled vocabulary. On-line Review, Abingdon, GB 11(1987) 4, pp. 243-253.

[8] Burkart, M.: Neue Thesaurusansätze - Frische Wind in alten Segeln? Nachr. Dok. 39 (1988), pp. 207-208.

[9] Panyr, J.: Thesaurus und wissensbasierte Systeme - Thesauri und Wissensbasen. Nachr. Dok. 39 (1988), pp. 209-215.

[10]Rohou, C.: La Gestion Automatisee des Thesaurus Etude Comparative de Logiciels. Documentaliste 24 (1987) 3, pp. 103-108 (French).

[11] Rolling, L.N.: Computerized Management of Multilingual Thesauri. In: Intern. Scientific symposium on multilingual thesauri. Berlin, W 1973, pp. 39-51.

[12]Taube, H.: TINAS - Das technische Information - Nachweis - und Auskunft-System. Nachr. dok. 32 (1981) 3, pp. 121-125.

[13]Burkart, M.: PROTEM - a software program for construction, updating and handling of thesauri and other kind of vocabularies. Nachr.Dok. 39(1988) pp. 249-252.

[14]Pott.B.: Das Thesaurus Maintenance System (TMS). In: Traditionelle und moderne Informationssysteme für Wissenschaft und Praxis. Weinheim, DE 1988 VCH Verl., pp. 233-242.

[15]Strauch, D.: PC faehige Software zum Aufbau und zur Pflege von Dokumentationssprache. In the same source as [14], pp. 243-348.

[16]Henzler, R.G.: Erfahrungen mit Methoden und Modellen zur maschinellen Thesaurusentwicklung. In: Dahlberg, W. Klassifikation und Erkenntnis. 1979, Frankfurt, DE pp. 100-126.

[17]Lukas, E.: INDEX - Ein Programm zur Erstellung von Wörterbücher und Dokumentationssprache auf Personal Computer. Nachr. Dok. 39 (1988), pp. 253-256.

[18]Thoenssen, B.: Automatische Indexing und Schnittsstellen zu Thesauri. Nachr. Dok. 39 (1988), pp. 227-230.

[19]Koerner, H.P.. etc.: Sehen und Agieren mit dem Cicero-Thesaurus. Nachr. Dok. 39 (1988), pp. 263-265.

[20]Rostek, L. etc.: Modelling a Thesaurus in a Frame System with a Graphical Interface, Nachr. Dok. 39 (1988), pp.217-226.

[21]Mazur, Z.: Organization of the inverted files in a distributed information retrieval system based on thesauri. Information processing and management, Oxford, GB 22 (1986) 3, pp. 243-250.

[22]Mazur, Z.: On a Model of distributed information retrieval system based on thesauri. Information Processing and Management, 20 (1984) 4, pp. 499-505.

[23]Yu, Y.: Design of a multilingual on-line term-bank with Chinese characters. Proceedings Intern. Congress on Terminology and Knowledge Engineering 1987, pp. 393-402.

[24]Yu, Y.: An On-line Multilingual Terminology Data-bank Including Chinese Data. Intern Report. 1989, p. 11.

[25]Mauch, H.U., Yu, Y., Samulowitz, H.: Map-DacS - a microcomputer-aided workstation for the building up and use of data-banks with Chinese characters. Nachr. Dok. 38 (1987) pp. 73-76.

[26]IRB: FINDEX Facet-Oriented Indexing System for Architecture and Construction Engineering. IRB Verlag, DE p. 304.

[27]IRB (1986): FINDEX Bau jetzt auch in chinesisch. IRB Aktuell No.11, July 1986, p. 12.

[28]GID: Descriptor-Liste zum Bereich Informationswissenschaft und praxis. 1987, DE p. 109.

[29]Simon, H.R., James N.: Infodata and other Services of the GMD Information Centre. Intern Report, 1988 p. 55.

[30]IBM Deutschland GmbH: STAIRS/VS-Handbuch. Teil A: Die Abfragesprache.

[31]Crueger, I. (1982): Information Retrieval mit STAIRS-Eine Einführung in die Abfragesprache anhand von Beispielen. GID-Publikation 1982, p. 81.

Annex 3.3.1

3.3.1.1 Thesauri

3.3.1.1.1 Standardized Guidelines

3.3.1.1.1.1 Monolingual

E   ISO. Documentation - Guidelines for the establishment and development of
    monolingual thesauri. Gen/ve: ISO, Aug. 1974, p. 13, A4 (ISO 2788-1974).
    (DIS 2788-1984, p. 65).

F   ISO. Documentation - Principes directeurs pour l'etablissement et le
    developpment de thesaurus monolingues. Geneve: ISO, Aug. 1974, p. 13, A4
    (ISO 2789-1984).

D   DIN. Richtlinien fur die Erstellung und Weiterentwicklung von Thesauri.
    Berlin: Beuth. p. 12, A4 (DIN 1463, Mar. 1976).

D   DDR. MINISTERIUM FÜR WISSENSCHAFT UND TECHNIK.
    Einsprachiger Informationsrecherchethesaurus - Struktur, Zusammensetzung,
    Darstellungsform. Berlin: Staatsverlag der DDR, 1976, p. 8, A4 (UTGL RGW
    174-75).

E   BSI. Guidelines for the establishment and development of monolingual thesauri.
    London: BSI, 1979, p. 36, A4 (BS 5723: 1979).

E   ANSI. Guidelines for Thesaurus Structure, Construction and Use. New York:
    ANSI, 1980, p. 18, 215x276 (ANSI Z 39.19-1980).

F   AFNOR. Documentation. Regles d'etablissement des thesaurus en langue
    française. Paris: AFNOR, 1981, p.20, A4.

S   ICFES; FID/CIA. Documentacion. Directrices para el establecimiento y
    desarrollo de tesauros monolingues. Bogotà: ICFES, 1980, p. 71 (Norma
    Colombiana 1476).

R   SEV. Tezaurus informacionno-poiskovvj odonjazycnyj: Struktura, sostav i
    forma predstavlenija [Monolingual thesauri: structure, composition, form of
    presentation]. Moskva: SEV, 1975, p. 7, A4, (ST SEV 174-1975).

R   GOSSTANDART. Sistema standartov po informacii, bibliotecnomu i
    izdatel'skomu delu. Tezaurus informacionno-poiskovjy odnojazycnyj. Pravila
    razrabotki, struktura, sostav i forma predstavlenija [System of Standards
    "Information, Libraries and Publishing". Monolingual Thesaurus for
    Information Retrieval. Rules for development, composition, structure and form
    of presentation]. Moskva: Gosstandart, 1981, p. 16, A5 (GOST 7.25-80).

3.3.1.1.1.2 Multilingual

E ISO. Documentation - Guidelines for the establishment and development of multilingual thesauri. P. 53, A4 (ISO/DIS 5964, 1983).

F AFNOR. Principes directeurs pur l'etablissement des thesaurus multilingues. Paris: AFNOR, A4 (NF Z 47-101-1977).

3.3.1.1.2 Non-Standardized Guidelines

AIRCHINSON, J.; GILCHRIST, A. Thesaurus Construction. A Practical Manual, London: Aslib, 1972, p. 95, 138x210.

BIELICKA, K.A. Fundamentals of development of disciplinary and subdisciplinary thesauri for SINTO. (In Polish) In: Aktual. probl. inform. i. dok. 24 (1979), No. 3, pp. 47-48.

CERNYJ, A.I. Obscaja metodika postroenija tezaurusov [General methods for thesaurus construction]. Naucno-techniceskaja Informacija. Seija 2 Moskva 5 (1968), pp. 9-32.

COMMITTEE ON SCIENTIFIC AND TECHNICAL INFORMATION (COSATI). Guidelines for the development of information retrieval thesauri. Washington, D.C.; Government Printing Office, 1967.

FID/CLA. Documentacion. Directrices para el Establecimiento y Desarollo de Tesauros Monolingues [Guidelines for the Establishment and Development of Monolingual Thesauri]. Bogotà, Columbia FID:CLA ICFES 1980, pp. XII+71 = FID 582.

GRIN'OV, S. Compiling a thesaurus. In: Fachsprache 1 (1979) No. 4, pp. 154-161.

IAEA-INIS. Guidelines for the development and maintenance of the INIS Thesaurus. Vienna: IAEA, s.a.

IZWTI. Mehrsprachiger Informationsrecherchethesaurus; Zusammensetzung, Struktur und Darstellungsform [Multilingual documentation thesaurus. Composition, structure, presentation]. Berlin: ZIID, 1975 (NTV 3-75).

IZWTI. Regeln für die Erarbeitung mehrsprachiger Informationsrecherche-thesauren [Rules for the construction of multilingual documentation thesauri]. Berlin: ZIID, 1976 (NTV 15-76).

IZWTI. Regeln für die Erarbeitung einsprachiger Informationsrecherchethesauren [Rules for the construction of monolingual documentation thesauri]. Berlin: ZIID, Dec. 1975 (NTV 9-75).

LEATHERDALE, D. Construccion de vocabularios controlados. documentacion 54 (Jul. 1981) pp. 3-18.

LESKA, K. Thesaurus construction principles. (In Polish) Warszawa: Pr. OIN PAN 1978, p. 284.

MACCAFFERTY, M. [comp.]. Thesauri and thesaurus construction. London: Aslib, 1977.

MONTI. Pravila razrabotki odnojazycnyh informacionno-poiskovyh tezaurusov [Rules for the preparation of monolingual thesauri]. Moskva: MONTI, 1975, p. 14, (NTP MONTI 9-1975).

MONTI. Pravila razrabotki mnogojazycnyh informacionno-poiskovyh tezaurusov [Rules for the preparation of multilingual thesauri]. Moskva: MONTI, 1976, p. 6, (NTP MONTI 15-1976).

MONTI. Tezaurus informacionno-poiskovyi mnogojazycnyj: sostav, struktura i forma predstavlenija [Multilingual thesauri: composition, structure and form of presentation]. Moskva: MONTI, 1975 p. 3, (NTP MONTI 3-1975).

NORDFORSK. ARBEIDSGRUPPE FOR THESAURUS SPORMAL. [Rules for developing thesauri in Nordic languages]. Stockholm: Nordforsk, 1970, p. 20.

PET. Rules for Thesaurus Preparation. Washington, D.C.: U.S. Department of Health. Education and Welfare, Sep. 1969, p. 20, 147x230. (ERIC).

POPOWSKA, H. Construction of thesauri according to the methods of A.F. Sokolov. (In Polish) In: Aktual. Probl. Inform. Dokument. 24 (1979), No. 6, pp. 21-26.

SPRINGL, W. Die Erarbeitung eines mehrsprachigen Informations-recherchethesaurus für das Fachgebiet Schwarzmetallurgie [Elaboration of a multilingual IR thesaurus for the subject-field of steel metallurgy]. In: XI. Kolloquium über Information und Dokumentation v. 14. bis 16 Nov. 1979. Institut für Informationswissenschaft, Erfindungswesen und Recht d. TH Ilmenau. Ilmenau 1980. pp. 26-31.

TOWNLEY, H.; GEE, R. Thesaurus-making: grow your own word-stock. London: Deutsch, 1980, p. 206, ISBN 0-233-97225-0.

UNESCO. Guidelines for the establishment and development of monolingual thesauri. Second revised edition, Paris: Unesco, 1981, p. 64, A4 (PGI-81/WS/15).

UNESCO. UNISIST Guidelines for the Establishment and Development of Multilingual Thesauri. Revised text. Prep. by D. Austin and J. Waters. Bibliographic Systems and Standards Office. The British Library, London. Paris: Unesco 1980, p. 85 (PGI 80/WS/12).

UNESCO. UNISIST principes directeurs pour l'etablissement et le developpement des thesaurus multilingues. [Guidelines for the establishment and development of multilingual thesauri] Prepared by D. Austin and J. Waters, translated into French by D. Menillet. Paris: Unesco 1980, p.88 (PGI-80/WS/12).

WERSIG, G. Thesaurus-leitfaden. Eine Einführung in das Thesaurus-Prinzip in Theorie und Praxis [Thesaurus guidelines. An introduction to thesaurus principles in theory and practice]. München/New York: Verlag Dokumentation Saur KG, 1978, p. 346, A5 (DGD-Schriftenreihe, Band 8).

ZIID. Methodische Rahmenregelung zur Erarbeitung einsprachiger Informations-recherchethesauren [Methodological rules for the preparation of monolingual thesauri for information retrieval]. Berlin: ZIID, 1977.

3.3.1.2 Indexing

3.3.1.2.1 Standardized Guidelines

E   ISO. Documentation - Methods for examining documents, determining their subjects, and selecting indexing terms. Geneva: ISO, Jan. 1981, p. 6, A4 (DIS 5963).

D   DIN. Indexierung zur inhaltlichen Erschliessung von Dokumenten - Begriffe. Grundlagen. Berlin: Beuth, 1983, p. 5, A4 (Vornorm DIN 31623 Teil 1).

D   DIN. Indexierung zur inhaltlichen Erschliessung von Dokumenten - Gleichordnende Indexierung mit Deskriptoren. Berlin: Beuth, 1983, p. 17, A4 (Vornorm DIN 31623 Teil 2).

3.3.1.2.2 Non-Standardized Guidelines

FID. Principles of the Universal Decimal Classification (UDC) and rules for its revision and publication [Principes de la Classification Decimale Universelle (CDU) et regles pour sa revision et sa publication] Grundsatze der universellen Dezimalklassifikation (DK) und Regeln fur ihre Revision und Veroffentlichung. 5th ed. The Hague: FID, 1981, p. 35 (FID Publ. 598).

IAEA-INIS. Manual for indexing. 4th rev. ed. Vienna: IAEA, 1978, p. 70, (IAEA-INIS 12).

IZWTI. Komplex der Informationsrecherchesprachen des Internationalen Systems für wissenschaftliche und technische Information; Anforderungen, Zu-sammensetzung [Complex of information retrieval language used by the International System for Scientific and Technical Information. Requirements, composition]. Berlin: ZIID, 1975 (NTV 7-75).

IZWTI. Informationsrecherchesprachen. Normativ-technische Dokumente und methodische Materialien [Information retrieval languages. Standardized-technical documents and methodological materials]. 2 vols. Berlin: ZIID, vol.1: 1931, p. 82; vol.2: 1983, p. 68.

JONKER, F. Indexing theory, indexing methods and search services. New York: Scarecrow Press, 1964, p. 124.

MORIN-LABATUT, G. Manual for the preparation of records in development of information systems. Ottawa: IDRC, 1982 (Report IDRC-TS-40e).

SOERGEL, D. Indexing languages and thesauri. Construction and maintenance. Los Angeles: Melville, 1974, p. 632.

UNESCO. Guidelines for indexing principles. Paris: Unesco, 1975.

Annex 3.3.2

Letter symbols

Hierarchical relationships	E	F	D	
	BT	TG	CB	broader term
	NT	TS	UB	narrower term
	BTG	TGG	CA	broader term generic
	NTG	TSG	UA	narrower term generic
	BTP	TGP	SP	broader term partitive
	NTP	TSP	TP	narrower term partitive
Associative relationship	RT	TA	VB	related term

Equivalence relationships				
	USE	EM	BS	use
	UF	EP	BF	used for
	USC		BK	used combination
	UFC		KB	used for combination
Scope note	SN	NE	D	scope note

Annex 3.3.3

Card file

For the recording of terminological data to be included in thesauri, card files are used as well.

Example: ZIID. Methodische Rahmenregelungen zur Erarbeitung einsprachiger Informationsrecherchethesauren [Thesaurus guidelines. An introduction to thesaurus principles in theory and practice]. Berlin: Zentralinstitut fdata-bank.

1 term	2 descriptor	3 non-descriptor
4 notation or subject code	5 Russian	
	6 English	
7 use (descriptor) notation or subject code of descriptor		
8 used for (non descriptor)		
9 BT		
10 NT		
11 RT notation or subject code of RT		
12 source		
13 definition /explanation		
14 frequency of use		
15 recording agency	16 date	17 recorder

3.4 General System Design for SPARK Information Pilot System

Zhou Dingheng

3.4.1 Introduction

Township and Village Enterprises (TVEs) are rising abruptly in China. They are full of vigour and vitality. In terms of both output growth and employment creation, TVEs have become the most dynamic element in China's economy. They play a crucial role in expanding the supply of consumer goods to the domestic market and create increasingly significant exports. They enable some of the farmers to engage in industry without leaving the farmland to enter the cities. By 1986, non-state industry accounted for 37.8% of the gross output value of industry in China, of this, 21,3% came from TVEs. TVEs output is 450 billion Yuan in 1987, surpassing the country's agricultural output. Annual growth for TVEs is about 30%. The total work-force are 85 million farmers. By the year 2000, it will be possible for rural enterprises to absorb at least 35 per cent of the rural labour force and yield an output value of 1500 billion Yuan, or 70% of the country's gross rural social output. Until recently, they are largely ignored by support services and still suffering from inadequate access to technology, qualified staff and business-oriented information.

The spark program was launched by the State Science and Technology Commission (SSTC) in 1985 and is implemented throughout China under the leadership of SSTC and the counterpart, the local Science and Technology Commissions (STC's). It seeks to harness the resource of China's technology sector to help upgrade technical standards in the rapidly growing rural non-state industrial sector. Spark takes its name from the adage that "one single spark can start a prairie fire".

Spark Information Pilot System (SIPS) is an important part of the spark project. The main purpose is to help an existing ST. information system reorient its focus to medium and small enterprises. The Institute of Scientific and Technical Information of China (ISTIC) and three other areas are selected as participants in SIPS. As a pilot system, the demonstration effects of the project would be maximized through implementation in one province (Jiangsu province) with an advanced TVE sector, one province (Jilin province) where TVEs are currently underdeveloped and one area (Chongming island) of "spark concentration".

3.4.2 TVEs Information Needs

Any sound planning must be based on proven fact and figure. Therefore, the starting point for planning a scientific and technical information network, whether on local, national or international level is a comprehensive survey about the user. The better the nature of user is understood, the greater is the likelihood that any system designed to serve them will be satisfactory and effective. In order to design a good information system fitting the user needs effectively, we have to conduct a user needs survey.

During the period from October to December last year, we visited Jingsu province, making a first-hand investigation on TVEs in the five locations of Nanjing, Suzhou, Wuxi, Changsu. We called together a fact-finding conference, which was attended by TVEs managers, information scientists working for TVEs, and we listened attentively to their report and collected a great deal of material. At the same time, we sent out questionnaires to 509 TVEs in Jilin province making sample investigations. From user surveys, we found that TVEs are eager for the following information:

- marketing
- advanced processing technology
- new product and technical transfer
- qualified scientists and technicians
- patent, standard, product catalog and product sample
- raw material and equipment

  and they enjoy the following information transfer forms and media:

- data-base
- technical consulting
- exhibition
- on-job training
- technical publication
- video tape

3.4.3 System Structure

From the user survey, we derived a strong idea that TVEs are eager for information, but they have a very week overview of information. In order to achieve the maximum of system effect and efficiency, SIPS must combine the advanced information technology (computer, data-base and telecommunication) with the information transfer form (medium) preferred by TVEs. Publication, video tape and training class are still very important information transfer forms and media. Technical consulting will play a vital role in SIPS. In nine cases out of ten, it is impossible for TVEs to access the data-base and publications in existing information systems or SIPS directly. The technical consulting groups will become the interface between the SIPS and TVEs and collect or search the

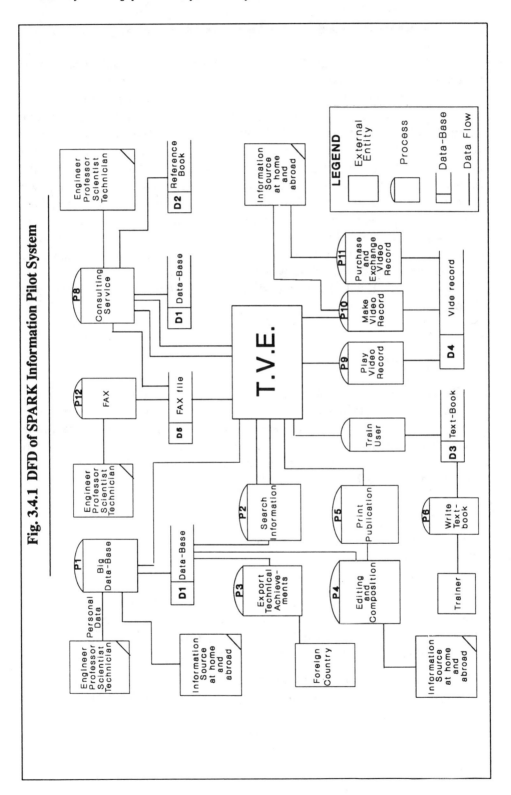

Fig. 3.4.1 DFD of SPARK Information Pilot System

information which is needed by TVEs and process or repackage it into a form feasible for TVEs.

Figure 3.4.1 shows the data flow diagram of SIPS, which describes what must be done by this system and how data flow among the different parts. In term of functions, the SIPS can be divided into the following components: computer and data-base (sub)system, publication (sub)system, audio-visual (sub)system, information consulting services (sub)system, fax (sub)system, user training (sub)system. SIPS will be a hierarchical system matching with the existing information system, that is to say, this system can be divided into three levels: the national level, provincial center and county information station. The system will be established in the existing information institutes at the above-mentioned three levels. A special working group of information systems on spark science and technology will be formed within the existing information institutes. In this way, the existing facilities can be fully used and save investments and accelerate the process of the establishment of the system.

In this paper, I will focus our discussion on data-base, computer and telecommunication system.

3.4.4 Specification on SIPS

In SIPS, the computer is chiefly applied to the data-base and partially used in the compilation and composition as well as the management task. What is going to be described in this article is only the specification of the computer and data-base system. The relationships between computer and data-base are closely related to each other. Some indices are referred to be a comprehensive index.

The following data-bases are planned to be established in SIPS:

1. User Registration Data-base
2. Data-base for the Spark product
3. Data-base for the Appropriate technology
4. Data-base for the Spark export product
5. Data-base for Personnel

As for the marketing and raw material information which is needed eagerly, but is ever changing, they are not suitable for creating a data-base without computer network, so that we use telefax and publication to provide them timely.

The specifications of the computer and data-base system are as follows:

1. The SIPS is oriented to township enterprises and the vast rural areas. Therefore the system is required to be able to process Chinese, which is a mandatory condition. At first, the information retrieval software in the data-base must be Chinese retrieval software. The operating system also should be a Chinese operating system as much as possible. In the meantime, it should have the

Chinese utility and Chinese input and output facilities (Chinese display terminal, Chinese printer, etc.).

2. In the experimental stage of the SIPS (1989-1991), the data-bases with 100,000 records each will be established respectively in the two provinces of Jinlin and Jiangsu and therefore the corresponding computers must be installed there. A data-base with 100,000 records will be established in the ISTIC, thus the total entries will be 300,000. Because most of the data-bases are the factual ones, the length of entries are long. It is assumed that there are 2000 Chinese characters in each entry, each Chinese character taking two bytes. In addition, they will contain the operating system and some utilities, therefore the total external storage capacity should not be less than 3600 mega bytes.

3. A considerable number of factual data-bases should be established in the system. In order to be convenient to use for the broad Information workers in the small and medium enterprises, a policy of combination of the manual and automatic indexing and combination of the controlled words and the free words is adopted. The retrieval software of the data-bases must have the capability of automatic indexing. The indexing capability should be established for some fields and should better have the capability of full-text retrieval.

4. There are about 46400 small and medium enterprises in the experimental areas of SIPS. Among them, there are 1200 in Jilin province, 38,000 in Jiangsu province, 1200 in Chungming county. The provincial institutes of scientific and technical information in Jilin and Jiangsu, in the meantime, must serve the other small and medium enterprises within their provinces. ISTIC must serve 15 million of the small and medium enterprises in the whole country. Therefore it must be considered that the system should have the capability that provides on-line retrieval simultaneously for the multiusers, and the response time should not be longer than 10 seconds. The response time of on-line retrieval is a complex function that is decided by factors like the speed of computer processing, the speed of magnetic disk access, the Max. I/O throughput, the file structure of data-base, the searching algorithms used by data-base software etc. In order to guarantee the response speed, the computer must have a certain processing speed at first.

5. The system must have the capability of protection, so as to prevent the unauthorized person from using the resource and data of the computer system. The use of the computer resource by users should be controlled by the computer operating system through login and password. The DBMS should be able to control which users can use which files, which fields of record and to control the right of reading, writing, deleting and amending the record, etc.

6. The system must have functions of keeping account, performing statistics and billing---it must be able to give the time of each on-line retrieval for each user, the time that is taken by CPU, the number of hit records, the number of pages or lines that are printed and it should be able to make accumulated statistics.

7. In order to be convenient for the information exchanges between the units within this system and between this system and the other information system, the data items which are chosen to be used in this system should refer to National and International standards as well as broad-adopted specifications. The tape and floppy disk formats which are used for the data exchange should also comply with the national and international standards.

8. The system must have the features of being easy to learn and being "user friendly"; in the meantime, it has the function of "help".

9. The data-base management system must have the capability of opening several files simultaneously, and should allow several users of the same file at the same time.

10. The software must support the following data-base size parameters:

Entity	Mandatory	Desirable
No. of data-bases (files)	20	no limit
No. of records in data-base	0.5 million	2 million
Max. size of record	4000 bytes	60,000 bytes
Max. size of field	4000 bytes	10,000 bytes

11. The mandatory capabilities for data-base query processing include:

> 1) searching on string, word roots and truncated words (both left and right truncation);
>
> 2) boolean operation AND, OR, and NOT;
>
> 3) range operations $=, >, <, >=, <=$.

12. The system should have the capabilities of being easy to establish and to alter the input screen format, the display screen format and the printing format.

13. The system should have the function of on-line data input, batch input, on-line updating, batch printing.

14. The last point is the most important one: SIPS is a distributed system which consists of national level, provincial level, municipal and county level. The input process and storage of data must be reasonably distributed and work must be reasonably divided. The mini computer or the super-micro computers may be adopted at the provincial level; the micro computer may be adopted at the county levels. The micro computer may be used not only for data entry and processing, but also as an intelligent terminal. As for the data communication mode, the remote terminal mode (private or dialing line) or the floppy disk exchange mode may be adopted. What kind of specific mode should be adopted depends on the data transmission volume, the condition of telecommunication circuits, the urgency of information delivery and the charge criteria of the telecommunication circuit.

3.4.5 Preliminary Consideration on the Computer Network

In order to save investments, it makes sense to take advantage of existing computer systems in ISTIC, making full use of them and expanding them. At present, there are two computers in ISTIC: IBM 4381 M-12 (main memory 16 MB, fixed disk 6500MB) and VAX 11/750 computer (main memory 4MB, fixed disk 800MB). The IBM 4381 computer is mainly used for on-line information retrieval. Currently a western language data-base with more than two million records is already established, using the CDS/ISIS software. The VAX 11/750 computer is chiefly used in the system of library automation and for on-line retrieval in a chinese language data-base with a Chinese version of TRIP software. In the long range, we plan to set up an on-line retrieval system on the IBM 4381 computer, in which the Chinese data-base system is included. However, at present, the IBM 4381 computer cannot process Chinese, so that, for the time being, we created a Chinese data-base on the VAX 11/750. They are all fully loaded of records. It will be necessary to expand the fixed disk to accommodate the SIPS.

At the country level, we prepare to use Micro computers (e.g. IBM PC/AT, IBM 386) for collecting data, creating a locally used data-base and at same time, use them as emulating terminals (or intelligent terminals) connecting with national level or provincial level computers through dial line and X.25 network.

As for the provincial level, with the mandatory requirement that they are mini or super micro computer systems and must be able to process Chinese, there are only very few computer systems which can be chosen. We prefer to choose the micro VAX 3600 computer system which can be used as a stand-alone system or in a distributed network, and achieves a higher level of price/performance. Its main features are as follows:

Operating system:	CVMS (Chinese version of VMS)
Maximum memory:	32MB
CPU speed:	2.6--3.0 MIPS
BUS:	industry standard Q-BUS
Maximum disk storage:	2.5 GB
Communication devices:	Ethernet
	synchronous
	asynchronous
	DEC net
	HDLC

In a networking environment, they can tie in mainframes from IBM and other vendors, keeping a wide-used data-base on the central computer and provincial-used data-bases on micro VAX 3600 systems. We use a network to transfer information back and forth as needed. Using micro VAX 3600 as network manager, we can pull a cluster of PC's together into one local area network. Instead of transferring data by floppy disk, we can share data electronically over the network. The micro VAX industry-standard Q-BUS provides I/O for options developed by Digital and other vendors. Options are high speed laser printers, asynchronous and synchronous communications devices, D/A and A/D converters. The decisive factor is that the information retrieval software TRIP is only running on VAX computer.

TRIP (stands for Text Retrieval, Input and Presentation) is a comprehensive information retrieval and data-base system for applications that handle large amounts of text documents. TRIP contains functions for data entry, free text searching and presentation of text. It also includes data-base design, administration of user and access rights. The Chinese version of TRIP has been jointly developed by PARALOG company (Sweden) and ISTIC successfully. It can handle the following data types:

1) **Text**: is used for free text in sentences and paragraphs. When the records are indexed, for every word its position is noted in inverted file (the number of the paragraph within the text field, the number of the sentence within the paragraph, and the number of the word within the sentence).

2) **Phrase**: is used for short text elements, e.g. name, addresses, codes of products. The individual phrase consists of sub-fields. The number of sub-fields allowed within a phrase field is unlimited. When the records are indexed, the complete phrase, as well as its individual words are noted in the inverted file with its position: the number of the sub-field within the field and the number of the word within the sub-field.

3) **Number**: is used for numeric information, both integers and real numbers, each number in a sub-field of its own. At indexing, the position of each value is noted (the number of its sub-field within its field).

4) **Date**: is used for dates, the primary form is year-month-day.

5) **Time**: is used for time of the day, expressed in hours, minutes and seconds.

6) **String**: is used for a string of characters of any kind.

The TRIP software has the following features:

- The length od record and field is unlimited, the number of fields and sub-fields is also unlimited.
- In TRIP, you can search in several data-bases in parallel (up to 30 files at a time).
- Data control: when you have completed the data entry form and send data to it, TRIP will check that there are no impossible data, the fields that must contain something are not empty and entered data conform with the rules laid down when the data-base was designed. If the TRIP detects a mistake of that kind, the record will be shown again, with a message telling you what kind of error was made, and the cursor will be in the field where the mistake was made.

- Global updating: global updating is a useful means of making an identical change to a group of records, using one updating order. In this way, we can save a lot of time to update the data-base.
- In the TRIP system, there is a template for the creation of the thesaurus.
- TRIP system can assign data-base access right to user. The system distinguishes between reading and writing right only, writing comprising the rights to alter and delete records of the data-base.

The national public data network (X.25) will be put into operation by the end of July this year. For the time being, it consists of 3 nodes (Beijing, Shanghai, Guangzhou) and 8 PAD's (Shenzhen, Nanjing, Tianjin, Xian, Wuhan, Chengdu, Shenyong et.). It will be expanded to every provincial capital in the near future. We should take advantage of X.25 network to save investments. Figure 2 shows the SIPS computer network. Further details have been considered.

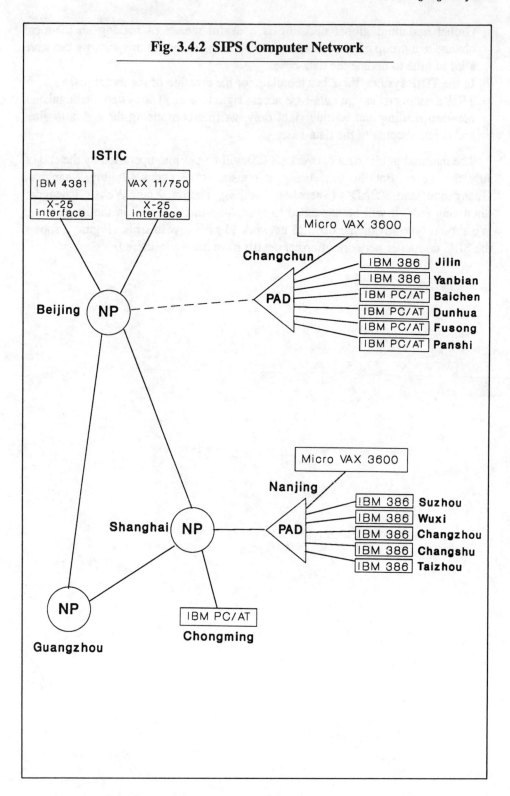

Fig. 3.4.2 SIPS Computer Network

4 Considering the Communications Options

Summary

The present section refers to communications technologies and techniques supporting information systems. The papers address a wide spectrum of solutions and stress the importance of the use of appropriate technologies against the tendency towards the indiscriminate use of "state of the art" technologies which, in some cases, do not represent the most effective solutions.

The examples presented range from the distribution of printed materials for the dissemination of information, to the use of Packet-Radio and PACSAT systems for distribution of information in rural areas. A specific section is dedicated to the use of Packet Switched Data Networks for national and international networks. Particular importance is given to the adherence to standards through a paper on access of data-bases in OSI environments.

4.1 Technology Broker System for SMEs in FRG

Helmut Gall

4.1.1 The Organization of Chambers of Commerce and Industry in FRG

First of all I should like to give a brief description of the German Organization of Chambers of Commerce and Industry, stressing what it does especially on behalf of small business.

To understand the organization one needs to know that there are sixty-nine chambers of commerce and industry in the Federal Republic, each of which is concerned with the economic interests of its particular region. However, their influence rises above the merely local sphere by virtue of their membership in the Association of German Chambers of Commerce and Industry, which is known by the initials of its German name DIHT, and has its headquarters in Bonn.

The Chambers are public-law bodies. Membership is compulsory for all enterprises of industry and commerce. They are self-administering, not government agencies and not a lobby for just one branch or just a special size of firm. They are not employers organizations with bargaining in wage negotiations. They represent and defend the economic interests of all their members and are committed by law to objectivity and neutrality.

All this makes chambers of industry and commerce an independent and very important source of advice on economic issues to governments, parliaments, law courts and other institutions at all levels. This is their primary task. Their second important aim is to provide services to all industrial and commercial firms, especially to SMEs.

In fulfilling these tasks, the chamber in their role of the self-administering organization of commerce and industry are supported by the enterprises and the business community they represent, who form the plenary assembly and contribute specialist knowledge and the fruits of practical experience. In addition, the DIHT has 20 specialist committees and 60 working groups looking after the interests of a total of 1,5 million German business enterprises. The bulk of these comes under the category of small business. Further support is given by 45 German Chambers of commerce abroad. These chambers are voluntary associations, organized bilaterally by German and foreign businessmen. Their task is to promote economic relations between FRG and the respective host countries.

What, then, does the organization do for small business in particular? Basically the aims and the task are two-fold. From the point of view of general economic policy, the chambers are espoused to the principle of a social free-market economy. Internationally, they advocate freedom of world trade and fight against subsidies and protectionism.

Besides this, the organization gives small and medium-sized business "help for self-help" (e.g. on the field of INNOVATION).

4.1.2 Innovation-Aid for SMEs

For the last ten years the Chambers of Commerce in the Federal Republic of Germany have offered firms in their regions a new service in the advice on innovation.

Surveys of member firms had repeatedly revealed a high level of innovative potential, especially among small and medium-size enterprises, but showed that problems were frequently encountered when it came to translating potential into marketable products and processes.

The first question was therefore what assistance could be offered, given that traditional management consultants services in the FRG had so far come up with no suitable response to the problem. Having recognized the usefulness of having a special innovation aid service in the vicinity of the potential innovative firms, the next question was:

- whether the Chambers of Commerce should be prepared to go beyond their traditional forms of fostering economic development and provide technological innovation advice and, further more,
- whether much greater importance was bound to attach in future to improving the services offered by the Chambers in this respect.

In other words: should the innovation aid, offered by the Chambers be regarded as a logical addition to the "traditional" services already offered in such fields as exporting, transport, vocational training and aid to industry, and are public law entities the right kind of organization to assume such responsibilities?

There are three factors which would seem to indicate that the Chambers are particularly suited to run an innovation advice service.

They would seem to be suitable because of:

- their regional structure covering the whole of FRG;
- their physical proximity to potential innovative firms;
- the confidence placed in them by their member firms.

The last of these factors is especially important. Another reason why the Chamber would appear to have a special responsibility for technological innovation is that

- government aid alone cannot be expected to enable firms to overcome many of the obstacles in the way of innovation and that
- there is a need for industry and its self-help-organizations to take the initiative themselves.

It is precisely because state innovation aid can be no more than a means of helping firms to help themselves that the Chambers of Commerce and Industry in the Federal Republic have a special role to play as an intermediary between government and the economy, given that they have a legal obligation to foster commercial activities in their particular regions.

Because of their close knowledge of the needs of their regions and individual firms, and - last not least - because of the confidence placed in them by their members, the Chambers can take the initiative, provide aid and act as an intermediary wherever e.g. central government cannot play an effective role (either because this does not come within its sphere of competence or for some other reason), or where other organizations are not sufficiently close to the firms in question. Due to the support received from the Federal Ministry for Research and Technology for five different pilot projects, the development of Chamber of Commerce innovation advice centers during the last 12 years was very rapid.

Generally speaking, innovation aid is available free of charge to members and the service has been well received by them. The innovation advisors are being worked off their feet.

The current situation is that 60 of the 69 local Chambers of Commerce in the FRG are served by 35 innovation advice centers run either by the Chambers themselves or in collaboration with other organizations. Deliberate policy decision was taken not to prescribe a fixed form of organization (e.g. the form being laid down by the DIHT) for these advice centers. It was assumed that practical experience would show which form of organization was best suited to providing effective innovation aid to the member firms. The traditional forms of advisory service using the Chamber's own staff is increasingly being replaced by various forms of specialized advice, either from the Chamber's own specialist staff or via outside private innovation consultants.

Many Chambers of Commerce are currently backing up their specialist advice by use of data-bank-terminals. A special working group has been set up to study problems relating to data-bank-information. A working group "Innovation" under the auspices of DIHT in Bonn organizes regular exchanges of view and experiences among the Chambers' innovation advisors.

We are planning to improve the range of services offered by the Chambers of Commerce whenever small and medium firms suffer under unfair conditions.

We are planning to improve the range of our service in those areas in which there is no likelihood of private consultants coming up with comparable services on a uniform regional basis.

4.1.3 The "CCI-Technology Exchange" (IHK-Technologiebörse): Innovation by Information

As regards innovation-aid, special importance attaches to this function as small and medium size enterprises without research and development departments of their own are finding it increasingly difficult to maintain their competitive position by going in for new, improved and lower-cost products and processes. In our time, which is a time of far-reaching information, SMEs have a great demand for information on market modifications and on the development of new technologies.

Some firms try to acquire technical innovations by way of licensing agreements, while others have patents, licenses and also unpatented technical know-how to dispose of to the highest bidder. In order to activate this supply-and-demand potential and bring it into more widespread use is the aim of our IHK-Technologiebörse. The Technological Exchange of the Association of German CCI's stimulates this supply and demand potential.

Technology Transfer, Innovation through Information. is the objective the Technological Exchange has set itself. This initiative was launched by the DIHT in 1982 at the Hannover Fair. We want to provide the firms with a platform on technical know-how through a catalogue, but also thanks to a data-bank via electronic support. The inscription in the catalogue is free of cost for those firms associated to the CCI; the catalogue is sent on payment of a small protection charge. We have reached our 15th edition: it contains 2000 technological offers and demands. We have also published an extract of this catalogue listing the 300 novelties.

We work on the basis of a questionnaire in which the interested party describes the innovation, the economic advantages of the latter, the fields of application, the progress of work, the products already introduced on the markets and possible outlets for the offer. After a technical control, a copy of the questionnaire is sent to Bonn, where it is processed on a computer and it is then included in the catalogue. The offer is maintained in the catalogue for 2 years. All inputs are included in three international Hosts.

If our Technological Exchange meanwhile has become the most important one in Europe, this goes to prove that many firms want to turn innovations into practice, that there is a real need on the market for this type of service by the CCIs.

The Exchange is but a preliminary stage before co-operation can take place between two firms; it is not a platform for marketing nor for mergers between firms. Besides the computerized-paper catalogue which appears twice a year (15th Edition April 1989) all the 2000 offers and demands are stored in a data-base called BUSINESS for worldwide on-line access via the Hosts DATA-STAR, Switzerland and the Host GENIOS in Hamburg, FRG. I'll give you details on this later on.

All in all this technology exchange which 7 years ago was started as a trial by 18 Chambers of Commerce met with a great deal of interest. The IHK-Technologiebörse has completed its experimental phase and has become the most comprehensive collection of this kind in Europe. The organizers are convinced and encouraged in their view that in the field of innovation alternative aid patterns do exist apart from the usual government-aid (especially from the mentioned point of view of self-help).

4.1.4 Support from Distributed Data-Base Systems

Now that the Technology Exchange is running well in the FRG, the CCI also wishes to promote contacts with foreign firms in the field of technology. Co-operation projects already exist with Canada, Austria, France. A planned co-operation with VECTRA will be the first example for cross-boarder co-operation by means of distributed data-base system. I'll come back to this point later .

Owing to this expansion towards foreign countries, we now publish an English version of the Catalogue and of the Input of the data-base.

The English version "Technological Innovations from Germany" is distributed by the worldwide network of 45 German CCIs abroad. As we learned in this symposium there are already a whole series of efforts in your country especially to help SMEs and I feel that, thanks to the present symposium, it will be possible to establish contacts and to give new ideas to similar initiatives in your country based on distributed data-base system and, not to forget, as well on paper media like this catalogue. Our experience is that the electronic publication of our technology exchange will not replace the paper information via catalogue. On the contrary the demand for the paper catalogue has even grown as a result of the data-base version!

In the last part I will explain to you this scheme showing our Technology Exchange as a technology-transfer instrument, based on a paper catalogue and supported by a distributed data-base system. The data-base infrastructure we use for this purpose is by no means a sophisticated computer network! It just considers the very different hardware outfit of our innovation-advice centers in FRG and abroad. But we are sure, that it will become a fast growing network, because its component parts are already used for different purposes in the day-to-day tasks of a CCI innovation-advice center. The needed hardware (AT-PC industrial standard) and the software components (e.g. relational data-base system dBASE IV) you can buy next door in our country.

What I mentioned before concerning the setting up of the innovation advice centers in general, is still more important in case of our data-base system. Also in this field a deliberate policy decision was taken not to insist on a fixed organizational structure, assuming that practical experience would reveal a form of organization that will be best suited to afford effective innovation assistance to member firms. On this last picture I would like to show you the development and the actual status of our data-base supported Technology Broker System.

It all started with a small problem in connection with the edition of the English version of our catalogue. The problem was the manual computer-input of rather difficult technical texts (offers and inquiries) in English delivered as paper printouts by our translation office. We developed a program, which

- enables the translation office to produce the English version on a floppy-disk, which
- enables us to roll-in (to store) this non-paper version to our computer system.

And as a computer does not care whether an input is given in English or in German language, the solution of this small problem enabled not only our translation office but as well our 69 Chambers of Commerce to leave the paper-form method.

The above mentioned program which is based on a compiled relational data-base system (dBASE IV) with mask-controlled input permits to deliver also the German offers and demands on a floppy-disk.

The Chamber of Commerce Organization in France has established a similar Technology Exchange Service, called VECTRA, which operates nationwide over the so called MINITEL (Videotex-) System. Our plan to co-operate with

VECTRA will be facilitated by the fact, that VECTRA uses exactly the same data-base system for the data-input (Floppy-disk exchange or Remote Data-Transmission). On the basis of a well developed DatexP-Network the next step will be of course the Remote Data-Transmission of all inputs into our system.

Besides the already mentioned On-line Hosts DATASTAR and GENIOS the non-paper output of the complete Technology Exchange is also available via leased-line connection with 2 CCI Computer Centers.

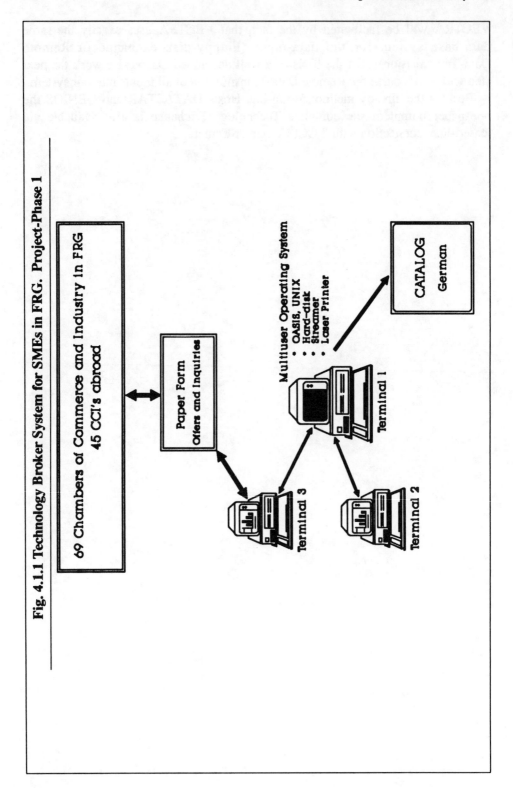

Fig. 4.1.1 Technology Broker System for SMEs in FRG. Project-Phase 1

69 Chambers of Commerce and Industry in FRG
45 CCI's abroad

Paper Form
Offers and Inquiries

Multiuser Operating System
• OASIS, UNIX
• Hard-disk
• Streamer
• Laser Printer

Terminal 1

Terminal 2

Terminal 3

CATALOG
German

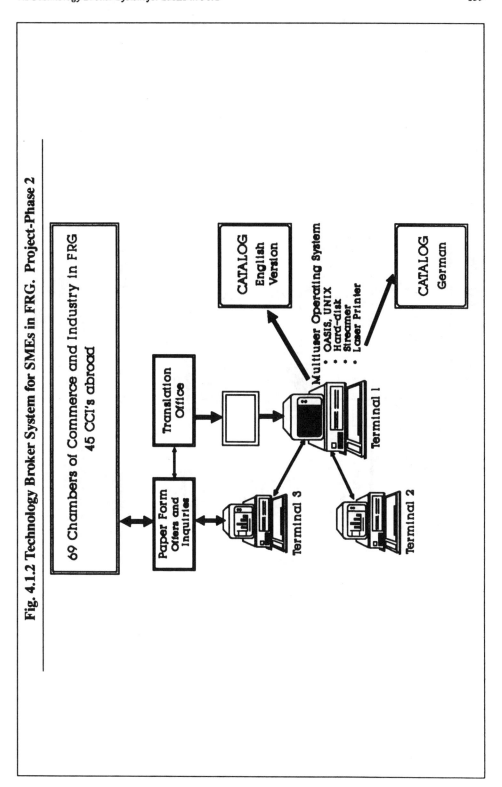

Fig. 4.1.2 Technology Broker System for SMEs in FRG. Project-Phase 2

Fig. 4.1.3 Technology Broker System for SMEs in FRG. Project-Phase 3

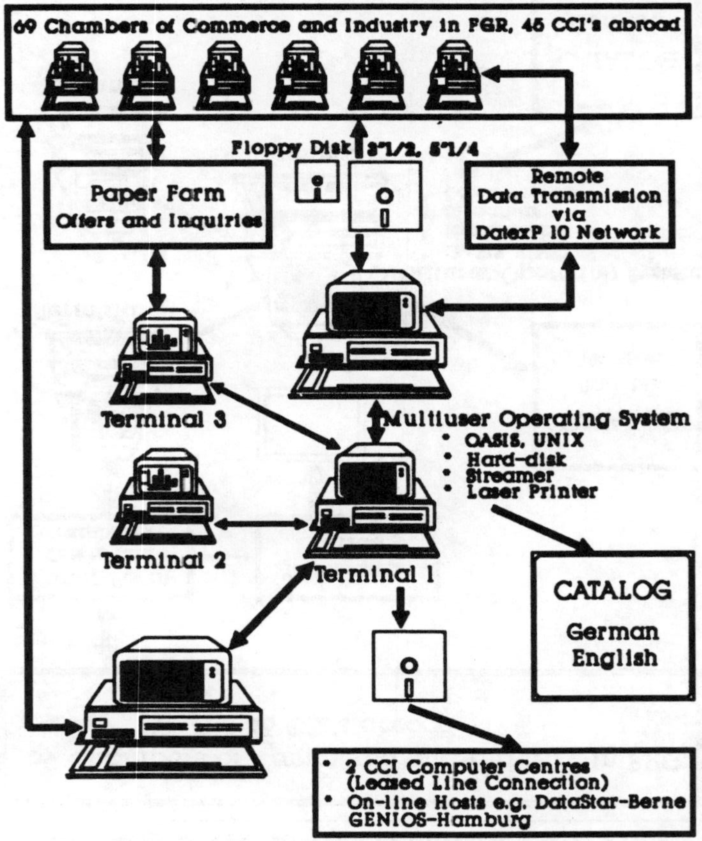

69 Chambers of Commerce and Industry in FGR, 45 CCI's abroad

Remote
Data Transmission
via
DatexP 10 Network

Floppy Disk 5¼, 3½, 3¼

Paper Form
Offers and Inquiries

Multiuser Operating System
• OASIS, UNIX
• Hard-disk
• Streamer
• Laser Printer

CATALOG
German
English

Terminal 1

Terminal 2

Terminal 3

• 2 CCI Computer Centres
  (Leased Line Connection)
• On-line Hosts e.g. DataStar-Berne
  GENIOS-Hamburg

4.2 Data-Bases and Information Distribution for Rural Industries

Henry R. Norman

Dr. Hyung Sup Choi, the former Minister for Science and Technology in the Government of Korea, has made the wise observation that in the effort to achieve technological self-reliance, "priority must be given to the sound and efficient utilization of available foreign technologies and that one must avoid engaging blindly in such noble but certainly financially unrewarding exercises as reinventing the wheel" [1]. The Japanese certainly didn't waste time reinventing the wheel. Instead, they redesigned it and produced high quality cars that threatened to capture the American market until quotas were set, watches that competed successfully with those made in Switzerland, and cameras that Germans buy. Masao Fujioka, President of the Asia Development Bank, writes of the spectacular success story of Japan, "What is often overlooked is the fact that Japan introduced the most suitable technology, not necessarily the most advanced one, and Japan adapted it to local conditions to meet market demand" [2]. This paper will describe communications and information technologies that will in my judgement help meet the present need for rural communication in China and build on what already exists rather than depend on early access to the "most advanced". It will also suggest that whatever the level of technology used, an information resource must be active and not passive if it is to be of maximum effectiveness. It must also respond to the needs of the people who will use it and not simply inflate the institutional pride of those who maintain it.

4.2.1 Meeting Communications Needs

4.2.1.1 The High Cost of a Communications Infrastructure

Global communications today depend increasingly on geo-stationary satellites positioned more than 22,000 miles in space. Designing, building, and launching these satellites is an expensive business, as one satellite can cost as much as $100 million. It is also a very risky business; last year alone at least four satellites failed for various electronic and mechanical reasons after reaching orbit. Understandably, insurance premium run to 21 percent of the value insured [3]. In addition, the satellites depend on highly sophisticated ground stations and good telecommunications systems all of which are very expensive.

It is anticipated that 6.6 trillion Yuan will be spent in China on Telecommunications to the year 2000 [4]. This enormous investment will undoubtedly pay off as it has elsewhere. Parker W. Borg, Deputy Director of the

Bureau for International Communications and Information Policy of the U.S. Department of State, has observed, "Recent economic studies on the relationship between telecommunications availability and economic growth in the Philippines and Costa Rica established cost/benefit ratios of over 5 to 1 and in some sectors 48 to 1" [5].   However, even after this massive effort service to rural areas is still unlikely to permit easy and inexpensive access to satellite communications to search remote data-bases.   While it may not be a concern in China that individual homes have telephones even in the next century, a modern communications capacity depends on the supporting infrastructure of a general telecommunications system.

In the United States it is anticipated that by the mid 1990's data traffic will take up over half of the communications capacity of AT&T, with voice reduced to less than half. Even today, American Airlines, the third largest carrier of air passengers in the United States and the most profitable airline, now earns more money from its computerized reservation service than from its traditional airlines business [6]. Nearly half the electronic information sold in the United States is financial information used for transactions such as stock or commodity trades [7].

4.2.1.2 VITA's Information Dissemination Service

The organization I direct, Volunteers in Technical Assistance (VITA), has been engaged in the dissemination of technical information to requesters from developing countries for 30 years. One of the avenues VITA uses to reach people in developing countries with technical information is a weekly broadcast over the Voice of America.   This program, which describes practical small-scale technologies and invites people to write for further information, brings in more than a thousand letters each month to VITA's headquarters in suburban Washington, D.C. Letters come from business persons, farmers, students, government officials, etc. Each one is answered, without charge, with the highest quality information available. Many are handled by VITA Volunteers, selected from VITA's computerized skills bank, who do whatever research is necessary to answer the inquiry.

The hunger for information this service demonstrates is not confined to urban areas anywhere in the world. VITA, a small organization in Washington, D.C., is able to reach thousands of people in remote places and inspire them to write to us about their needs.   This connection is possible because all that those many thousands of people require is a transistor radio a radio that runs on batteries and does not need to be plugged in to the electricity grid, which probably doesn't reach them anyway. A small self-contained radio permits a dialogue between people on opposite sides of the world. This is indeed suitable technology for rural areas.

4.2.2 Alternatives to Conventional Communications Technologies

The poor state of communications in the rural areas as well as many urban areas of the Third World countries has long been a concern to VITA. We know that there can be no development without communications and, as we have seen, an investment in communications pays off well. We also know that development cannot wait until poor countries have the resources to extend conventional telecommunications networks to all of their citizens. This has fueled our search for alternative systems that are low in cost, reliable, and can be put into operation now, with currently available technology.

VITA is involved in the universe of technology, but its emphasis is on the applications of technology rather than the technology itself. Vita introduces and assists in the assimilation of technologies, whether they be high or low, that are appropriate to the actual conditions that exist in the place where they are to be used, and designs applications that can be used effectively with the skills available. Of the 5,000 VITA Volunteers who assist with these and other VITA activities, more than 1,400 are graduate engineers; some 1,200 hold doctorates; and 650 serve on the faculties of major universities.

With the help of VITA Volunteers and others, VITA has begun aggressively to promote the use of packet radio and low orbiting, satellites, two communications technologies that we feel meet the requirements of people in remote areas. VITA has also actively explored applications for computer-based information storage systems. These various technologies are described below.

4.2.2.1 Packet Radio

In Ethiopia in 1985, VITA carried out what is thought to be the first packet radio demonstration in a developing country, at the request of the relief agency CARE. Distribution of food during the famine was seriously hampered by breakdowns in communication, which was largely by radio, and CARE asked VITA to explore alternatives.

The technology VITA settled on was packet radio communications. Packet radio is a system that enables computers in places distant from each other to send data through radio transmission. Each station in the network consists of a personal computer, a radio transceiver, a terminal node controller (TNC, a modem-like device), a printer, and a whip antenna. In swift bursts of energy, the TNC breaks the message into small pieces (packets) that are transmitted by radio to the receiving computers. There, another TNC decodes the packet, which appears on the computer screen and can be printed. The packets are error-free since the TNC not only forms the packet, it adds address and error-checking codes. The receiving TNC will reject the packet if for any reason there is an error and the sending TNC will repeat the packet as often as necessary until it is received exactly as sent.

This versatile technology is relatively low in cost. Despite its level of technical sophistication, one TNC unit costs only $100 to $300 and an entire communications center costs about $5,000 or less. System computers can be used for other purposes when the TNC unit is not receiving or sending, and data can be stored for printing during off hours. Systems can be assembled from existing components with few additions.

Permission to carry out the demonstration in Ethiopia was obtained from the Ethiopian Relief and Rehabilitation Commission, which is charged with responsibility for the distribution of relief supplies. Since the government had long banned amateur radio, sideband radios had to be located and repaired, and then installed at the CARE offices in Addis Abeba. The two VITA Volunteers sent to the country succeeded in doing this and with the Terminal Node Controller (TNC) they linked the radio with a computer. A simple whip antennae was also attached.

In the town of Dire Dawa, a rural feeding station operated by CARE some 300 miles from Addis, another "communications center" was set up duplicating the equipment of the first. The transmission of complex data was completed without a single error and without benefit of telephones. If necessary, it could also have come about using a battery or solar panels instead of conventional electricity.

VITA has since carried out demonstrations of packet radio communications in several countries as well as innumerable times in the United States. A number of other groups, including enterprises within developing countries, are now implementing packet radio networks. These "networks" may have as few as two centers or they can be made up of large numbers of centers. There can be sub-networks and networks of networks as data are refined up through the system with appropriate software programs so that they reach decision makers with the information necessary to make well informed choices.

China has already developed an effective system in which large factories assist small ones in a variety of ways. Packet radio networks could expand this system more broadly and permit conferencing within the network to share knowledge and experience. The large factories are more likely to be knowledgeable about foreign markets and design requirements. Access to such information at no cost could be helpful to small factories seeking to export.

4.2.2.2 Low-Orbiting Satellites

VITA's interest in packet radio technology was an outgrowth of our pioneering activities in a low earth-orbiting satellite technology (LEO), known as PACSAT, that uses packet radio communication systems. These began five years ago when a Delta rocket was launched from the Vandenberg Air Force Base in California carrying a unique experimental digital communications package. VITA Volunteers in five cities in three countries designed the package, which was built by the Spacecraft Engineering Research Unit of the University of Surrey in Great

Britain. Messages have been exchanged routinely since that time between VITA and the university via the satellite.

A more sophisticated satellite, presently being built by the Surrey group, will be launched in November of this year. By late 1991 two more satellites will be in orbit, completing the system. Each one of these will be capable of supporting up to 500 ground stations. The satellites will act as orbiting "mailboxes". When one is within receiving distance of a ground station, the station uploads or transmits messages for storage in the satellite's memory and similarly downloads or retrieves messages. The satellite will then carry the new messages from the ground station to their destination.

Because the PACSAT satellites will be in low earth orbit, they will pass over most points on earth at least twice a day. Depending on the location of the source and destination stations, a complete query response cycle is possible within 24 hours. The entire message transmission and retrieval system is automatic, so that field personnel can enter their messages and then concentrate on their other activities.

The National Research Council of the National Academy of Sciences in the United States in a report on Microcomputers and Their Applications for Developing Countries described the advantages of PACSAT under the heading "A New Model for Communications Via Satellite" as follows:

- Ground stations can be relatively inexpensive...because the satellite is only a few hundred miles in orbit, as opposed to many thousands of miles, and because the choice of operating frequencies (Very high frequencies--VHF, or ultra high frequency-UHF) does not require the use of parabolic "dish" antennas, but only simple vertical "whips". Because the system is portable, it is useful for applications such as disaster relief and monitoring supply logistics for refugee camps. Stations can be run on battery or solar power, so independence from the vagaries of electrical power is possible.
- The system does not depend on the existing telecommunications infrastructure with its attendant technical and institutional problems, though clearly it would require regulation in its use for communicating within a country to and from rural areas and towns and villages that will never have reliable international data communications capability.
- It uses sophisticated "packet switching" techniques making high-quality, error-free communication possible.
- It allows for automatic operation, so that the user need not be present to upload or download messages.
- It provides low-cost communication capability for those groups and organizations that cannot now regularly use the international system.
- While the satellite's on-board memory would be too small to make resident any substantial data-base for on-line searching (in addition to the limited 10-15 minute time "window" per pass), messages describing the boundaries of such

searches could easily be transmitted to another party on the system with access to those data-bases who could more easily carry out the search. Given current costs, use of an intermediary organization for this purpose would be advisable even in the present situation.
- South-south communication would be facilitated, lessening dependance on the industrialized nations [8].

4.2.2.3 Information Storage and Retrieval Systems

The technologies discussed above have not generally been commercially exploited because most telecommunications technology is developed for instantaneous message delivery and simultaneous, two-way communication. In planning an information system and the communications necessary for information dissemination, I think we have to go back to the comments cited earlier by Japan's Fujioka, who said "...Japan introduced the most suitable technology, not necessarily the most advanced one".

Rural industries in developing countries would seem to have little need at present for "instantaneous message delivery." Most remote data-bases are bibliographic so delays in obtaining the full text of a document let alone the expense reduces the value of immediate communication. Reliable, inexpensive, and simple systems appear to be a greater priority and a 24-hour turn-around time does not create serious problems.

When we turn to the data-bases themselves, a combination of technologies, some ordinary and some advanced, would seem to offer the greatest benefit for the least cost. Some micro fiche and even paper may be appropriate under existing circumstances in rural areas. However, while these should not be excluded, limiting an information resource to them would seriously curtail the potential value of the data-base. Technologies such as CD-ROM and other advanced storage technologies are important.

The Board on Science and Technology for International Development of the National Research Council has described CD-ROM as follows:

- CD-ROM or compact disk/read-only-memory is one of the latest technological advances in the high-volume, low-cost information storage devices. It uses laser technology to record and play back large amounts of information on a small, very durable disk. Use of CD-ROM permits distribution of information to the most appropriate geographic or organizational location, and makes it possible to collect and store information at the most appropriate point for subsequent distribution either upward (such as forwarding requests for information) or downward (such as distributing search results to users).
- The chief advantage of CD-ROM is that one disk can store about 250,000 pages worth of information (about the amount of information contained on 1500

floppy disks). While the initial mastering costs are relatively expensive, duplication costs are relatively low. This means that once a data-base is mastered it can be copied and distributed to several locations. CD-ROM is particularly advantageous where telecommunications is impractical or impossible. The stand alone CD-ROM system eliminates the need for on-line frequent use of the data-base is made, or in remote areas where telecommunications linkages and computer time usage charges. Users receive unlimited access for a fixed fee.

- Many commercial bibliographic data-bases are now available on CD-ROM. For instance, the U.S. National Agricultural Library's Agricola archival disk, which contains 2,5 million records, is available for about $4,000. A subscription to the current disk, which contains close to a half million citations to publications from 1983 to present, costs $1,750 per year and includes quarterly updates. Grolier's Electronic Encyclopedia, which contains 21 printed volumes, takes only 1/5 of a CD-ROM and is available for about $200.
- To use CD-ROM, one must have a personal computer, an operating system, and a cd player. The search software incorporated into the records on the disk performs all the search tasks now possible on the major online systems [9].

Making a master of a CD-ROM disk as recently as a year ago could have cost $10,000 with copies at $45 to $52. Now a master can be made for as little as $2,500 and copies for $8 to $12 in quantities of 50 to 200 copies [10]. It is expected that in the early 1990's erasable optical disks will be available so that data may be added, deleted, or revised, thereby eliminating one important constraint of CD-ROM [11].

4.2.2.4 Applications

The packet radio network of ground stations may be used separately or linked with the PACSAT satellite system depending on local needs and the wishes of the government. These applications can perhaps best be explained by describing some recent VITA initiatives.

In February of this year VITA entered into a contract with the Department of Health of the Philippines to set up a network of seven packet radio communications centers and to design a larger network of 120 centers. It is anticipated that ultimately more than 600 centers will be established. The Department concluded after a demonstration VITA conducted last year that the technology was particularly well suited to the country, which has more than 7,000 islands and a poor telecommunications system.

Rural health centers will be grouped into provincial networks, which will themselves be part of district networks, and, finally, the districts will be part of the national network. At each level data will be collected and organized by management information software to provide appropriate data for health officials to effectively use their resources and to improve the health of Filipinos throughout the country.

An important part of the agreement in the Philippines, which is being financed as part of a World Bank loan, is the training of a local firm to install and maintain the equipment. The Department of Education has indicated interest in a network for the school system and several private groups in that country have also made inquiries. The local firm is negotiating a 100-center contract with the Philippines Airlines to install systems in all of the country's airports.

In Jamaica, where Hurricane Gilbert was the worst natural catastrophe ever suffered, a combined terrestrial/satellite system is planned. At the time of the disaster a difficult situation was made worse by the lack of communication around the country. A packet radio communications system will soon be in place as a result of generous contributions from the IBM Corporation and CITICORP/ CITIBANK. In a future disaster, information on real needs can be gathered from around the island and communicated by PACSAT to the outside world regardless of the state of the normal telecommunications system.

An example of PACSAT used alone is a proposal advanced by the Technical Education Research Centers (TERC) Inc., in Cambridge, Massachusetts. Through its program of Network Science, TERC involves students in telecommunications-based, collaborative investigations in scientific subjects, such as a recent program in the United States on acid rain. Outstanding scientists professionally involved in acid rain research collaborated in this activity, giving students an unusual opportunity to participate in science and to gain a personal view of scientific processes.

TERC and VITA will collaborate to extend the program to the developing countries. Personal computers at sites throughout the world will transmit messages to PACSAT as it passes over. When will be received and posted on VITA's electronic bulletin board; TERC's computer will automatically read these messages and responses will be made as appropriate [12].

4.2.3 A Practical, Low-Cost Communications/Information Resource

The system that VITA proposes for consideration is a rural network of information centers equipped with packet radio communications equipment. Entire data-bases on CD-ROM in subjects of importance would be purchased with update subscriptions. Intermediaries in various countries would be used to do occasional searches using the PACSAT satellite to communicate.

This system is reliable, costs relatively little (much of the equipment is used interchangeably), and permits the economical training of personnel and the development of an information culture. It can easily assimilate new technologies coming on-line and will itself become an integral part of any future telecommunications capability. It can be used in local, regional, or national networks based on geography, subject matter, or specific purposes such as health, education, disaster communications, etc. Computer conferencing can be encouraged so that intellectual resources and experiences can be shared throughout the country. Indigenous data-bases can be developed either discretely or by revisions to purchased international data-bases. Finally, much of the equipment required could be manufactured within China either or license or designed domestically.

The critical element of the proposed system is that it is active rather than passive in its response to the needs of the community it serves. "The information transmission business and the information storage business are not the same as the information understanding business. An understanding business is a service that makes data and information useful, applicable, and approachable" [13].

The biggest problem in information today is not its availability, but the glut of data: how to manage the avalanche of information so that its selection, organization, and accessibility encourage and enable its use. An information system is not a library in which documentation is catalogued uncritically. An active information system isn't even limited to just providing information. For example, in many countries the technique of incubator industrial parks is popular. Much like ordinary industrial parks physically, incubators concentrate small beginning businesses in a location that also has both services the entrepreneurs might not be able to afford to set up themselves such as computers, telex, facsimile, etc., as well as advisers including accountants, lawyers, marketing people, and others. Incubators are often connected to universities where expertise is available.

The purpose is not just to make information available, but to help entrepreneurs understand it and use it so they can create new wealth that will benefit themselves and their communities.

This is much like the present Chinese system of large factories helping small factories described above. Imported data-bases may not have the orientation desired by China. My understanding of present Chinese priorities is that export is most important and that efficiency and quality to make Chinese products competitive on the world market are critical. This must be done in the context of Chinese form of socialism, which encourages individually owned factories. While the purpose is not unique, the environment in which it is being carried out is without precedent. Access to information is important, but the ability to adapt that information to the needs of China and to make it easily available to collective factories and others is of paramount importance.

VITA's experience in providing technical information free of charge to requesters in developing countries for 30 years might be instructive. The service was free, but reactive and passive; i.e., we responded to people who heard of us and wrote to us. About ten years ago we became more active and sought to introduce technologies through long-term programs in Third World countries. At the same time, we started a course in information management that has now trained over 200 people in more than 40 countries. Seven people from China have taken the course.

The number of inquires received increased as VITA became more active. The Voice of America broadcasts that began three years ago sky-rocketed the number of requests to unprecedented numbers. We are now engaged in the development of communications facilities with packet radio and PACSAT and there is little doubt the number of inquiries will jump dramatically as more people become aware of the availability of information and the communications capacity to ask for it and receive it.

4.2.4 Conclusions

Communications are essential to development, but it will be many years before rural areas of developing countries are served by adequate telecommunications. If they are not to fall even further behind, an alternative to modern tele-communications must be placed in service for at least the next decade. Networks of packet radio centers are ideal for this purpose with un international communications capacity available through PACSAT, the low earth orbiting satellite system.

This system can well serve the development of rural industry in China by expanding the present practice of large factories helping small factories and intensifying their interaction through computer conferencing. The use of data-bases on CD-ROM disks will provide a base for a highly interactive information system that can be adapted to the real conditions in China and give an enormous boost to the development of rural industry.

References

[1] Choi, Dr. Hyung Sup, "Popularization of S&T Agencies'" Tech Forum, July/August 1985, Asia-Pacific Tech Monitor, p. 22.

[2] Masao, Fujioka, "Alleviating Poverty Through Development: The Asian Experience," Development 1988: 2/3, Rome, Italy, p. 29.

[3] Burgess, John, "Risky Business of Satellites," Washington Post, September 15, 1988.

[4] "Telephone Company Diversifying into Variety of Business Through New Units" Japan Economic Journal, October 5, 1985, p. 31.

[5] Borg, Parker W., "Miami Conference on the Caribbean," November 30, 1988, p. 5.

[6] Ibid.

[7] Schiller, Zachary, "The Information Business," Business Week, August 25, 1986, p. 35.

[8] Microcomputers and their Applications for Developing Countries, Westview Press, Boulder/London 1986, p. 35.

[9] "CD-ROM," Bostid Developments, Volume 8, No. 1, 1988, p. 20.

[10] "CD-ROM Developments, The Outlook is Improving," Center for Advanced Learning Systems Tech Bulletin #2, U.S. Department of Labor, February 1989, p. 3.

[11] Mortensen, Erik, "CD-ROM Debate: What is Its Potential Value?," The Office, May 1988, p. 144.

[12] "The Low Altitude Satellite Project: First Steps Toward Global Education", The Technical Education Research Centers, Inc., Cambridge, Massachusetts, February 1989, p. 6-7.

[13] Wurman, Richard Saul, Information Anxiety, Doubleday Press, New York, New York, 1989.

4.3 Data-Base Access in the OSI Environment

Ma Yingzhang, Zhao Xiaofan

4.3.1 Introduction

The OSI Reference Model (OSIRM) has been extremely successful in providing a fundamental architectural framework for the development of OSI standards. It established functional relationship between standards for the various OSI layers and defined a core set of concepts which are common to standards in all layers. The ultimate goal of OSI standardization is to specify mechanisms that support the operation of distributed information processing activities in a networked systems environment. The Application Layer, the highest layer in the OSIRM, lies at the boundary between communication and processing aspects of distributed processing. It contains functions that are directly related to the specification and coordination of distributed processing activities.

The RDA is one of the OSI standards in the Application Layer for supporting the application development of distributed data-base.

4.3.2 Remote Data-Base Access

RDA is a Specific Application Service Element (SASE) in the Application Layer of the OSIRM and defines the interworking between two program components in different end systems, where one controls a data-base and the other requires access to the data-base. The RDA standard defines the behavior of the system components and the format and meaning of all messages exchanged between the programs.

The following aspects have been defined:

- A general model for access to remote data-base;
- The abstract interactions between a pair of users;
- The services for supporting the above communications and the mapping to the services of Association Control Service Element (ACSE), Remote Operation Service (ROS) and Commitment, Concurrency and Recovery (CCR) which are needed by the transactions management;
- The protocols for supporting the above services;

The RDA standard uses the semantics defined in other data-base standards. The archetypical use of RDA is for supporting the access to the physically remote data-base by users at workstations. The more complicated use is the distributed data-base system. The major topics in this paper are based on the client-server working model in the workstation usage as shown in Fig. 4.3.1.

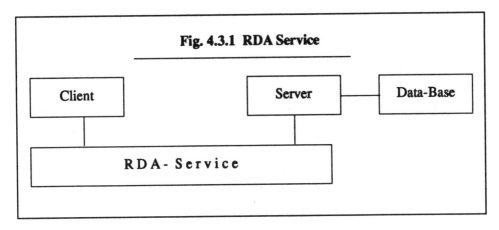

A client is Application Entity (AE) which creates the Application Association and requires service provided by a data-base. A server is an AE which respond to the created Application Association and provides the service of data-base. A more detailed structure of Fig. 4.3.1 is shown in Fig. 4.3.2.

The client Application Process Invocation (API) includes an executable process of a program, which is responsible for data processing. The RDA communication element is a software component on behalf of the client process and the server process. At the data-base end, the server process is translating the protocol message into data manipulation procedure calls and transmitting the result back using the RDA communication service. The interface, i.e. DBL (Data-Base Language), between the server process and the data-base is functionally equivalent to the DML (Data-Base Manipulation Language) defined in the data-base standards, e.g. Network Data-Base Language (NDL) and Structured Query Language (SQL).

The only requirement of RDA is the conformance to the communication protocol, i.e. exact formats and procedures of the messages exchanged over the communication connections. No particular component or interface is needed within the client or server end systems. It provides the independence to the client system (workstation) and the server (data-base). The implementation on the workstation should be capable of interacting with any data-base conformable to the standards. On the other hand, the standardized data-base should be capable of interacting with any user at any workstation conformable to the standards. The separation of the client and the server implementations means that the user can switch between different data-bases without adjusting their working mode.

The following concepts are essential for RDA:

- Associations is represented by Application Association and defines relationships between the client and the server from its establishment to release.
- Resource Handling, by using r-open and r-close commands, opens and closes any named data resource.

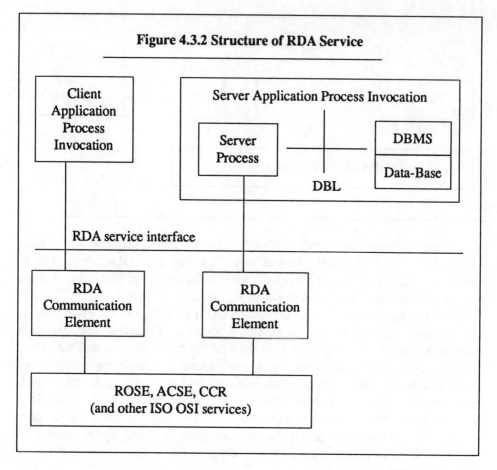

Figure 4.3.2 Structure of RDA Service

- Transaction is a logically integrated processing unit depending on the client API and has the property of being atomic from the point of view of all processes not involved in the transaction. An API can only execute one transaction at a time, but a data-base server may concurrently execute several transactions for different API's.
- Data Manipulation facilities are supported by the RDA in two independent ways, i.e. single statemer.ts and repeated operations.
- Data Representation for exchange of argument or result is not defined in the RDA, but the data values must be agreed between the partners and the data types must be defined by the Abstract Syntax Notation 1 (ASN.1), another OSI standard.

Four groups of RDA service elements have been defined:

- ACSEs provide the establishment and release of the Association between a pair of application processes.
- Remote Operation Binding provides the context control functions.

- Remote Operation Invocations are asynchronous between the clients and the servers.
- Transaction Management and Recovery is optional for the RDA.

4.3.3 Relationship Between RDA and OSI

In Fig. 4.3.3 the simplest form of a distributed information processing task is used to explain the relationship between RDA and OSI, where SAO stands for Single Association Object and SACF for Single Association Control Function.

The client application process consists of the client process, which has the RDA job to accomplish, plus the AE that handles the communications. The Server application process contains a server process, the data-base management system

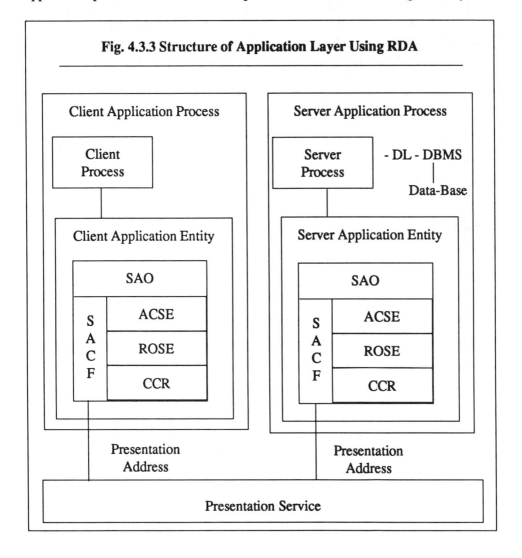

Fig. 4.3.3 Structure of Application Layer Using RDA

(DBMS) and an AE. The Server process is the link between the communication and the data-base. Both AEs contain an ASO which contains an SACF and components of ROSE, ACSE and CCR.

Each association object has a Presentation Address, which is used to establish the Association between them. If the client process had established Associations with more than one remote server, the AE would contain more than one SAO and a Multiple Association Control Function (MACF). The communication capabilities of the AE are modeled as a set of Application Layer Service Elements. There are service elements already defined for ACSE and CCR.

Establishing an instance of cooperation between the APIs creates an Application Context, which is loosely defined as a shared understanding of the semantics of the protocol and user information that may be exchanged.

Support of the ACSE is expected to be included in all connection-oriented applications. These elements establish and manage an Association, which is an instance of cooperation between real open systems. It is not necessarily the case that an Association supports a single pair of APIs. It is possible for one pair to release an association for reuse by another pair. However, at any instance in time the Association supports just one API in each real open system.

In RDA, the services to be supported are those defined by ACSE, CCR and ROSE OSI Standards. The RDA defines a specialization of those services and has no protocol of its own. The RDA protocol is effectively defined by the composition of ACSE, CCR and ROS protocols, and the RDA Application Context, established at the BIND Time, is the composition of the ACSE, CCR and ROSE contexts.

4.3.4 RDA and Distributed Data-Base

A distributed data-base is a coordinated body of data that is partitioned into separated data-bases, each managed by its own DBMS. Coordination across the components is managed by a distributed DBMS (DDBMS) which is itself distributed. The DDBMS is aware of the component data-base nodes in the system.

The RDA may be used to provide a standard method of accessing DDB or to support their internal communications. Figure 4.3.4 shows the use of relational RDA for the internal protocol within a distributed data-base system. An application program calls a DDBMS component in its own end system, which communicates with the Server Process in other end system via the two client Application Processes, each of which is the client for a single data-base server.

Of course, there may be more than two remote data-bases serving the DDBMS, and some of the remote data-bases may themselves be distributed data-base systems. At present the support provided for distributed data-base in RDA is rather less than is required for a full implementation.

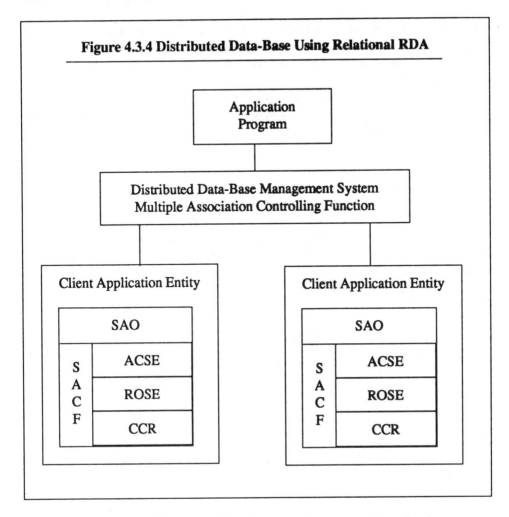

Figure 4.3.4 Distributed Data-Base Using Relational RDA

There are many problems, too: first, there are still some outstanding issues open in distributed data-base, such as:

- The update of the global scheme when a new site is added to or one of the sites which is a component of the DDB is disconnected from the DDB;
- The data inconsistency caused by the data duplication in the system;
- The CCR of the distributed transaction.

Second, SQL, the interface between the data-base and the users, is under development. SQL2 is upward compatible with the SQL. It defines some useful facilities for RDA, e.g. the structure of some tables which notionally exist in the data-base, i.e. they may be viewed or exist in a dictionary, and contain the scheme.

In addition, a temporary table is useful in RDA too. It is created by a single user entirely for his own use in that interactive session. At the end of the session, when the user logs off the system, the table is deleted. During the session no other user has access to the table. A temporary table is used in the execution of tasks involving data at more than one site. Data relevant to the task may be sent to the other site and used for a sequence of transactions, or as a table participating in complex join functions.

Third, RDA itself is still under development for applications because the Application Layer of the OSI standards is naturally dealing with the complex data processing problems in the real world.

4.3.5 Present Situation and Further Work

The distributed data-bases based on microcomputers in the LAN environment have been developed for several years in China and prototype systems have been put into operation in some applications. On the other hand, the remote data-base access software based on some specific system, e.g. IBM CICS, is also under development for the State Economics Information System.

In the China Seventh Five-Year-Plan (1986-1990), the RDA research and development is a key project besides the China OSI Project and the China PDN Project [10], which will provide the supporting OSI environment for the RDA and other OSI applications. SQL will become the State Standard around the end of this year and SQL2 is under development, too. In the China Eight Five-Year-Plan (1991-1995), the implementation of the RDA, SQL and SQL2, and the improvement and enhancement of the China OSI and PDN Projects will be key projects.

At present, the client-server (workstation-data-base) model is recommended for the small and medium enterprises in China for their maintaining and accessing the data-bases relevant to each other. The real distributed data-base development should be well planned and organized in phases before the integrated distributed information processing system is developed.

References

[1] ISO 7498, Information Processing Systems - OSI - Basic Reference Model, 1984.

[2] GB 9387, Information Processing Systems - OSI - Basic Reference Model, 1988 (in Chinese).

[3] ISO 9545, Information Processing Systems - OSI- Application Layer Structure.

[4] ISO 9579, Information Processing Systems - Remote Data-base Access.

[5] ISO 9807, Information Processing Systems - Network Data-base Language (NDL).

[6] ISO 9075, Information Processing Systems - Data-base Language SQL.

[7] ISO-ANSI, Working Draft of SQL2.

[8] ISO/TC97/SC21 N1927, RDA Tutorial.

[9] Stefano Ceri, et al, Distributed Data-Base Principles and Systems.

[10]ZHAO Xiaofan, "Present Situation of OSI Standards in China", Computer Networks and ISDN Systems, Vol. 16 (1988/89), pp. 83-88.

4.4 Networks and Protocols for Information Systems

Bernard M. Lebouteux

4.4.1 Networks Built

4.4.1.1 Characteristics of Networks Built with Dedicated Lines

Access to data-bases started twenty five years ago with terminals on dedicated lines, direct connections or via leased lines of the GSTN (General Switched Telephone Network) with modems at each extremity. Data-bases were built with sophisticated software like IDS or FORTE and generally not designed as higher level data-bases. Further steps to improve the use of dedicated lines were to build multipoint lines, to connect a cluster of terminals instead of one terminal per line, and now to make local connections by means of high speed BUS such as ETHERNET.

This network organization has the following characteristics:

- access is limited to a physical population of DTE's (Data Terminal Equipment), an arrangement which possibly exempts from problems of access control, user identification and billing. However access control is necessary with applications managing data owned by specific users.
- inclusion of a new user requires equipment extension and investment in the network.
- problems linked with long dedicated lines:
  * cost and poor rate of use
  * transmission problems and lack of security: interworking of two stations depends upon one line
  * transmission errors must be tackled by error detection and recovery procedures, for instance error detection by host giving echo of each character transmitted by terminal has been frequently used
- protocols of layers two and three are generally linked to manufacturer software especially in the case of multipoint lines
- protocols of higher levels are those of the manufacturer software and the application designers, they differ from one application to another.

In case of dependence of a local data-base on data-bases of higher level data transfer by long dedicated lines is costly and lacks security. If the need of updates is only periodic one may consider such transfers by tape or disk transportation if transportation time is compatible with update requirements.

Fig. 4.4.1 Connections Via Dedicated Lines

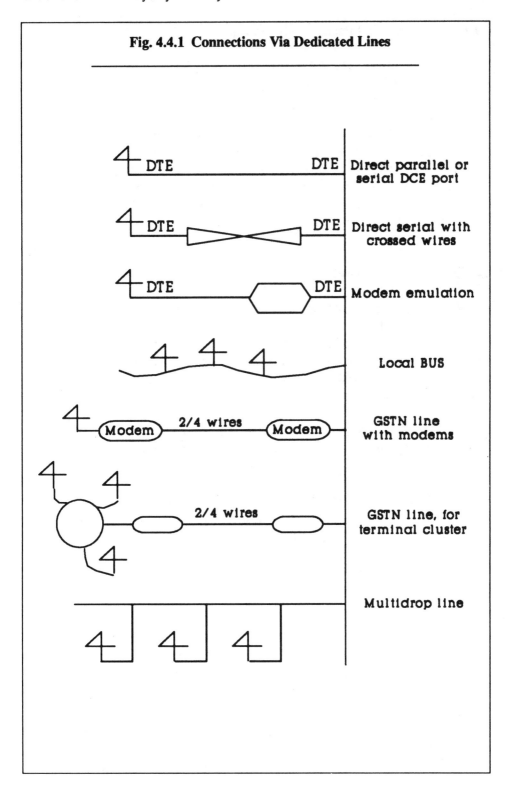

4.4.1.2 Transmission Interface Between Equipment

4.4.1.2.1 The CCITT V - Series

Let us see more precisely what is a connection between computers or computer and terminal. The CCITT recommendations of the V series deals with DTE/DCE and modem to modem interfaces. DTE (Data Terminal Equipment) means a computer or terminal and DCE (Data Communication Equipment) a modem. We distinguish two families V24 and V35. In these families two transmission modes, the asynchronous (or arythmic) mode, and the synchronous mode lead to two options of operation, especially in the V24 family.

4.4.1.2.2 The V24 Family

The V24 Rec. defines signalling for a set of interchange circuit numbers in the 100 series and the 200 series between DTE and DCE. Rec. V10 and V11 define electrical characteristics of the signals on interchange circuits. ISO 2110 defines connector and pin assignment for each circuit among twenty five pins.

Several V - recommendations define each a type of V24 modem and for each type the V24 circuits used for baseband interchanges with the DTE and the modulation on the line exchanged with the distant modem. From a user point of view V24 modems differ essentially by transmission rates (bits per second), use of 2 or 4 wires lines, adaptations to leased or switched telephone lines, synchronous or asynchronous capabilities. Telephone digital voice channels at 64 Kbs are able to transmit a V24 modem modulation like voice modulation. For instance we have used for years V29 modems (9,6 Kbs, synchronous) between Paris and French overseas departments. I must add that in case of use of satellite lines the modems must have tuning capabilities in order to take into account the transmission delay in the synchronizing procedure. Manufacturers provide modems able to meet the requirements of several V.. definitions by strapping adaptation.

4.4.1.2.3 The V35 family

The wideband modems family is intended to use sixty to one hundred eight kilohertz group band circuits. Use of GSTN is excluded, synchronous mode is nearly the rule and two senses of transmission are separated. V35 wears electrical interface characteristics and ISO 2593 is the connector and pin assignment specification for V35 and V36. G703 applies to physical/electrical characteristics of V37 modem. V35 connectors are however different between American and

European equipment. I must point out that models V24 or V35 connectors may be compatible at the pin level and incompatible by the type of connection bolting.

4.4.1.2.4 Baseband Adaptators

On short telephone lines with metallic continuity basic square modulation may be transmitted without use of carrier modulation. In that case the DTE/DCE interface is in conformity with a V. rec., V29 for example. But between DCEs baseband modulation is exchanged on four wire lines with previous coding in order to preserve signal shape and synchronization. HDB code (High Density Bipolar Code) is the most used. There is no CCITT standard for baseband exchanges on dedicated lines. These baseband adaptors are currently called baseband modems although they don't use carrier modulation.

Baseband modems are not exceptions to modems: they are widely used as low price equipment for synchronous transmission in a town. We use also such adaptors between DTE and multiplexers extracting data channels at 19.2 or 9.6 kbs from digital 64 kbs voice channels.

4.4.1.2.5 Direct Connections

Two DTEs may be connected by direct interchange circuits on distances of some meters. If none of the DTEs has ports tunable to a DCE configuration one has to use a cable that makes some exchanges and short circuits between wires. The required number of wires is not twenty five but a reduced number. In NTI premises for instance asynchronous terminals are connected to a PAD by four wires up to forty meters at 9.6 kilobits. Distance is reduced when speed increases. Such connections at 19.2 kbs may reach ten meters. For higher speeds cables must be armored. For synchronous mode one of the DTEs must be able to provide a clock. Modem emulators are available for direct connections exceeding twenty meters for the range of speeds around forty Kilobits. They provide clocks when necessary.

4.4.2 Access to Data-Bases

4.4.2.1 Access by GSTN Technical Features

Compared to leased lines the existing (opposed to ISDN) telephone switched network offers some specific features:

1. The transmission line is obligatorily made or two wires with the following consequences:

- modems use two carriers, one for each sense of transmission for full duplex exchanges
- as this obligation is combined with a smaller bandwith modem manufacturers have been lead to offer either sophisticated modems/reduced capabilities
  * unequal data bit rates in the two senses e.g. 1200/75, V23
  * half duplex transmission with specific procedures for sense reversing (V27 ter, 2400b/sec. and also V23)
  * use of echo annulators (V26 ter, V32)
- used modems are of the V24 family.

2. Proper interface must be provided to establish the telephone call on calling and called extremities. These interfaces are standardized by CCITT V25 and V25 bis recommendations which cover:

- relation between DCE and DTE (modem and data equipment) and between DCE and GSTN
- calling and answering functions on GSTN with manual or automatic operation.

Automatic call repetition is generally not recommended on GSTN and care must be taken to avoid frequent automatic call repetition.

3. Electrical troubles come from telephone switches, and for asynchronous mode error recovery procedures like MNP are useful. I must mention that in FRANCE transmission at 1200b/s crossing several digital telephone switches was difficult before general synchronization of digital switches. Synchronous procedures associated with X25 have error recovery features.

4.4.2.2 User's and Operational Points of Views on GSTN Access

This type of access is cheap and highly used from terminal to data-base where telephone tariff is low and transmission duration short. It is rarely used from data-base to data-base and transmission of important files is excluded without protection against errors. Data-bases are equipped with automatic answering modems and access is open to any telephone customer as soon as he knows the numbers to be called. Telephone network does not deliver the calling line identity to the called system and protection from undesirable users is usually necessary and commonly provided by passwords. If information delivery is free of charge a password may be common to all users. If there is a billing procedure or management of personal data each user must be identified by his password. For instance it must not be allowed that enterprise A makes fancy updates in data belonging to enterprise B. A calling station may be identified by the use of disk containing specific data prepared by a data-base management center. Reception of a new user will not require new hardware implementation in the network. The number of callable ports must be only statistically adjusted to the traffic. Tables for management of access authorization must be updated for each change of user.

Asynchronous transmission speed will be chosen in the range 300/300, 1200/1200, 1200/75 according to GSTN possibilities and user's location. Synchronous procedure may be envisaged but equipment is more expensive: synchronous modems, X25 ports and X25 software for instance. See V32, V27 ter. A data-base may have automatic answering modems and for the calling parts one may choose between:

- manual operation: the telephone terminal makes the call and switches the line on the modem as soon as modem modulation is perceived. Normal use of the line is telephone and   exceptionally data transmission.
- automatic calling modems (called number registered by the modem)
- terminal software transmitting commands to the modem for the telephone call.

Protocols generally use ASCII asynchronous transmission and are defined by data-base designers. Cost may be high and quality very poor on long distances. In spite of this and of the lack of calling line identification the use of GSTN must be considered a major facility for access to D.B. GSTN access is widely used in local area where telephone tariff is low and quality acceptable.

4.4.2.3 ISDN

In the next years ISDN will not be available everywhere. That would require the replacement of many recent telephone switches. But ISDN may be taken in consideration in some local areas if the opportunity is detected.

4.4.2.4 Telex Network

There are data-bases, especially message handlers, designed for telex terminals. Possibilities for information retrieving are so poor that I have excluded the telex network from this speech. However it may be taken in consideration.

4.4.3 Access Through Packet Switched Data Networks (PSDN)

4.4.3.1 Principle and Importance of Access by PSDN

Access from users to DB situated in a foreign country is mostly made through Packet Switched Data Networks (PSDN). This international type of access is schematically the following (see Fig. 4.4.2):

- an ASCII asynchronous terminal calls through the GSTN the nearest PAD entry to its national PSDN, this entry is equipped with automatic answering modem
- the PAD (Packet Assembler Disassembler) makes a first user identification for network services billing
- the PAD receives from the terminal the data necessary to send a call request packet through the PSDN
- call is established through one or several PSDNs. If several are involved we can distinguish:
  * the calling network supporting the PAD
  * the transit networks
  * the called network supporting the requested DB generally connected with X25 procedure.
- the DB accepts the call and starts the dialogue, generally by customer's identification
- during the dialogue 1) PAD receives DB packets and transmits to terminal corresponding sequences of asynchronous characters 2) PAD gets characters from terminal and assembles them in packets along tunable rules (characters subset, time-out, number of received characters)
- the calling network establishes call record for user billing and computation of shares owed to other involved networks.

This diagram may be considered as a standard for international access to DB although it has not actually lead to a really standardized procedure. To situate its importance let me give some indications on the worldwide spread of PSDN's.

The French International Packet node (NTI) manages ninety five data country codes (DCC) and routes from and towards around three hundred data network identification codes (DNIC), of which thirty are for networks of USA. In EEC there are more than:

- 100,000 X25 customer dedicated lines
- 12,000 asynchronous customer dedicated lines
- 60,000 identified asynchronous users accessing PADs by GSTN.

In FRANCE there are more than four million of VIDEOTEX terminals accessing via the national PSDN TRANSPAC around four thousand data-bases, the biggest of which is the telephone directory.

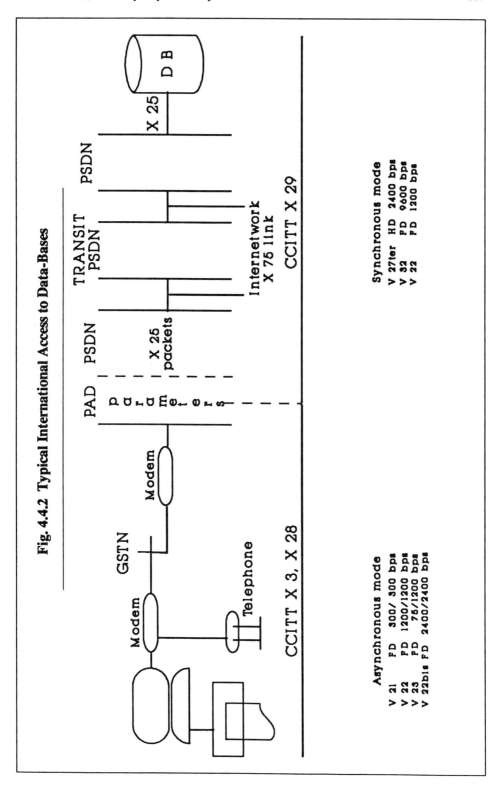

Fig. 4.4.2 Typical International Access to Data-Bases

4.4.3.2 Advantages of the Packet Procedure

4.4.3.2.1 Principles of Packet Procedure

4.4.3.2.1.1 Packet or Communication Level

Data flow is sliced in pieces along a maximum length, often 128 cctets. Each packet is transmitted from terminal to switch or from switch to switch with a serial number and acknowledgment is required. By delaying acknowledgment the receiving side controls the transmitting source and adjusts the flow to its own capabilities. A missing serial number reveals a loss signaled to user by RESET packet. On each X25 link each communication is identified at packet level by a logical channel number (LCN) allowing to have several independent communications established on the same link. Transmissions for each communication are interlaced.

Main objective is to offer establishment of a virtual transmission channel with a distant DTE whose address is given in call-request packet. However PSDN offer permanent virtual channels between two DTEs.

4.4.3.2.1.2 Frame or Link Level

Packet to be transmitted is included in a serially numbered frame. The resulting sequence of bits is subject to computation of a frame checking sequence which is joined to the frame. Receiving side computes again the FCS and checks identity with received FCS. So it is checked that no bit has been altered in the transmission, and in that case acknowledgment is given in answer. If frame is not correctly received it is discarded. Transmitting side waits for acknowledgement and if not received before a time-out makes a second transmission and so on until it gets acknowledgement or reaches a tunable maximum number of frame repetitions. If transmission is unsuccessful after N2 retrials all established communications are cleared.

The security against link failures may be improved by the MLP (multilink procedure) which uses several lines for transmission and is not disconnected as long as one line is in state of operation.

4.4.3.2.2 Advantages of Packet Procedure

- Speed adaptation between DTEs (flow control)
- Protection against errors and losses (frame control)

- Transparency to user data (program loading is possible)
- Several communications on the same line (interlacing)
- Worldwide interconnection because of worldwide standard.

Owing to these advantages the X25 packet switched procedure is the most used for connection of DTEs to public data networks by dedicated lines. However some switched line data networks are in operation in Europe and Canada. The european PSPDN will soon extend their possibilities by opening X32 service which allows packet mode terminals to access network via GSTN. In France such services are available since 1986 for X32. V27ter HD 2.4 kbs; 1988 for X32. V32 FD 9.6 kbs

4.4.3.3 Access by PAD and GTSN for Asynchronous Terminals

The asynchronous interface through a PAD defined by CCITT Rec. X.3, X.28, X.29 was designed to offer access from existing terminals to newly installed PSDN's. It is still highly used by terminals calling PAD entries through the GSTN. Most part of above quoted CCITT rec. deals with PAD parameters, 22 of which were defined in 1984. Short classification of them reveals:

- 2 parameters for user to PAD dialogue (PAD recall character and PAD service signals receipt)
- 3 for transmission procedure (BREAK translation, line speed, parity)
- 4 for flow control tuning (X-ON/X-OFF, padding after CR and LF)
- 17 concern editing facilities.

Some of these parameters interfere with local tunings of the terminal: parity, local edition or via echo, line feed insertion after CR. When a terminal calls a DB through a PAD, the DB recognizes the PAD presence by the PAD protocol code inserted in the user data field of the incoming call packet. At the beginning of the session the DB generally starts by tuning the PAD parameters by means of an X29 message. The terminal, via X28 dialogue may also alter the parameter values and can duplicate some effects by local tunings. A user calling regularly the same DB solves only once the problems raised by parameters and local tuning management and has a high rate of successful calls. But in case of scarce calls to scattered DB there is a long list of traps handicapping the accessing user. For instance:

- terminal or PAD parity does not fit host parity
- tuning of number of stops is inconsistent between terminal and modems
- in a previous call host has altered the parameters values
- previous user has modified terminal of PAD tunings
- host does not understand X25 BREAK translation (INTERRUPT packet)
- PAD does not insert bit "more" in full packets
- host wants to tune more parameters than PAD managers or there is discrepancy in the reverse sense

- PAD does not obey X-ON/X-OFF
- difficulties to obtain transparency, for instance for software loading thorough PAD asynchronous procedure.
- PAD and PSDN give standardized detailed codes in case of call failure or disconnections. This is of no utility if terminal does not deliver these codes or if user has no guide for their understanding.

We can add that user has a subscription to network administration and one subscription, for each not free of charge DB. So this type of access frequently requires a period of acquaintance between host and user. In EEC the EUSIDIC association representative of users scarcely accessing PAD's stresses the difficulties raised by the PAD's to sophisticated possibilities. These difficulties may be partly solved by the use of elaborated terminals able to register all the procedure for call establishments. The MNP procedure gives protection against asynchronous mode possibilities for transmission errors (V42). So does X-PC. Specific software allows transparency and software loading.

4.4.4 Videotex

4.4.4.1 An Example of Easy Operation

In spite of their graphic and coloring capabilities the Videotex services appear of very easy operation from user's point of view. I shall try to give commentaries on protocol features from the example of the French Teletel Service.

4.4.4.2 Billing and Identification Procedures

The Teletel procedure for service billing is the following:

- the information service is paid in proportion of the connection duration and each data-base is invited to choose its place in a given range of levels of cost per minute. The DB's have X25 connection to TRANSPAC PSDN.
- French Telecommunication office pays data-bases according to total connection time and chosen cost level,
- the Minitel terminal calls through GSTN a specific kind of PAD, called in French PAV or Point for Access to Videotex, and receives on its telephone billing counter periodic pulses whose periodicity fits with the DB cost level majored by network costs (Telephone and TRANSPAC).

Where information is public there is no need of user identification for access control purposes neither for billing purposes. This is the general case. For private

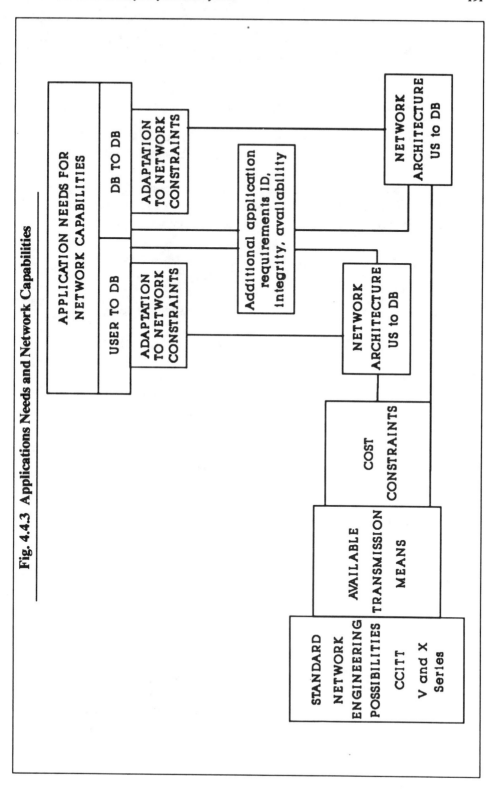

Fig. 4.4.3 Applications Needs and Network Capabilities

Table 4.4.1 Applications Needs and Network Capabilities

Geographic area covered and terminals distribution:	available transmission supports and power supply conditions.
Transfers total volume and distribution in sessions and messages per period:	transmission speed, modems, calling facilities, mean time between disconnections.
Data integrity:	error recovery, transmission procedure.
Transparency:	transmission procedure.
Access restrictions, personal data:	terminal and user identification.
Billing necessity:	user id.,call recordscollection and processing.
Dependability:	back-up means, network supervision guidelines for fault localization and service restoration.
Occasional or specialised end-users:	calling facilities, restricted choice of options, terminal ergonomy.
Graphic and colours requirements:	incidence on transferred volumes and speed to display.
User's assistance:	help desk, guide and tools for diagnostic, network indication for call faileure ordisconnection, terminal transparency to these codes, user's guide, terminal indication for local disconnection.

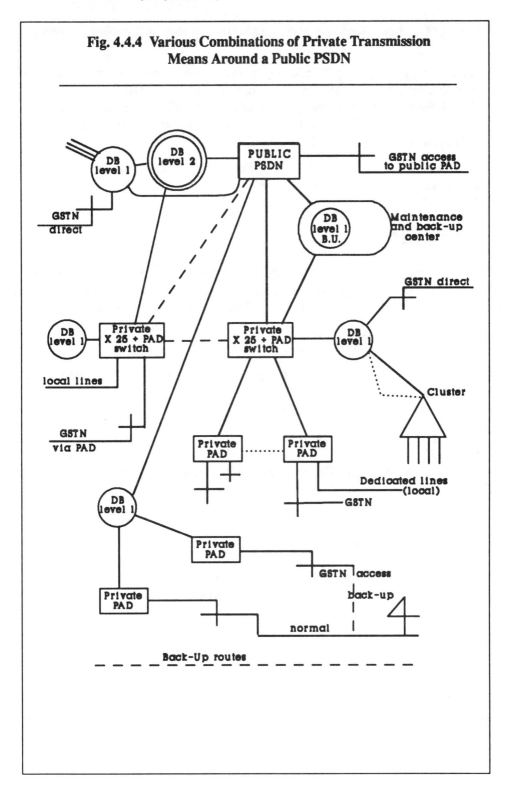

**Fig. 4.4.4 Various Combinations of Private Transmission
Means Around a Public PSDN**

and free of charge data-bases access authorization may be checked by several ways:

- Minitel terminal uses public access whose billing periodicity is reduced to network service billing and exchanges passwords with the DB.
- Local cluster of Minitels use a cheap private PAV offering several ports. This PAV is a PSDN X25 customer and identified by the PSDN, this id is given to DB in the incoming call packet.

PSDN may also include calling and called X25 ports in a common closed user group to which external accesses are forbidden.

4.4.4.3 Calling Procedures

The GSTN called number to PAV entry is a short one: 4 digits. When accessed by a terminal the PAV requests the mnemonic of the called data-base or offer consultation of Teletel services directory. Terminal operator has not to deal with

- long insignificant network user numbers
- changes of network user number of DB

Following the example of the national service all small size private PAV offer this service for a reduced number of mnemonics, around 100. For call establishment a specific key is used for:

- shifting from telephone interface to modem interface when called modem tonality is received
- to clear connection from DB and return to PAV offer for a new call
- to clear the GSTN connection to the PAV

4.4.4.4 Facilities Given by Specific Keys

A set of specific keys with clear indication of their use is available on the Minitel keyboard with the purpose of easier dialogue. These keys send sequences of two characters.

4.4.4.4.1 For Message Reduction

Characters are not retransmitted by PAV as soon as received but only after activation of a send message key, until activation of this message key may be erased or amended (editing facilities). Dedicated keys are offered for corrections (erase) and jumps to next or previous fields. PAV manages the characters in a field and DB manages jumps from field to field.

4.4.4.4.2 For Information Retrieving

Keys facilitate jumps to next or previous pages or to directory of choices.

4.4.4.5 Standards for Consultation

Two types of information selection are privileged in the Teletel host: menu and keywords:

4.4.4.5.1 Menu

A head page gives a list of possible choices and the rank number or the mnemonic to key for each choice. A first choice may lead to a page offering more detailed options and so on in an arborescent structure.

4.4.4.5.2 Keywords

The user names its choice and the DB makes alphabetic search through its data entries. For example the french Railways data-base for travel timetable requests following data:

> departure town: PARIS
>
> arrival town: BRUXELLES or BRUSSEL
>
> date: 12 04

This example shows possible difficulties if orthography is not strictly established. The DB may have to recognize several orthographic possibilities for the same object: BRUXELLES and BRUSSEL. The concerned French DB recognized the two names. In this example a system of "menu" would have led to successive levels for departure and arrival towns: choice of countries, then choice of province before choice of towns. One might imagine also a list of town names beginning by a first alphabetical character requested from the terminal.

4.4.4.5.3 Mnemonics

Each detailed rubric of a DB may be given a mnemonic allowing user to·
short-circuit the arborescent tables. A regular user is so able to access directly the
desired information. The existence of privileged procedures and of standard
specific keys has given birth to standard software tunable to fit with most frequent
DB structures. Nearly ready-to-use tools for Teletel data-bases exist.

4.4.4.6 Remarks on Procedure-Standardization

A review of F300 CCITT Rec. or of CEPT Rec. on VIDEOTEX provides a useful
list of frequently used functions whose standardization would help users of DB.
The idea of specific keys with clear indication printed on them is to be considered.
Cancellation of character combinations for specific functions is necessary for
transparency.   The use of specific software makes the necessary bit stuffing.
Ready to use software is a cheap means to check the DB main features utility for
final users. CCITT T61 and T100 give an idea of management of sets of characters
and pictorial, graphic and color features.

4.4.5 Synthesis

The main component of a distributed data-base project is the definition of "which
data for which users". From such a definition must be extracted the requests to
network services or possible complementary services. Owing to actually available
transmission means and cost constraints the application definition may be led to a
compromise for easier to meet requirements and to take into account some network
weaknesses on such features as user-id., data integrity, unexpected disconnections
and network availability. The network management design on its side must make
provision for network supervision, fault localization and operation restoration.

5 The Case of China: General Framework and a Specific Situation

Summary

This section is dedicated to the situation of the information systems in China. After an overview on the progress in the development of computer-based retrieval systems over the past ten years and a description of the unsolved issues in this area, a possible structural organization is defined and in this framework ISTIC is positioned and its main activities and objectives are described.

Finally an interesting survey on the users needs in the Chong Ming County (Shanghai) is presented and many aspects of the possible implementation of a pilot experience in this county are addressed .

5.1 Status and Development of Computer-Based Information Retrieval Systems in China

Gao Chongqian, Zhang Fenglou

5.1.1 Introduction

China initiated its research on the computer-based information retrieval in an organized way in 1975, when a Takachiho 4100 Chinese Character information processing system with a TK 70 mini-computer was imported from Japan by the Institute of Scientific and Technical information of China (ISTIC) to conduct experiments on the computerized information retrieval and the Chinese Character processing technique. In July 1975, on the initiative of the ISTIC and the Beijing National Library, a working group was formed to compile a Chinese thesaurus of subject terms. The result of this project, which involved the joint efforts of 1370 experts from 500 organizations in four years, was a large comprehensive Chinese Thesaurus of Subject Terms, covering 108,568 subject terms in 3 volumes subdivided by 10 sub-volumes. The work has laid the foundation of the national Chinese character information retrieval system. Up to now, the development of China computer-based information retrieval systems has undergone two important phases:

- Phase I is prior to 1986. This was an organization phase, mainly in carrying out the "sixth five year plan" for setting up the national computer-based retrieval system for scientific and technical information.
- Phase II is from 1986 to now. This is a phase of establishment and development, mainly carrying out the seventh five year plan for setting up the national computer-based information retrieval system for scientific and technical information.

The following basic principles were adopted in organization and establishment of the system to smoothly implement the above two programs:

- Reduction of investment and avoidance of repetition in data-base processing and data-base creation.
- Facilitation to realize industry-based data-base creation and service.
- Adaptation to the situation of organizational reform in the country.
- Information retrieval service on an easy, speedy and economical base.

The national scientific and technical information retrieval system composed of the national information center, the professional information centers at the Ministry level and the information retrieval subsystems established at the level of provinces and autonomous regions. It is planned in the coming three years to connect through the public communication network more than ten large, medium and small computer systems from different Ministries, to provide nation-wide information services to users in the Ministries, the provinces, autonomous regions, and municipalities directly under the Central Government, the municipalities separately listed under the national plan, and the major coastal cities, and open cities. Thus, a national scientific and technical information retrieval system will hopefully begin to take shape by 1992. The development of China's computer-based information retrieval system over the past ten years is characterized by the fact that it started its first step with the introduction and utilization of the foreign commercially available bibliographic data-bases and establishing user terminals to access the international on-line information retrieval services. Experience shows that it is only through practices and not planning that it is possible to train personnel to become technically competent and thereby easier to establish the Chinese Character information retrieval system once they are able to digest and absorb currently available techniques of advanced countries.

5.1.2 Status of System Establishment

In the last decade, the development of national information retrieval system has achieved accountable progress due to emphasis from the government, which was shown in a survey made at the end of 1988 by the State Commission of Science and Technology on the automation of scientific and technical information and library process. The following is a summary of the survey:

- More than 120 computer systems, excluding the microcomputers, have been installed for application in information retrieval and library automation, with a total 129 GB disk capacity. The computer resources and their distribution is shown in Table 5.1.1. The changes are shown in Table 5.1.2.
- Over 65 foreign commercially available data-bases were imported, including CA, WPI, INSPEC, GRA, Georef, OA and MEDLINE, etc. from which more than 30 searchable data-bases have been created, with a total number of 17,000,000 records. The details are shown in Table 5.1.3.
- Near 300 bibliographic, factual and numerical data-bases were created, in which 90 are data-bases in Chinese characters with a total number of 800,000 records. The details are shown in Table 5.1.4.
- Over 10 retrieval application packages and data-bases management software were imported or developed in cooperation with foreign institutions, including CDS/ISIS, STAIRS, MINISIS, BIRDS and UNIDAS, etc. Over 100

Table 5.1.1 Computer Resources and Distribution

computers	A	B	C	D	others	total
large (a)	11	2	2	1	0	16
medium (b)	12	3	3	7	1	36
small (c)	24	10	32	11	4	81
total	47	15	37	19	5	123

Where:
A: computer systems installed in the professional information centers of ministries and commissions.
B: computer systems installed in the information centers at level of provinces and autonomous regions.
C: computer systems installed in the university libraries.
D: computer systems installed in the institutes within the Chinese Academy of Science.
a: large computers refer to those with memory over 4 MB and disk capacity over 3000 MB.
b: medium computers refer to those with 2 to 4 MB memory and 1000 to 3000 MB disk capacity.
c: small computers refer to those with memory below IBM and disk capacity below 1000 MB.

**Table 5.1.2 Comparison of Computer Staff
and Resources in Two Phases**

Phase	Staff	Mainframes	Disk Capacity	Computer Types and Number of Sets	
1985	900	40	23 GB	VAX 11 Series	16
				WANG VS Series	15
				M Series	12
				PDP 11 Series	15
				IBM 4300 Series	10
1988	4000	123	129 GB	HP 3000 Series	10
				DPS Series	9
				ACOS Series	4
				DUAL Series	4
				UNIVAC 1100 Series	1

microcomputer-based aapplication packages with functions such as editing, composition, information retrieval and library automation, like acquisition, cataloguing, journal management and circulation, have been developed by Chinese institutions.

- Over 60 user terminals to access international data-bases have been installed in some 30 cities, which link with ten major world information retrieval services, including DIALOG, ORBIT, STN, ESA, etc.
- About 10 CD-ROM data-bases, including Book in print plus, AGRICOLA, ASFA, Bibliofile, ERIC, LISA, LSC, GRA, MEDLIN, etc., have been imported, with over CD-ROM drivers installed.
- 28 national standards for documentation work have been formulated, including 7 in the field of data-base creation.

5.1.3 Technical Implementation of Information Retrieval System

In the past over ten years, in order to speed up establishment and services of the information retrieval systems, the following technical problems have been tackled with great emphasis.

Table 5.1.3 Foreign Data-Bases Imported and their Utilization

Phase	Imported Data-Bases		Utilization		Search Profiles
	Data-Bases	Records	Creation	Records	
1985	52	25 million	9	4.28 million	16,000 profiles
1988	65	37 million	36	17 million	60,000 profiles

5.1.3.1 Pattern of Data-Base Creation and Service

According to the requirement of the overall plan, the data-bases which have been created or are under creation, can be grouped into four categories:

1) domestically made bibliographic data-bases,
2) library holdings data-bases or departmental management data-bases,
3) factual and numerical data-bases,
4) data-bases created on the basis of foreign-made bibliographic tapes.

Table 5.1.4 Data-Bases Creation

Types of Data-Bases	Number of DB's	Number of Records	Percentage (%)	Coverage
Domestically made bibliographic data-bases	98	800,00 in Chinese 150,000 in English	32%	patents,standards, proceedings,disser. journal papers, technical reports, etc.
Library holdings and management data-bases	62		20%	library holdings, union catalogues, journal catalogues catalogues, library management catalogues, etc.
Factual and numerical data-bases	102		34 %	organization,corp., on-going projects, technical markets, products, reports, scientific data, etc.
Data-Bases from foreign-made information sources	30	1.7 million	12 %	WPI, CA, GRA, INSPEC, Georef, INIS, METADEX AFSA,COMPEND.,TULSA API,MARC,MEDLINE, WAA,IRRD,POSR,etc.

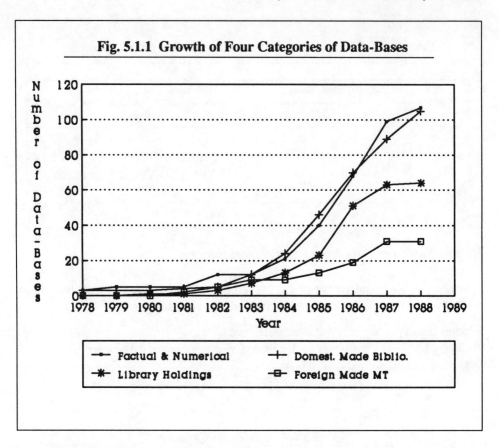

Fig. 5.1.1 Growth of Four Categories of Data-Bases

It can be seen from Fig. 5.1.1 that bibliographic, factual and numerical data-bases developed most rapidly and took three-quarters of the total number of data-bases ever created. Figure 5.1.1 also shows the development trends of the four categories of data-bases. Generally speaking, the above data-bases are created in different patterns according to each specific situation.

- Data-Bases created by the joint efforts of horizontal cooperation, that is created by different Ministries of organizationally parallel departments. This pattern is suitable to create factual and numerical data-bases, public-oriented and with trans-departmental or multi-disciplinary nature.
- Data-Bases created by the joint efforts of vertical cooperation, that is created within one big department but by hierarchically different organizations. The pattern is suitable to create discipline-oriented data-bases.
- Creation and service of data-bases are integrated in one organization. This pattern is suitable for information centers at the national level, which possess strong manpower and rich information resources, like the Patent Information Center, the Standardization Information Center, and are usually liable to create public-oriented comprehensive bibliographic data-bases.

Practice shows these patterns are suitable and feasible for different situations in China. Therefore, the principle, which was used to direct the process of data-base creation, can be summarized as unified planning, incorporation by disciplines, division of labour with individual responsibility and distributed creation and service of data-bases. As a result, a number of important bibliographic data-bases have been built and made available to the public.

5.1.3.2 Design of Chinese Character Retrieval Software

From 1980 on, in spite of the fact that progress has been made in the development of microcomputer-based retrieval package, China still lacks experiences in the development of retrieval software capable of processing the Chinese Character information on mainframes. Therefore, the following measures have been taken in an attempt to solve this problem.

- Retrieval application packages in the English language have been imported at the same time when the bibliographic data-base imported from abroad, and then either were used directly on the mainframe or later modified to handle the Chinese scripts. This is what is called the modification mode, which intends to modify the existing retrieval application software in western languages in a way capable of processing the Chinese scripts.
- Development of the retrieval application package capable of handling the Chinese scripts on specific mainframe, like Wang VS, UNIVAC 1100 etc. This is known as the self-development mode, which is implemented independently or with the joint efforts of the related departments using the same mainframes or the related computer institutions, under supervision by the State.
- Sophistication and popularization of a broad spectrum of retrieval application package capable of handling the Chinese scripts on the microcomputers. This is known as microcomputer oriented mode, which aims to develop software with functions of inputing, editing, information retrieval and library management and so on, operating on local microcomputer systems.

5.1.3.3 On-Line Retrieval Networking

In 1988, the Ministry of Post and Telecommunication had built up an experimental public data communication network called the CHINAPAC, based on the imported French TRANSPAC packet switching network technique and set up three nodes in Beijing, Guangzhou, and Shanghai and 8 concentrators in cities of Beijing, Tianjin, Shenyang, Chengdu, Wuhan, Nanjing and Shenzhen. This is the first facility to provide public data communication service to the public in China. Presently, conditions are being further improved, along with a general improvement of the telephone service in the major cities of China. There may be now several options for user terminals to access the international data-bases or to link up with domestic mainframes. Firstly, user terminals and host mainframes can be linked via the nearby nodes or concentrators. Secondly, the PADX installed in the ISTIC can be used as a switching node to connect user terminals with the CHINAPAC or other world-wide networks. Thirdly, it is expected that more host systems will be available in the near future to provide on-line information retrieval service to their users via dedicated or dial-up telephone lines.

5.1.3.4 Development and Utilization of Foreign-Made Information Resources

In recent years, at least four kinds of information media are available to utilize the foreign-made data-base resources, that is the commercially available bibliographic data-base magnetic tape, the international information retrieval services, the abstracting and indexing journals and the CD-ROM data-bases. All these information media are being used in China for information retrieval, though in differing degrees of utilization.

- For most systems which have imported the foreign-made bibliographic data-bases, the utilization mode is usually direct loading of the data-bases into the system using the retrieval application packages either introduced from abroad or modified locally, and to provide SDI or on-line retrieval services to their users. While in some systems, library catalogs are printed and subfiles are down-loaded for use on microcomputers.
- In order to reduce the cost, pre-processing of the search strategy, down-loading of small files and post-processing of the search results are usually implemented by users who access the international data-bases.
- CD-ROM data-base is a new-emerging information media for utilization of the foreign-made information resources and is likely to be more acceptable and have a higher market than the bibliographic tapes in the coming future.

5.1.3.5 Research on Supporting Techniques for Bibliographic Data-Base Retrieval

Automatic indexing of literature in the Chinese language and machine translation are two new types of supporting techniques for the computer-based information retrieval systems. The critical problem in automatic indexing of literature in the Chinese language rests on the feasibility of automatic segmentation and extraction of Chinese words. There are two sides to this argument. Without automatic segmentation of words, it is impossible to produce subject terms, let alone to say high-quality of indexing results. Automatic indexing experiments are currently underway and progress has been made since the 1980's in some universities and institutions. About 40 papers have been presented to symposium or published, and have been helpful in promoting the research in this regard.

Machine translation in China has a history of over 30 years. It was reported in 1988, that accuracy of the computer-aided translation of titles from English into Chinese in a few systems has reached 70%. It is a significant progress towards practical use. If we say that automatic indexing is the pre-processing technique for data-base creation, which assigns subject terms instead of manual labour, then machine translation is the post-processing technique for the information retrieval system, which helps convert the retrieved results from the foreign language into the native language. The integration of these two techniques with the information retrieval would hopefully make an intelligent information retrieval system feasible.

5.1.4 Future Prospects

From the viewpoint of system construction, the foundation of the architecture of a national information retrieval system has been basically laid. The remaining tasks should be to provide various forms of information services for public use as rapidly as possible. However, the following technical problems still remain to be solved.

5.1.4.1 Quality Control of Domestically Made Data-Bases

Figure 5.1.1 shows that data-bases in China have experienced a rapid development since 1984, particularly with the total number of factual and bibliographic data-bases which have increased more than twofold. The problem of quality and insufficient coverage of the data-bases prevent the service of data-bases from being practically usable outside a small circle. It is a very technical task to improve the quality of data-bases, to train the technical staff in indexing and information services, to strictly implement the related national standard, to clarify the division of labour and to assure the information sources for data-bases creation. It makes sense to increase the number of data-base only once the quality of the data-base can be assured.

5.1.4.2 Capability of Supplying Primary Documents

Presently, due to the fact that policy on document acquisition and division of work is not clear among many information centers and libraries, resulting in a duplication of library holdings or incomplete coverage, it is hard for services of primary documents to be provided for data-base creation and service. It is now a task of top priority to adjust the irrational distribution of sources throughout libraries and information centers as soon as possible, and to replenish their library holdings according to each specific situation and to strengthen the work of the union catalogue and the service of inter-library loans.

5.1.4.3 User Marketing

The users' information need is the basis for the building of an information system. An information system lacking users will not be able to survive. At present, the information retrieval systems in operation in China are generally facing the problem of under-utilization. The critical problem of user marketing rests on understanding the users' need and developing their information consciousness. It is possible to provide various forms of information services to specific users only when their information needs are fully understood. Utilization and absorption of information are dependent on users' information consciousness. Thereby, it is important to popularize the information services and to train the information users, and to create a number of data-bases urgently needed by society and to organize the exportation of domestically-made data-bases useful world-wide and with Chinese characters.

5.1.4.4 Development and Application of the New Information Technology

Application of CD-ROMs as a new media of information has been initiated in recent years in China and will most likely have an impact on information retrieval pattern both with traditional systems and computer-based systems. In comparison with the magnetic tapes. CD-ROMs are easy to use, low cost and require less complicated equipment. It is most likely that CD-ROMs will take the place of most of the magnetic tapes in establishing small information retrieval systems. On the other hand, on-line information retrieval services, if used together with the CD-ROMs in a reasonable way, will remain an acceptable and efficient facility for information service because of its faster updating and broader coverage.

It can be expected that China will meet the day, where centralized information retrieval systems based on a large amount of data-bases with functions such as automatic indexing, machine translation, and distributed information retrieval systems based on CD-ROMs and microcomputers, could continue to develop side by side.

References

[1] Computerized Information Retrieval in China in Retrospect and in Prospect, Gao Chongqian, Proceedings of the First Beijing International Symposium on Computerized Information Retrieval, October 21-25, 1985.
[2] The Development of Data-Base in China and the Suggested Policy, Gao Chongqian, The Second Beijing International Symposium on Computerized Information Retrieval, Dec. 7-11, 1987.

5.2 The Institute of Scientific and Technical Information of China

5.2.1 Introduction

Founded in October of 1956, the Institute of Scientific and Technical Information of China (ISTIC) is the national information center for science and technology and acts as the central organization in documentation, retrieval, and information research. It is presently under the leadership of the State Science and Technology Commission (SSTC). ISTIC provides various services to the whole country. Amalgamated with ISTIC, the Department of Scientific and Technical Information (DSTI) of SSTC is a government agency responsible for planning and coordinating the national scientific and technical information resources and services. The Chongqing Branch of ISTIC was established in 1960 for suiting the needs of development. The specific objectives of ISTIC are:

- Collecting Chinese and foreign information materials extensively as well as selectively according to national priorities and document distribution, in order to meet the information needs in the fields of national economy, science and technology.
- Processing and cataloguing the materials collected, and disseminating information by publishing retrieval journals, translations and information research publications.
- Offering both manual and computerized information retrieval services by using various retrieval tools and means, developing Chinese/foreign language bibliographic data-bases suitable for China's own situation, and establishing national on-line retrieval network to make full use of domestic and foreign S&T information resources.
- Analyzing and studying foreign and domestic S&T information, reporting S&T achievements, developments and trends, and providing policy-making organizations with comprehensive and strategic information on major issues in national economy, science and technology.
- Providing reading-room, reference, translation and reproduction services, audio-visual material production and showing services, as well as special services for specific purpose and major research projects.
- Recording, processing and reporting major domestic S&T achievements, organizing exchanges and extension, tracking the developments of science and technology in China and reporting new developments to the authorities concerned.
- Carrying out research on information theory, policy, management, and methodology, and study on the application of modern information technology in China.

- Promoting international cooperation and exchange in the fields of scientific and technical information.
- Directing the Chongqing Branch to share some of the tasks listed above, prepare secondary literature, and provide information services to Chongqing metropolis in order to support the development of its economy, science and technology.

5.2.2 Facilities

5.2.2.1 Building

Embodying the modern, scientific and flexible design idea, the new building (its usage began in Autumn 1987) with a total floor space of over 60,000 square meters consists of the main part of five stories and the auxiliary part of two stories both above and under the ground. The document stacks in the basement of the main building have two floors of totally 16,000 square meters. Equipped with systems of advanced program-control telephone, close-circuit television, mechanized conveyer, automatic monitoring control, automatic fire protection etc., the building provides facilities for carrying out all kinds of scientific and technical information services, such as document storage, reading, consultation and retrieval, copying and microfilming, computer network, telecommunication, information analysis and research, audio-visual shooting, processing and showing, publishing, administration, and so on.

5.2.2.2 Major Equipment

- IBM 4381 computer
- VAX 11/750 computer
- Various kinds of microcomputers and terminals
- Monotype laser photo-typesetter
- SP-8 high-speed Chinese character printer
- Complete set of equipment for audio-visual shooting, editing, cutting, transcription and dubbing.
- All kind of machine for photocopying, microfilming, and printing.

Table 5.2.1 Collection Of Materials
(up to the End of 1987)

Item	Unit	Amount
Foreign S&T literature	Copy	750,000
Foreign S&T periodicals	Kind Copy	15,711 1,528,000
Microform S&T materials	Copy	1,393,000
Retrieval books	Kind Copy	1,200 217,000
Reference books	Copy	27,000
Foreign catalogs	Piece/copy	85,000
Foreign S&T films	Copy	1,531
Domestic S&T films	Copy	336
S&T videotapes	Cassette	4,353
Domestic S&T literature	Copy	398,000
Domestic S&T periodicals	Copy	345,000
Domestic catalogs	Piece/copy	5,000

Table 5.2.2 The Percentage of Foreign
S&T Literature by Language

Literature	English	Russian	Japanese	German	French	Other
Document	67%	14%	8%	8.4%	1.4%	1.2%
Periodical	60%	12%	15%	8%	8% (with others)	
Retrieval book	69.7%	27.2%	3.1%			
Reference book	50.4%	11.8%	37.8%			

5.2.3 Service

5.2.3.1 Acquisition Service

ISTIC has been collecting all kinds of Chinese and foreign information materials extensively as well as selectively for many years, and so far has relations with domestic information organizations at all levels and over 1,700 organizations in 58 foreign countries.

5.2.3.2 Reading Service

The Division of Literature Service has seven reading rooms with a total of 1,000 seats for readers, namely: the reading rooms of Chinese Periodicals, Foreign Language Periodicals, French Literature, Domestic and Foreign Conference Proceedings, Appropriate Technology Materials, Microforms, and Reference Books. A room for Japanese literature is available as well. All new domestic and foreign periodicals and documents are provided for open-shelf reading.

The central circulation desk is equipped with calling-book device. In the Microforms Reading Room there are microform readers and printers and positive and negative photocopiers and transcription machines are available to users.

The Library of Product Sample and Trade Literature has an exhibition hall showing domestic and foreign product samples and trade literature.

5.2.3.3 Retrieval Service

5.2.3.3.1 Manual Retrieval

There are two sections of card catalogues on the third floor for manual retrieval of literature.

The foreign literature card catalogues section consist of:

classified catalogs subdivided into:
- classified natural science catalogs
- classified social science catalogs
- classified reference book catalogs
- classified newcomer literature catalogs
alphabetical catalogs subdivided into:
- western language alphabetical catalogs
- Japanese alphabetical catalogs

- Russian alphabetical catalogs
organizational code name catalogs subdivided into:
- organizational code name catalogs in western language
- organizational code name catalogs in Russian
- organizational code name catalogs in Japanese
- catalogs of conference proceedings in foreign languages

The domestic literature card catalogs section consists of:
classified Chinese literature catalogues including:
- classified Chinese dissertation catalogues
- classified S&T achievement catalogues
- classified Chinese reference book catalogues
- classified document catalogues
Chinese alphabetical catalogues
domestic conference-proceedings catalogues
catalogues of dissertations in Chinese
Chinese dissertation author catalogs

In the Retrieval Room there are over 200,000 retrieval books for open-shelf reading. The Library of Product Samples and Trade Literature has microfilms of American trade literature for retrieval and reading.

5.2.3.3.2 On-Line Retrieval

The international on-line retrieval service was set up in October, 1983 with the support of UNESCO and the Chinese PTT. The service consists of four terminals connecting with ESA-IRS in Italy, DIALOG and ORBIT in USA, STN in the Federal Republic of Germany, and ECHO in Luxembourg. The system can allows the access to 500 data-bases through the five above mentioned networks. So far the service has been extended to 23 sub-terminals in the provinces, cities and autonomous regions of China via domestic leased-lines and PTSN system.

5.2.3.4 Consultation Service

The Division of Literature Service, entrusted by users through telephone, letter or face to face talking, provides users with SDI service and retrieval of domestic and foreign literature.

The Division of Retrieval and Referral Service allows the retrieval of domestic and foreign literature and data manually or using the international on-line retrieval systems.

The Division of Domestic Science and Technology Exchange provides information on scientific and technical achievements in China.

The Library of Product Samples and Trade Literature can contact foreign companies to supply information about products according to users' requests.

The China Techno-Economic Information and Consulting Services Inc. provides both Chinese and foreign users with technological and economic information consultation service, carries out investigations and studies on special subjects entrusted by users and offers intermediary service for domestic and foreign enterprises aimed to technical and economic co-operation.

5.2.3.5 Document Reproduction Service

The China Scientific and Technical Documents Microform Corporation, equipped with advanced document reproduction machines, undertakes the work of xeroxing, microfilming, enlarging and copying all kinds of documents.

5.2.3.6 Translation Service

The Translation Department of China Techno-Economic Information and Consulting Services Inc. has organized a large large group of experienced translators both from ISTIC and from private companies to offer translation service in many languages such as English, Japanese, French, German, Russian, Spanish, Italian, etc.. The division can also provide interpreters for technology exchange and trade negotiation. High-quality typing service is offered as well.

5.2.3.7 Audio-Visual Service

The Library of Audio-Visual Materials is responsible for:

- collecting, translating, editing and showing domestic and foreign scientific and technical films and video tapes;
- shooting and recording major scientific and technical achievements, new technology, new products, and newsreels concerned;
- shooting and editing "Spark Science and Technology" programs sponsored by SSTC and broadcasted on China Central Television.

Equipped with advanced means, studios and a theatre, the Library provides all kinds of services concerning audio-visual materials.

5.2.3.8 Information Awareness Service

In order to disseminate scientific and technical information, ISTIC edits and publishes many publications such as:

- Management Science Abstracts (monthly)
- Information Science Abstracts (monthly)
- Bulletin of Chinese Dissertations (bimonthly)
- Bulletin of Scientific and Technical Books and Periodicals Published in Taiwan (bimonthly)
- Bulletin of Proceedings and Papers of Academic Conferences held in China (monthly)
- Bulletin of Research Results in Science and Technology (monthly)
- Brief Reports of Science and Technology in China (irregular)
- International Exchange in Science and Technology (monthly)
- Trends in Foreign Science and Technology (monthly)
- Bulletin (irregular)
- Science and Technology and Progress (irregular)
- Scientific and Technical Information Work (monthly)
- Journal of the China Society for Scientific and Technical Information (quarterly)
- Bibliographies of foreign S&T collections

5.2.3.9 Exhibition Service

The exhibition area, which occupies about 900 square meters, presents scientific and technical literature, product samples, trade literature, achievements, technology, equipments, and so on.

5.2.3.10 S&T Achievement Spread Service

The Division of Domestic Science and Technology Exchange, authorized by SSTC and with the name of SSTC Administration of Scientific and Technical Achievement, is responsible for national management of S&T achievements. Its main tasks are:

- registering and managing major scientific and technical achievements within the whole country, editing Bulletin of Scientific and Technical Achievements, spreading and exchanging significant achievements;
- building up data-bases of major scientific and technical achievements and appropriate technology outputs, compiling the Corpus of Scientific and Technical Achievements in co-operation with the concerned organizations;
- organizing fairs and exhibitions to introducing and spreading valuable S&T achievements;
- researching and selecting important issues and announcing the results through "Brief Reports of Science and Technology in China".

5.2.3.11 Information Analysis and Research Service

The Scientific and Technical Documents Press mainly publishes S&T publications as well as books and literature dealing with science and technology. The publications are mainly retrieval publications, translations, reports, and research publications. Main fields of interest are S&T theory, practical use, and policies, management of science, appropriate technologies, new technologies, etc. Advertisement service is also provided.

5.2.3.12 Computer Service

The computer service includes:

- designing and implementing all kinds of information processing and library automation systems;
- offering the use of IBM 4381 and VAX 11/750 systems to external users;
- editing books, magazines, advertisements, and other publications in Chinese and western languages;
- developing software applications;
- installing CDS/ISIS information retrieval software, setting up data-bases and offering training to the users;
- data inputting in Chinese and western languages;
- on-line retrieval of data-bases such as INSPEC, ENERGY, EI-Meeting, etc., and SDI service;
- consultation of computerized libraries and information systems.

ISTIC is building up several data-bases. They are:

- Data-Base of Scientific and Technical Achievements in China;
- Data-Base of Appropriate Technology Outputs in China;
- Chinese Academic Conference Proceedings Data-Base;
- Data-Base of Collected Periodicals in Occidental Languages;
- Appropriate Technology Data-Base;
- Data-Base of Chinese Periodical Union Catalogues;
- Data-Base of Chinese Dissertations;
- Data-Base of Abstracts of Learned Journals Published by Chinese Societies;
- Data-Base of Collected S&T Documents in Western Languages.

5.2.3.13 Training Service

The training service provided by ISTIC includes manual and/or on-line information retrieval and indexing; microcomputer applications; editing; etc. ISTIC holds the Postgraduate Training Course on Computer Science which is sponsored by UNESCO and by the British Culture Council.

5.2.4 International Exchange and Co-Operation

5.2.4.1

ISTIC has, as representative of China, joined the following international organizations and information systems:

- UNISIST , Universal System for Information in Science and Technology;
- UNESCO/PGI, United Nations Educational, Scientific and Cultural Organization/General Information Programme;
- FID, International Federation for Documentation;
- ASTINFO, Regional Network for the Exchange of Information and Experience in Science and Technology in Asia and the Pacific;
- INNERTAP, Information Network on New and Renewable Energy Resources and Technologies for Asia and the Pacific.

5.2.4.2

ISTIC has established, through formal inter-governmental agreements, co-operation relationships in the fields of science and techology with 14 countries, namely: United States of America, Canada, Brazil, France, Britain, Sweden, Denmark, Federal Germany, Hungary, Poland, Korea, Japan, the Philippines and Australia. Informal collaboration programs with scientific and technical institutions, libraries and corporations in nearly 30 countries are operational as well.

5.2.4.3

The international exchange and co-operation programs include:

- mutual visiting and observing between S&T;
- sending and receiving specialists for lecturing and consulting;
- holding academic conferences, workshops and training courses;

- carrying out co-operative research projects;
- exchanging S&T information materials;
- establishing and developing data-bases and on-line information retrieval systems;
- organizing exhibitions and audio-visual presentations.

Along with the further implementation of the open-to-the-world policy and improvement of conditions, ISTIC will undertake more activities in the international exchange and co-operation.

For information, please contact:

Zhou Shusen
Chief
Division of International Relation and Co-operation
ISTIC
P.O. Box 3827
No.15, Fu Xing Lu
Beijing, 100038, CHINA
Tel: 801 4020
Telex: 20079 ISTIC CN
Fax: (01) 801 4025

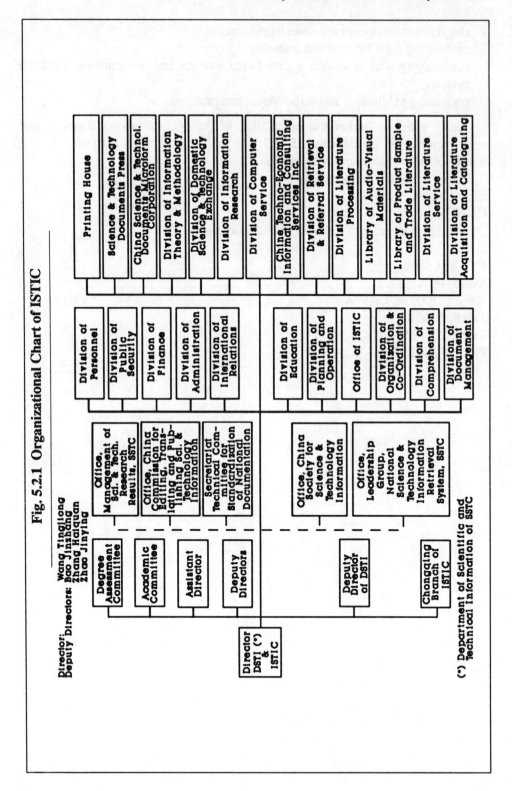

Fig. 5.2.1 Organizational Chart of ISTIC

5.3 The User Survey and Design Conception of Information System for the County of Chong Ming (Shanghai)

Baowei Fang

5.3.1 Introduction

Chong Ming, the third biggest island in China is one of the ten counties of the Shanghai Municipality, and is situated at the mouth of the Yangtze River, with an area of 1100 Square kilometers and a population of 750,000.

Spark Plan is a national scientific and technical development plan started in 1986. The plan aims to spread sciences and techniques to the countryside, generate the changing of industrial structure of rural areas, promote the technical progress of small and medium enterprises and develop the economy of the region. As the biggest county of Shanghai, Chong Ming, with more than 1000 enterprises and over 1000 kinds of products, is a key county of the Shanghai Municipality in the development of the Spark Plan project.

Since the Spark Plan projects were carried out, the significance of an effective and prompt information system within Chong Ming island has been noticed.

In 1988, the authorities of Chong Ming government decided to set up a Spark Information Pilot System (SIPS) by using a loan from the World Bank to help the completion of Spark Plan Projects and the development of the local economy in the county.

5.3.2 The User Survey of Chong Ming Sips

As part of the system design, a user survey was carried out from July to Dec. 1988, to determine the information needs of the system users. Because the Chong Ming enterprises will be the essential part of the system end users, the survey, therefore, focused on them.

The survey consisted of three stages:

A. Basic data was collected from the documents and statistics of Chong Ming government.
B. An investigation was taken up by a sealed questionnaire of 33 questions. About half of the Chong Ming enterprises were questioned and 373 effective responses were received.
C. Based upon the result of the first two stages, over 30 experts, managers and officers of Chong Ming were interviewed to get more details on the requirements of Chong Ming SIPS.

5.3.2.1 General Situation of Chong Ming Enterprises

There are more than 1000 enterprises with over 1000 kinds of products in the county of Chong Ming, about 80% of these enterprises are township and village enterprises (TVEs). These enterprises can be divided into 20 industries. In 1987, the average output and net profit of an enterprise was 3.2 million yuan and 0.3 million yuan respectively.

Tables 5.3.1, 5.3.2 and 5.3.3 show the distribution of industrial employees and outputs of the Chong Ming enterprises.

Table 5.3.1 The Distribution of Industries

Industries	%
Electrical Appliances	10.0
Textiles & Clothing	17.3
Food and Light Industry	20.5
Mechanical Processing for Shanghai Factories	24.1
Construction	7.0
Chemical	6.5
Others	14.6

Table 5.3.2 Distribution of the Output

Output (Million Yuan)	< 0.5	0.5-2	2-5	5-10	> 10
%	31.1	36.7	17.0	6.8	8.4

Table 5.3.3 Distribution of the Employees

Number of Employees	< 50	50-200	200-400	400-600	> 600
%	15.2	44.7	25.6	8.6	5.9

Apart from this, 80% of products from Chong Ming enterprises are put on to the national or export market, and more than 80% of enterprises, have their technology transferred from Shanghai or other cities.

Thus the conclusion may be as follows:

A. Most of the Chong Ming enterprises are small and medium enterprises, township and village enterprises.
B. The 4 major industries of Chong Ming enterprises are mechanical processing, Food and Light Industry, Textiles & Clothing, and Electrical appliances.
C. Most of the Chong Ming enterprises have an extrovert character, tending to use information frequently.

5.3.2.2 Current Information Environment of Chong Ming Enterprises

A. Chong Ming is an estuary island of the Yangtze River, the ferry boat is the only means of travel to link the island with Shanghai. On the island, a manual operating switch-board is still being used as a main tool for connecting telephone communications. Thus, the information received by Chong Ming enterprises could be delayed for 2 or 3 days, when compared with the enterprises in other counties of Shanghai.
B. From Table 5.3.4, it can be seen that, more than 85% of enterprises in Chong Ming have benefited through using information during the last years, and therefore regard information as a valuable resource.

Table 5.3.4 Benefits of Using Information

benefits	very big	big	some	few	none
%	13.4	30.2	41.6	6.7	8.1

C. Only 6.9% of Chong Ming enterprises have information groups within their enterprises, and therefore have a systematic way of handling information. On the other hand, in 93.1% of enterprises, there is no person responsible for handling information, and information is used casually.
D. An information group with 5 staff members is located in the Science & Technical Committee of Chong Ming. The information group publishes a monthly information bulletin but has no public reading room, no computer and no telecommunication facilities. Obviously, being the information center of the county, the information group is unable to meet the information needs of Chong Ming enterprises.

Table 5.3.5 The Means TVE Assessed Information

Means	used by TVE / TVE questioned (%)
Information Adviser	52.6
Information Agency	28.2
Library	4.2
Information Announcing Conferences	23.7
TV & Broadcasting	17.8
Newspapers and Magazines	32.1
Private Communication	41.8
Government Authority	20.6
Foreign Trade Agency	24.0
Others	7.0

Table 5.3.6 Type of Information Required by TVEs

Type of Information	required by TVEs / TVE questioned (%)
Market Information	85.3
Management Information	33.9
Government Policy Information	23.3
Technical Information	67.9
Financial Information	17.7
Information on qualified Persons	13.5
Others	4.0

Table 5.3.7 Items of TVE Required Information Service

Used Items	Provided by TVE s/ TVEs questioned (%)
Product Samples	41.4
Product Specifications	28.7
Patent Document	29.1
Magazines and Newspapers	8.9
Technical Books	19.7
Engineering Drawings	30.9
Teaching by Experts	39.5
On-line Searching	1.8

E. The Institute of Scientific and Technical Information of Shanghai (ISTIS) is a large and well-equipped information center. It has a large quantity of documents and is equipped with modern facilities such as an IBM-4381 Computer, international on-line terminal and Facsimile etc., all of these might be enormous resources for the Chong Ming information system, but they are currently inaccessible to Chong Ming.

Table 5.3.8 Contents of Information TVEs Can Provide to SIPS

Contents	Providing TVEs / TVEs questioned (%)
Product Market Information	57.9
Supplying and Demanding Information on Materials	47.4
Technical Information	26.3
Financial Information	2.3
Others	18.8

5.3.2.3 Information Needs of Chong Ming TVEs

Tables 5.3.5, 5.3.6, 5.3.7 and 5.3.8 show the results of a set of multichoice questions in the questionnaire.

From the data used, the conclusion is reached that:

A. Information adviser, private communication and information agency are major channels of TVE accessed information; it reflects the fact that TVEs of Chong Ming are unable to use information effectively without guidance, therefore a well-organized and well-trained team of information advisers (information brokers) will be necessary for SIPS.
B. Market information is the main information needed and produced by TVEs , as it is information dependent on a time-limit, the SIPS must emphasize the need for the prompt transmitting of information.
C. Except for technical information, the information produced and needed by TVEs are all in the form of factual and numeric data, thus a factual and numeric data-base could be the main form of the SIPS data-bases.
D. The traditional service items such as product exhibitions, technical seminars, information conferences etc., will still play an important role in the SIPS.

5.3.3 The Design Conception of Chong Ming SIPS

According to the results of the users survey, an information system based on modern communications and computer technology is therefore suggested. The system consists of three parts: the county's information center, the facsimile network and an on-line terminal.

5.3.3.1 The Information Center of the County

The county's information center is the nucleus of the SIPS. As the majority of the Chong Ming TVEs are unable to handle information systematically, an organization is requested which will concentrate the management of information within the county. The information flow chart of the center is shown in Fig. 5.3.1.

A. Information acquisition.
   The center collects information produced by Chong Ming TVE and acquires information from systems outside Chong Ming as well. The information regarding the 4 major industries of Chong Ming TVEs, that is to say electrical appliances, textile and clothes, food and light industry, mechanical processing, should above all take precedence.
B. Information processing.
   The center is responsible for processing all information in-putting the data into

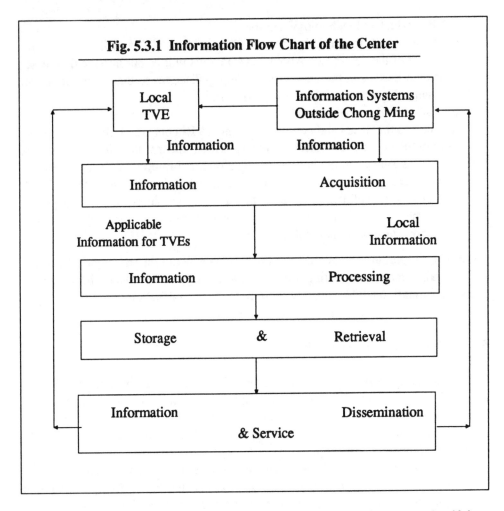

Fig. 5.3.1 Information Flow Chart of the Center

the system. The centralized processing of the information e.g., classifying, formatting etc, should ensure a high quality input and provide a prompt handling of information.

C. Information storage and retrieval

The center equipped with a super personal computer can set up data-bases to meet the requirements of the TVE. The data-bases to be established are:

* TVEs registry data-base.

   The data-base records all the basic data about TVEs within the county of Chong Ming. About 1,000 enterprises will be recorded.

* Qualified persons data-base

   The users survey show that the qualified people who can give instructions or provide guidance are of vital importance for TVEs development. Thus, a profile of these people should be created to guide the TVEs in finding the right person. These profiles are estimated as 1,000 records.

* TVE product and technology data-base

  The data of 4 major industries of Chong Ming TVEs will be the main contents of the data-base. About 7,000 records will be put into the data-base. All the data-bases will be established on floppy diskettes so that information can be exchanged with other information systems.

D. Information dissemination and service

  According to the needs and conditions of the TVEs concerned, the center relays information in various suitable forms, which means that in many cases, traditional service forms such as publications, exhibitions, consultations etc. will be used, and the contents of information delivered will be selected, rearranged or consolidated. In order to separate local information through the country, the center will also transmit information on Chong Ming TVE to other information systems at national level.

Another important function of the center is to carry out the training of the users. It is crucial, when implementing a system, that as users surveys have shown, a well trained information adviser team will promote the use of SIPS in a TVE.

5.3.3.2 The Facsimile Network

The facsimile network is the key part to the SIPS. FAX machines are installed in most information centers in the county and in the towns' industrial companies. These FAX machines are linked by a local telephone line or other lines, forming a facsimile communication network to transmit information exactly and rapidly within the Chong Ming county.

As a terminal of National Facsimile Information Exchange System, the FAX machine in the county's information center is connected to the Shanghai terminal in ISTIS, then to the national network station, Beijing, to form a nation-wide network. (see Fig. 5.3.2)

The information transmitted by the network is mainly time-dependent information such as market information and material supplies. The TVE pass the information to the county center through the facsimile network, the county center then sum up the received information and transmit it to the national network via Shanghai terminal. The national station can also transmit information to the TVE of Chong Ming in the same way. Thus, the facsimile network of SIPS can permit the TVE of Chong Ming to receive information 2 or 3 days earlier than that of the TVE in other county of Shanghai.

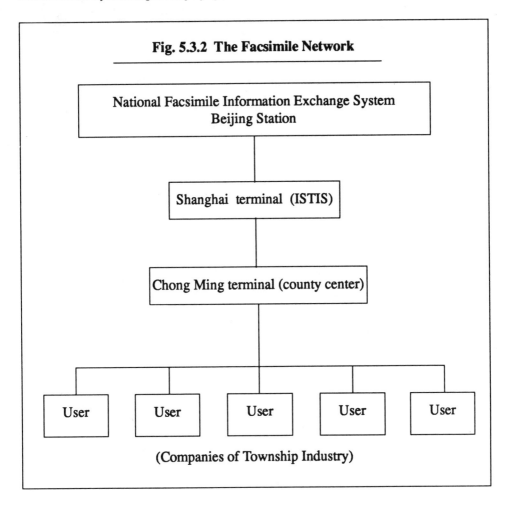

Fig. 5.3.2 The Facsimile Network

National Facsimile Information Exchange System
Beijing Station

Shanghai terminal (ISTIS)

Chong Ming terminal (county center)

User   User   User   User   User

(Companies of Township Industry)

5.3.3.3 On-Line Terminal

An on-line terminal is set up in the SIPS, it is an effective measure for the system to access the ISTIS data-base and other national data-base directly. As a terminal, a personal computer in the county information center can connect to the ISTIS computer through the telephone network, thus the data-base under the host computer of ISTIS can be searched on-line in the Chong Ming center; that means, the TVE of Chong Ming can share the enormous information resources of ISTIS through the SISP on-line terminal.

The Chong Ming SIPS is composed of the three parts mentioned above and is planned to be set up within three years. We can predict that the system will bring the development of the local economy and the progress of science and technology throughout the county.

6 Annexures

6.1 List of Participants

Bao Jinzhang
Deputy Director of ISTIC
15 Fu Xin Lu Lu
P. O. Box 3827
Beijing 100038
CHINA
Telex: 20079 ISTIC CN
Fax: (01) 801 4025
Tel: 8015544-2522
8014029

Chen Songsheng
Chief of the Division of Planning and
Operation of ISTIC
15 Fu Xin Lu
P.O. Box 3827
Beijing 100038CHINA
Telex: 20079 ISTIC CN
Cable: ISTIC
Tel: 801 4019

Renato C.L. Brea
ASA Teleinformatica S/C Ltda.
Rua Buenos Aires, 2-S/1407
Rio de Janiero - 20 070
BRAZIL
Tel: (55) (21) 263-4036 (Office)
(55) (21) 266-6555 (Home)
Fax: (55) (21) 552 1546

Fang Baowei
Head of Information Science Theory
and Methodology Department
Institute of Scientific and Technical
Information of Shanghai (ISTIS)
1634 Huaihai Zhong Road
Shanghai
CHINA
Telex: 30306 ISTIS CN
Tel: 374599 Ext. 55
Fax: (86) (21) 334913

Sergio Faustoferri
Information Systems Officer
International Centre for Science and
High Technology (UNIDO - ICS)
Via Grignano, 9
P.O. Box 586
34100 Trieste
ITALY
Telex: 46449 APH I
Tel: (040) 224572
Fax: (040) 224575

Helmut Gall
Re. Forschung & Technologie
Deutscher Industrie und Handelstag
(DIHT)
Adenauerallee 148
5300 Bonn 1
WEST GERMANY
Tel: (49) (228) 104540

Ge Songxue
Deputy Chief of the Division of
International
Co-operation of ISTIC
15 Fu Xing Lu
P.O. Box 3827
Beijing 100038
CHINA
Telex: 20079 ISTIC CN
Fax: (01) 801 4025
Tel: 8015544-2591
8014020

Karl Ganzhorn
Member of the U.N. Advisory
Committee for Science and Technology
for Development
Gluckstrasse 1
D-7032 Sindelfingen
West Germany
Tel: (49) (7031) 82022

Gao Chongqian
DSTI of SSTC
15 Fu Xing Lu
P.O. Box 3827
Beijing 100038
CHINA
Telex: 20079 ISTIC CN
Fax: (01) 801 4025
Tel: 8015544-2567 (Office)
8015544-3411 (Home)

Bernard Lebouteux
International Packet Switch Department
DGT-DTRE
Direction des Reseaux Exterieurs
Noeud de Transit International
12, rue Vivienne
75002 PARIS
Telex: 220 455 NTIFRA
Teletex: 933-1 42 60 52 27-DTRE NTI
Tel: (331) 42 60 51 25

Liu Yi
Division of the International Relation
and Co-operation of ISTIC
15 Fu Xing Lu
P.O. Box 3827
Beijing 100038
CHINA
Telex: 20079 ISTIC CN
Fax: (01) 801 4025
Tel: 8015544-2591 / 8014020

Henry R. Norman
President
Volunteers in Technical Assistance
1815 N. Lynn Street, Suite 200
P. O. Box 12438
Arlington, VA 22209
Telex: 440192 VITAUI
Cable: VITAINC
Tel: (703) 276-1800
Fax: (703) 243-1865

Louis J. O'Korn
Assistant Director
Information Systems, CAS
2540 Olentangy River Road
P.O. Box 3012
Columbus, OH 43210
Telex: 6842086
Tel: (614) 447-3600

Qu Weishuang
Deputy Chief Engineer of ISTIC
15 Fu Xing Lu
Beijing 100038
CHINA
Telex: 20079 ISTIC CN
Cable: ISTIC
Fax: (01) 801 4025
Tel: 801 5544 2553 (Office)
801 5544 4311 (Home)

Keith W. Reynard
Winkinson Consultancy Services
Stable Cottage Broad Lane
Newdigate Surrey RH5 5AT
UK
Telex : 934999 TXLINK G quote MBX
016881795
Tel: (44) 306 77 247
Fax: (44) 306 77 247

Wang Yalin
Chief
Division of Planning and Operation
of ISTIC
15 Fu Xin Lu
P.O. Box 3827
Beijing 100038
CHINA
Telex: 20079 ISTIC CN
Cable: ISTIC
Tel: 801 4019

Yang Ming
Jiangsu Province Science and
Technology
Information Institute
Suo Jin Cun Najing
CHINA
Tel: 653360-206

Yao Erxin
Assistant Director
State Science and Technology
Commission
54 San Li He
Beijing
CHINA

Yu Yongyuan
Gesellschaft fuer Mathematik und
Datenverarbeitung mbH (GMD)
Institut fuer Angewandte
Informationstechnik (F3)
Schloss Birlinghoven
5205 St. Augustin 1
WEST GERMANY
Telex: 889469 gmd d
Tel: (49) 2241 14-2720

Zhang Fenglou
Chief Engineer of DSTI of SSTC
15 Fu Xin Lu
P. O. Box 3827
Beijing 100038
CHINA
Telex: 20079 ISTIC CN
Fax: (01) 801 4025
Tel: 801-4020

Zhao Xiao-Fan
Computer Network Engineer
North China Institute of Computing
Technology (NCI)
P. O. Box 619
Beijing
CHINA
Telex: 222630 NCI
Cable: 2422
Fax: 2018902
Tel: 201-8902

Zheng Mingzhu
The Beijing Document Service (ISTIC)
15 Fu Xing Lu Road
P.O. Box 3811
Beijing
CHINA
Telex: 20079 ISTIC CN
Cable: 3725 Beijing
Fax: 8014025
Tel: 8014048

Zhou Dinheng
Division of Information Science and
Methodology
P.O. Box 3829
Beijing
CHINA
Telegram: ISTIC
Tele: 801 4003
Tel: 801-5544-2421

Zhou Longxiang
Academia Seneca
Institute of Mathematics
Zhongguancua
Beijing, CHINA
Tel: 283303

Zhou Shusen
Chief of the Division of International
Co-operation of ISTIC
15 Fu Xin Lu, P.O. Box 3827
Beijing 100038 - CHINA
Telex: 20079 ISTIC CN
Cable: ISTIC
Tel: 801 4019

OBSERVERS FROM ISTIC:

Gao Hengbao
Deputy Chief of Div. of Literature
Processing
Shen Rong
State Economic Information Centre
Beijing
CHINA

Xu Jifeng
The Institute of Informatics for
Management of SSTC
15 Fu Xing Lu, P.O. Box 3827
Beijing 100038
CHINA
Telex: 20079 ISTIC CN
Fax: (01) 801 4025
Tel: 8015544-2567 (Office)

Yang Zhongli
Deputy Chief of Library of Trade
Literature

Zhang Baoming
International Online Information
Retrieval Service (ISTIC)
15 Fu Xing Lu Road, P.O. Box 3811
Beijing - CHINA
Telex: 20079 ISTIC CN
Cable: 3725 Beijing
Fax: 8014025
Tel: 8014048

6.2 Abbreviations and Acronyms

ACSTD: Advisory Committee for Science and Technology for Development of the United Nations

CA: Chemical Abstracts

CCI: Chamber of Commerce and Industry

CCITT: International Telegraph and Telephone Consultative Committee

CD-ROM: Compact-Disk Read Only Memory

CEC: Commission of the European Communities

CSTD\UNCSTD: United Nations Centre for Science and Technology for Development

DB: Data-Base

DDBMS: Distributed Data-Base Management System

GSTN: General Switched Telephone Network

ISTIC: Institute of Scientific and Technical Information of China

MNP: Microcom Networking Protocol

PAD: Packet Assembler Disassembler

PC: Personal Computer

PSDN: Packet Switched Data Network

SIPS: SPARK Information Pilot System

SME: Small and Medium Enterprise

TVE: Township and Village Enterprise

UNESCO: United Nations Educational, Scientific and Cultural Organization